REDISCOVERING THE
BOOK OF MORMON

REDISCOVERING THE BOOK OF MORMON

Edited by John L. Sorenson and Melvin J. Thorne

Deseret Book Company
Salt Lake City, Utah
and
Foundation for Ancient Research and Mormon Studies
Provo, Utah

Library of Congress Cataloging-in-Publication Data

Rediscovering the Book of Mormon / edited by John L. Sorenson and
   Melvin J. Thorne.
     p. cm.
   Includes bibliographical references and index.
   ISBN 0-87579-387-8
   1. Book of Mormon — Criticism, interpretation, etc. 2. Book of
Mormon — Evidences, authority, etc. I. Sorenson, John L.
II. Thorne, Melvin J. III. Foundation for Ancient Research and
Mormon Studies.
BX8627.R397 1991
289.3'22 — dc20   90-29124
                                        CIP

Printed in the United States of America

10   9   8   7   6   5   4

CONTENTS

CONTENTS

PREFACE

During the 1980s, LDS scholars did a great deal of research on the Book of Mormon. The result was a bumper crop of serious scholarly studies that shed new light on this sacred scripture. For example, the first (1989) annual issue of a new periodical, *Review of Books on the Book of Mormon,* listed more than a dozen books and fifty articles of a scholarly nature. The second issue (1990) listed another impressive set.

Despite the insights these studies contain, most of them have remained unknown to anyone outside the academic fields of the authors, including scholars in other fields. The officers of the Foundation for Ancient Research and Mormon Studies (F.A.R.M.S.) have long felt that the results of these research studies ought to be made available to a larger audience.

This book begins to meet that need. It presents exciting new studies without the technical language that scholars sometimes use to communicate with each other in their specialized fields. No special background is required to appreciate these essays — just a desire to rediscover the value of the Book of Mormon by learning new things about it.

This collection of essays focuses on one type of recent research: studies demonstrating that the Book of Mormon contains complex patterns not previously recognized — patterns of style, ideas, history, and actions. Hugh Nibley has correctly observed that the Book of Mormon describes the Nephite civilization "with due attention to all the complex factors that make up an exceedingly complicated but perfectly consistent picture."[1] He has argued persuasively that one strong evidence of the authenticity of the Book of Mormon is that it interweaves dozens of complex stories and patterns with an uncanny consistency that is never caught in a slip or contradiction.[2]

Not only are many of these patterns complicated, they are so subtle or hard to detect that they become visible only through careful analysis. Once visible, however, these complexities help us appreciate better the power of the book and its messages for us. The essays in this book help to make some of these patterns clear.

A few examples will clarify what we mean. In one of the first pieces, Grant Hardy discusses the effect that Mormon had on the Book of Mormon in his role as editor. By his choices of what to include and what to leave out, Mormon shaped the book decisively. Hardy shows that Mormon's influence was both sweeping and consistent throughout the book. Once we see the patterns in what Mormon did as he edited, we understand better how he desired the book to affect us.

In another essay, John Tvedtnes shows another complicated pattern we had not seen before; he identifies traces of the Hebrew language that were left behind when the book was translated to English. There are dozens of places where, as Tvedtnes reveals to us, awkward or atypical English phrases give us clues that Joseph Smith translated these "Hebraisms" literally.

Stephen Ricks looks at King Benjamin's great assembly (Mosiah 1–6) and the way in which Benjamin's son Mosiah became the next king. He shows us how similar these events were to what is known about kings and their ways in the ancient Near East. Thus this part of the Book of Mormon accurately and consistently reflects the culture that it claims to come from.

William Hamblin discusses the Book of Mormon's descriptions of warfare. He gives us insights into how Lehi's descendants adapted their Israelite military heritage. The details he points out form a complicated but realistic picture without any of the contradictions that a modern writer would inevitably have fallen into.

The articles in this book teach us about unexpected concepts, images, or cultural facts in the Book of Mormon that become obvious once they are pointed out but that we were blind to previously. In this sense, these essays help us "rediscover" the Book of Mormon. In each case we gain new insights into the richness of the Book of Mormon and its messages for us. Each essay reveals unsuspected strands and threads that run through the Book of Mormon as through a huge, rich tapestry. These new studies reveal remarkable designs deserving our careful examination. When we look in greater detail at the tapestry and at the weavers' (writers') techniques and motives, we see their creation in new ways—we rediscover the book.

We also see new evidence that the book is the ancient record it says it is. These patterns are so intricate and yet so consistent that it seems highly unlikely that Joseph Smith (or any writer of his day) could have created them. By showing us these patterns, the essays in this collection focus on internal evidence and turn our attention primarily to the scripture itself. As President Gordon B. Hinckley has observed, key evidence for the truth and validity of the Book of Mormon "lies within the covers of the book itself."[3]

We heartily thank the authors who contributed these essays, whom we editors occasionally pressed with vigor. We also express gratitude to the officers and staff at F.A.R.M.S.

Our labors will be rewarded if this book sheds new light upon the Book of Mormon, Another Testament of Jesus Christ, and stimulates new appreciation and respect for it. We also hope readers will share our conviction that scholarly research is producing exciting new discoveries in the Book of Mormon and that scholarship is not a frill but a valuable activity in its own right.

John L. Sorenson
Melvin J. Thorne

Notes

1. Hugh W. Nibley, "The Book of Mormon: True or False?" *Millennial Star* 124 (November 1962): 276; reprinted in the *Collected Works of Hugh Nibley* 8:225.

PREFACE

2. Nibley considers this question in several of his writings. See in particular "The Book of Mormon: True or False?" in *CWHN* 8:219–42; and "New Approaches to Book of Mormon Study," in *CWHN* 8:54–126.

3. Gordon B. Hinckley, "The Cornerstones of Our Faith," *Ensign*, November 1984, p. 52.

AUTHORS AND EDITORS

Chapter 1

NEPHI'S USE OF LEHI'S RECORD

S. Kent Brown

In many places in the Book of Mormon, the authors refer to writings known to them but not included in the book. One of these is the record of Lehi. Nephi reported that he made "an abridgment of the record of my father" (1 Nephi 1:17), which he included on his own original (large) plates. An English translation of that abridgment was included in the 116 pages of manuscript translation lost by Martin Harris in 1828. Someday we will have that record restored; meanwhile, we can discover some of what it contained because both Nephi and Jacob included parts from it in their records.

The Book of Mormon consistently lets us know that, years after Lehi had died, Nephi had his father's record before him as he wrote his own record (our books of First and Second Nephi). Wherever bits of Lehi's record are found scattered throughout Nephi's account, they reveal a body of language, experience, and teachings so varied and deep and yet so consistent that we must believe that a real man, a genuine prophet named Lehi, was the source.

As we start to read 1 Nephi 1, Nephi tells us that he is making "a record of my proceedings in my days" (verse 1). Yet within a few verses he is borrowing from what Lehi had written:

> Now I, Nephi, do not make a full account of the things which my father hath written, for he hath written many things which he saw in visions and in dreams; and he also hath written many things which he prophesied and

3

spake unto his children, of which I shall not make a full
account. But I shall make an account of my proceedings
in my days. Behold, I make an abridgment of the record
of my father, upon plates which I have made with mine
own hands; wherefore, after I have abridged the record
of my father then will I make an account of mine own
life (verses 16–17).

Lehi's record must have been very important to Nephi, for
he not only used it as the basis for part of his record on the small
plates, he also presented even more of it on the large plates (see
1 Nephi 19:1). Fortunately, because Nephi, and Jacob, used it
as a source, we can learn much about Lehi's record from their
writings. By searching there, we can construct a likely picture
of how Lehi's record was made and what it contained.

When and on What Did Lehi Write?

Most of Lehi's record must have been completed by the time
Nephi made and started writing on the large plates. This would
be after arriving in the promised land. Nephi tells us that he
recorded on those plates "the [abridged] record of my father,
and the genealogy of his fathers, and the more part of all our
proceedings in the wilderness" (1 Nephi 19:2). Nephi could have
obtained the genealogy from the brass plates, where Lehi had
learned about it (see 1 Nephi 5:14). But his father's own version
of the events in the wilderness (for example, 1 Nephi 5:2–6,
which happened in Nephi's absence) would have had to come
from another source, most likely Lehi's own. Lehi probably had
begun writing his record while still in Jerusalem so that he could
include his visions there while they were still vivid (see 1 Nephi
1:16).

Notice how Nephi talks about their wandering in the wilderness after the discovery of the Liahona (see 1 Nephi 16:9–
17:5). He makes a series of statements that feature the word *we*
(except for the incident of the broken bow, which he tells in first
person singular, interrupting the main story). He seems to be
summarizing what happened without giving details. The text

simply gives the direction and length of their travels, plus the type of hardships in general that the family faced. He is satisfied with summaries like "we did sojourn for the space of many years, yea, even eight years in the wilderness" (1 Nephi 17:4). This part of Nephi's record is likely a summary of a more detailed, diary-like account probably either written or authorized by Lehi.

We have no way of knowing what material Lehi kept his record on, but probably it was perishable. A remark made by his son Jacob supports this view. Jacob notes, "We know that the things which we write upon plates must remain; but whatsoever things we write upon anything save it be upon plates must perish and vanish away" (Jacob 4:1–2). Jacob's experience with the brass plates had shown him the durability of metal plates. We can well believe that the experience of Lehi's family concerning records kept on perishable materials included the disintegration of Lehi's record.

Other hints also suggest that Lehi's record was not kept on metal. No mention is made of metal plates or engraving tools being brought from Jerusalem. Nor is there mention of ore being smelted in the wilderness to make either plates or tools. On the contrary, the party avoided making any fires (see 1 Nephi 17:2, 12). These hints point to Lehi's having used something other than metal for his record.

The most likely candidates, according to materials used in Lehi's day, would be animal skins, clay, wood covered with wax, or possibly papyrus. The Talmud specified the use of the skins of clean animals for writing the law, and the Hebrews were expert at dressing skins (see Exodus 25:5; Leviticus 13:48). Rolls, or scrolls, made from skins were used in Lehi's day (see Jeremiah 36:2; Ezekiel 2:9–10).

The Content of Lehi's Record

Nephi describes Lehi's record as containing "many things which he [Lehi] saw in visions and in dreams" and "many things which he prophesied and spake unto his children" (1 Nephi 1:16). Using this description of Lehi's record and examining the

5

instances in which Jacob and Nephi either quote from or para-phrase it can give us some idea of its content.

Although we naturally think of Nephi's book as being by and about himself, much of his record may have come directly or indirectly from Lehi's record. The beginning of Nephi's account seems to echo the opening lines of what Lehi had written. A statement telling how the prophet was called was normal for ancient writers; this came near the beginning of the record. He included information about the year, expressed in terms of when the local king took over the throne (for examples, see Jeremiah 1:2–10; Ezekiel 1; Zephaniah 1; and Zechariah 1). Of course, this is what we find in 1 Nephi 1:4–15. Directly after Nephi's opening statements about himself (verses 1–3), he puts in a note that the beginning of his story came during the first year of King Ze-dekiah's reign (1 Nephi 1:4). Next, as expected, we read that God called the prophet (verses 5–15). But, unexpectedly, the prophet is not Nephi but Lehi. It looks as if Nephi has used the standard opening format from Lehi's book but adapted it slightly to begin his own account. Adaptations of Lehi's record can be found often in Nephi's writings.

Nephi later says this about using his father's record, "Upon the [large] plates which I made I did engraven the record of my father, and also our journeyings in the wilderness, and the prophecies of my father" (1 Nephi 19:1). This verse is intended to describe some of the content of Nephi's large plates, yet in fact it also describes what is included on the small plates (the first part of our Book of Mormon record) in 1 Nephi and the first three chapters of 2 Nephi.

To illustrate, (a) "the record of my father" corresponds roughly to 1 Nephi 1–10; (b) the "journeyings in the wilderness" appears in 1 Nephi 16–18; and (c) the "prophecies of my father" would include 2 Nephi 1–3 and possibly 1 Nephi 10. The overall scheme is interrupted only by the account of Nephi's dream (1 Nephi 11–15) and Nephi's discourse to his brothers (1 Nephi 19–22), both of which digress from the main story that notably focuses on Lehi. Note, however, that Nephi's dream was

6

prompted by his father's dream, which Lehi had undoubtedly recorded in his own record. Among items that Nephi apparently borrowed from Lehi's record are the summary of Lehi's wanderings in the desert, paraphrases of and quotations from his dreams and visions, and parts of his teachings, doctrines, and blessings to his children.

Visions and Dreams

Preserved in the Book of Mormon are seven of Lehi's inspired dreams and visions. Nephi mentions Lehi's dreams and visions being in his record: "[Lehi] hath written many things which he saw in visions and in dreams" (1 Nephi 1:16). Lehi himself considered that he was "a visionary man" (1 Nephi 5:4).

The earliest vision recorded in the Book of Mormon is the one that probably began Lehi's own record. Nephi describes it briefly: "As [Lehi] prayed unto the Lord, there came a pillar of fire and dwelt upon a rock before him; and he saw and heard much; and because of the things which he saw and heard he did quake and tremble exceedingly. And it came to pass that he returned to his own house at Jerusalem; and he cast himself upon his bed, being overcome with the Spirit and the things which he had seen" (1 Nephi 1:6–7). Nephi gives nothing more of the vision's content, but it may have included Lehi's call to the role of prophet, for soon afterward Lehi began to preach to the people (see v. 18; also 1 Nephi 2:1).

Nephi begins his summary of Lehi's second vision, the vision wherein he sees a book, by emphasizing that "being thus overcome with the Spirit, [Lehi] was carried away in a vision, even that he saw the heavens open, and he thought he saw God sitting upon his throne, surrounded with numberless concourses of angels in the attitude of singing and praising their God" (1 Nephi 1:8). Lehi then saw "One descending out of the midst of heaven" and "twelve others following him" (1 Nephi 1:9–10).

Nephi continues: "The first came and stood before my father, and gave unto him a book, and bade him that he should read" (1:11). Lehi then read of Jerusalem's wickedness and of its impending destruction. This same warning was the core message of other prophets in Lehi's time at Jerusalem (see 1 Nephi 1:4). Although Nephi does not mention it here, at some point in the vision Lehi also learned that the Messiah would come and save humankind: Lehi "testified that the things which he saw and heard, and also the things which he read in the book, manifested plainly of the coming of a Messiah, and also the redemption of the world" (1 Nephi 1:19). Nephi also includes two apparent direct quotations from Lehi's record—his warning to Jerusalem (1 Nephi 1:13) and his psalm rejoicing in God's power and goodness (1 Nephi 1:14).

Speaking of his father's third vision, Nephi includes words from the Lord that were probably quoted from Lehi's record: "The Lord spake unto my father, yea, even in a dream, and said unto him: Blessed art thou Lehi, because of the things which thou hast done; and because thou hast been faithful and declared unto this people the things which I commanded thee, behold, they seek to take away thy life" (1 Nephi 2:1). In this same vision, Lehi also received the command to leave Jerusalem, the first step in the family's long journey (see 1 Nephi 2:2). Lehi's obedience eventually led him and his family to their land of promise halfway around the earth.

Lehi's fourth vision was about his sons returning to Jerusalem for the brass plates (see 1 Nephi 3:2–6). Here Nephi quotes Lehi's own words, "I have dreamed a dream, in the which the Lord hath commanded me that thou and thy brethren shall return to Jerusalem. For behold, Laban hath the record of the Jews and also a genealogy of my forefathers, and they are engraven upon plates of brass" (1 Nephi 3:2–3). Nephi and his brothers were to go to Laban and "seek the records, and bring them down hither" (1 Nephi 3:4), even though his brothers had already complained about the task.

The fifth vision showed the tree of life and possibly included the Messiah. Much of the vision was written in first person singular ("I saw"). This was thus a long direct quotation from Lehi's record. When Nephi introduces the story, he clarifies that

8

he is quoting: "He [Lehi] spake unto us [his family], saying: Behold, I have dreamed a dream" (1 Nephi 8:2). In addition, Nephi leaves no doubt when he stops quoting Lehi, for at the end he only summarizes the rest of his father's vision: "I, Nephi, do not speak all the words of my father. But, to be short in writing, behold, he saw other multitudes pressing forward; and they came and caught hold of the end of the rod of iron" (1 Nephi 8:29–30). This summary includes Lehi's warnings and urgings to Laman and Lemuel (except for a brief direct quote in 1 Nephi 8:34–35). He closes this paraphrase by saying: "All these things did my father see, and hear, and speak, as he dwelt in a tent, in the valley of Lemuel, and also a great many more things, which cannot be written upon these [small] plates" (1 Nephi 9:1).

In Lehi's original record, the material in 1 Nephi 10 (Lehi's teachings about the coming of the Messiah and the scattering and gathering of Israel) may well have followed directly the account of his dream of the tree of life and his exhortation to his sons. This can be seen from two facts: In the first place, just a few lines (1 Nephi 9:2–6) separate these two sections. In those lines, Nephi briefly discusses the plates mentioned in verse one, before resuming his father's account in chapter ten. In the second place, when we compare the content of these two parts (chapters 8 and 10) with the content of Nephi's vision of the tree of life (chapters 11–14), we see that the second part (chapter 10) plainly belongs together with the first (chapter 8). In Nephi's parallel vision, the prophecies regarding Israel's destiny and the Messiah (1 Nephi 10:1–16) go with his account of the tree of life, suggesting the same pattern for Lehi's dream of the tree and prophecy of the Messiah. So, we should conclude that the brief segment in 1 Nephi 9:2–6 was inserted between two sections that likely were continuous in Lehi's narrative.

I believe that the words written upon the compass or Liahona (see 1 Nephi 16:26) constituted Lehi's sixth specific revelation. (Since it was shared by all the others in the party, perhaps it should not be called a vision, strictly speaking.) On this occasion

Lehi had prayed to learn where Nephi should go to find food. The response came as words that appeared miraculously on the sacred ball. The Lord chastised Lehi and his family for complaining about their hardships in the wilderness (see 1 Nephi 16:24–25). Nephi wrote, "When my father beheld the things which were written upon the ball, he did fear and tremble exceedingly, and also my brethren and the sons of Ishmael and our wives" (1 Nephi 16:27). We see that, like the Urim and Thummim among the ancient Israelites, the compass-ball served as a means to receive revelation.

The last recorded vision of Lehi is mentioned in 2 Nephi 1:4: "I have seen a vision, in which I know that Jerusalem is destroyed; and had we remained in Jerusalem we should also have perished." The Lord, who had earlier told Lehi to prophesy that Jerusalem would be destroyed, now, in the New World, showed him the fulfillment of that prophecy.

The Desert Journal

The description of wandering in the wilderness (1 Nephi 16:11–17, 33; 17:1–6) also seems to have been paraphrased by Nephi from the record Lehi kept. Possibly Nephi himself made the original record of his family's journey in the desert (perhaps acting as scribe for Lehi), but the way Nephi speaks of this account makes it seem a record originally written by Lehi.

Nephi mentions the desert journal twice in 1 Nephi 19:1–2. In verse one, when listing the sources he used for the large plates, Nephi includes "the record of my father, and also [the record of] our journeyings in the wilderness, and the prophecies of my father." Note that Nephi mentions the desert journal between the items from Lehi. Only after stating what sources he employed from his father does Nephi say, "and also many of mine own prophecies have I engraven upon them" (1 Nephi 19:1).

Verse two presents a similar picture. Once again Nephi announces the sources he drew from in composing his record on the large plates: "The record of my father, and the genealogy of his fathers, and the more part of all our proceedings in the wilderness." Again Nephi associates the "proceedings" of the desert period with his father's account. Consequently, the desert journal almost certainly came from Lehi's pen. Years later, when Nephi was making his record on the small plates, this desert journal undoubtedly proved helpful in filling out Nephi's memory of hazy or forgotten details.

Doctrines and Prophecies

The material quoted or summarized from Lehi's records contains some of the most powerful doctrine and far-reaching prophecies in the entire Book of Mormon. Much of what we know about such basic gospel doctrines as loyalty in the marriage relationship, the Fall, the expected Savior, and the house of Israel, we learn from Lehi.

One doctrine often overlooked as being from Lehi is found in his son Jacob's teachings on fidelity in marriage (see Jacob 2:23–33). At first glance Jacob appears to be repeating instructions he received directly from the Lord, following the Lord's direction to declare "the word which I shall give thee unto this people" (Jacob 2:11). However, a more careful look at chapter two shows us that although the counsel concerning one wife indeed came from the Lord, Jacob was not the first to receive it. Lehi was the source for these directions.

For following what must be the Lord's own words (Jacob 2:23–33, with only the first part of verse twenty-seven being Jacob's statement), we find this: "My brethren, ye know that these commandments [concerning a husband's loyalty to his wife] were given to our father, Lehi; wherefore, ye have known them before; and ye have come unto great condemnation; for ye have done these things which ye ought not to have done" (Jacob 2:34). Clearly Lehi was the one who first received these beautiful teachings from the Lord. Jacob, then, mostly likely quoted from Lehi's record.

As we might expect in a book planned to be a witness of Jesus Christ, many teachings and prophecies that Nephi took from Lehi's record are about the Savior. For instance, although we have only a short summary of Lehi's preaching in Jerusalem, we learn that he prophesied not only of the destruction of Jerusalem but also of the coming of the Messiah and the redemption of the world, information gained in his vision of the book (see 1 Nephi 1:19).

A more complete account of the Savior's life and redeeming role in the plan of salvation is found in Lehi's later sermons. This knowledge apparently came to him in connection with his vision of the tree of life (see 1 Nephi 10). Nephi recorded an apparent direct quotation from Lehi's record about what the forerunner of the Messiah would say (see 10:8). Much more detail on this topic was given as part of Lehi's blessing to Jacob (see 2 Nephi 2). There we learn such important truths as the role of the fall in the plan of salvation, the necessity of commandments, and the reasons for and effects of the Atonement.

Many of Lehi's teachings and prophecies are found in the record of his last blessings and instructions to his family before his death (see 2 Nephi 1:1–4:12). This account, using Lehi's own words, is clearly a direct quotation from his record. Written in the first person, it is doubtless part of what Nephi referred to when he said that Lehi's record contained "many things which he prophesied and spake unto his children" (1 Nephi 1:16). In these last blessings, Lehi taught his children principles for successful living in the promised land and prophesied of a time when his posterity would reject their Redeemer and rebel against the principles of righteousness. They would then lose the lands of their inheritance and be "scattered and smitten" (2 Nephi 1:11).

Even after picturing these difficulties, Lehi assured his family that their descendants would survive the disasters. Eventually, a special seer would bring to pass "much restoration unto the house of Israel, and unto the seed of thy brethren" (2 Nephi 3:24). Lehi also prophesied that the record his people kept would spread to the survivors of his seed and then to all parts of the world (see 2 Nephi 3:18–21).

Another significant teaching, in Lehi's final blessing to his son Jacob, concerned "opposition in all things." Lehi began by indicating that the judgment must lead either to "punishment that is affixed [assigned]" or else to "happiness which is affixed" (2 Nephi 2:10). He then reasoned: "It must needs be, that there is an opposition in all things. If not so . . . righteousness could not be brought to pass, neither wickedness, neither holiness nor misery, neither good nor bad" (2 Nephi 2:11).

Lehi taught that without choices we are unable to be or feel righteous or unrighteous. Note the dramatic result that Lehi said would follow: "If these things are not there is no God. And if there is no God we are not, neither the earth; for there could have been no creation" (2 Nephi 2:13). According to Lehi, all of existence would cease and make no sense if opposition were removed. This observation led Lehi to say: "Wherefore, this thing must needs destroy the wisdom of God and his eternal purposes, and also the power, and the mercy, and the justice of God" (2 Nephi 2:12). Since Lehi had just previously been dealing with the redemption to come through the Messiah (2 Nephi 2:6–10), we should probably understand this series of passages in terms of the Redeemer's work. That is, if there exists no opposition, there is no reason for a redeemer who can bring about God's mercy and justice.

Closely related to the teachings about opposition is Lehi's understanding of the role of Adam and Eve in the drama of salvation (see 2 Nephi 2:15–27). Lehi insisted that two ingredients were essential in our first parents' situation—a choice, along with freedom to choose. There had to be "an opposition; even the forbidden fruit in opposition to the tree of life. . . . Wherefore, the Lord God gave unto man that he should act for himself" (2 Nephi 2:15–16).

For Lehi, the opposition facing Adam and Eve was necessary so that they could make the choice that could bring about mankind's mortal existence. In fact, if they had not been enticed to make that choice, which brought about both mortality and the ability to become parents, the earth would never have been peopled. This would have frustrated God's plan: "If Adam had not transgressed he would not have fallen, but he would have remained in the garden of Eden. . . . They would have had no children. . . . Adam fell that men might be" (2 Nephi 2:22–23, 25). So from Lehi we have the clearest explanation of why the fall was a necessary part of the plan of salvation.

We have seen repeatedly in Nephi's and Jacob's records that Lehi's account was a rich source of the knowledge the sons have given us. They owe to Lehi—and they acknowledge it—many precious items of revelation and instruction about the gospel. Neither son set out consciously to present and interpret his father's record for future readers. But they were so deeply and broadly influenced by their father that much of what we learn from them originated with Lehi. His life and teachings, as preserved in the sons' accounts, beautifully served their purpose in writing—"to persuade our children, and also our brethren, to believe in Christ, and to be reconciled to God" (2 Nephi 25:23). Because they turned to him for light, we benefit by the legacy a great prophet and patriarch left.

Chapter 2

MORMON AS EDITOR

Grant R. Hardy

The Book of Mormon, to the dismay of critics and believers alike, is a very complex book. This complexity disturbs critics because it makes it hard for them to believe that anyone in the nineteenth century could have written the book. This complexity also taxes the patience of Latter-day Saints who may be looking for simple, straightforward answers. But the Book of Mormon is neither simple nor straightforward. It presents itself as a translation of an ancient record. Furthermore, much of it is an abridgment of numerous sources compiled and edited by the prophet-historian Mormon.

The Book of Mormon is not like the *Congressional Record* — it does not try to include everything. Again and again, Mormon reminded us that he had to drastically condense his sources. "This book cannot contain even a hundredth part of what was done among so many people," he wrote, "but behold there are records which do contain all the proceedings of this people" (3 Nephi 5:8–9). Thus Mormon's concern over what to leave out must have been as great as his anxiety over what to include. On every page, he was making choices, and his decisions tell us a great deal about him — what he valued, what he believed, what he thought his readers ought to know. As we read the Book of Mormon, we must constantly ask, "Why is this story or detail included? What is being left out? Why do the events take this form or sequence?"

We can learn much about Mormon's priorities and purposes when we identify patterns in the type of details he chose to delete or include. For instance, his editing may be responsible for some of the more puzzling features of the Book of Mormon, such as its fascination with war (Mormon himself was a general) and its lack of attention to the law of Moses (Mormon, as a Christian, may have thought the space could be better used on other, more Christian topics).

Mormon's choices are most revealing when the message of his editing seems to contradict the facts that he recorded. Mormon's honesty as a historian sometimes forced him to include facts that did not exactly support the message he was trying to convey. This tension is frequent in the Book of Mormon as Mormon tried to make spiritual sense of historical events. For me at least, this tension is evidence that Mormon was an actual person, since we all face similar difficulties in making sense of our own lives.

In studying Mormon's editing, we are not striking out in an entirely new direction. Biblical scholars have had long experience with similar ancient edited texts in the Old and New Testaments. By looking at how they have approached the Bible as an edited text, we can gain insights into how we might study the Book of Mormon and what we might discover. In addition, if this type of analysis works on the Book of Mormon, that would be strong evidence that it too is a genuinely ancient text.

Biblical Editing

To consider the effect that editors had on the Bible, we must first determine what sources biblical editors used. This is difficult because, unlike the Book of Mormon, the Bible does not always admit its extensive editing. In any case the sources have long been lost. Nevertheless, by reading carefully and observing contexts, repetitions, sudden shifts in style and ideology, and passages where things do not fit together smoothly, we can make educated guesses about the original sources. In short, they look for rough spots in the text, or "seams" that do not quite fit together. Some examples might help to make this clear.

The original Greek in Philippians 2:5–11 is quite poetic, but the surrounding material is not. Most scholars are convinced that Paul was there quoting an early Christian hymn. In John 14:31, after two chapters of farewell discourse, Jesus said to his disciples, "Arise, let us go hence." But instead of leaving, he continued speaking for two more chapters. Perhaps the best explanation for this puzzling remark is that John used two separate accounts of Jesus' last discourse. When he combined them into one narrative, he did not quite smooth out this seam.

Another example in the Old Testament shows even more details that do not fit together smoothly. In the familiar story of David and Goliath, David was introduced as a "stripling" or a "youth" (1 Samuel 17:33, 56) whom his father had sent to the battlefield with provisions for his three older brothers (17:17–20). He was outfitted with Saul's armor (17:38–39), but instead chose to face Goliath with only his sling. Yet earlier in 1 Samuel, another version of the situation seems to exist. There David was first described to Saul as "a mighty valiant man, and a man of war" (1 Samuel 16:18), whom Saul summoned and made his armor-bearer (16:19–21). This was presumably why he was at the battlefield. (Notice that the story seems to start all over again at 17:12.)

In 17:15 someone appears to have tried to harmonize the two accounts by having David return home after serving Saul. But this runs counter to Saul's request in 16:22, which implies a more permanent arrangement. The explanation doesn't explain why in 17:55–58 Saul had no idea who David was when he saw him go against Goliath. One simple explanation of the discrepancies is that the author-editor combined at least two different accounts. The story reads fairly smoothly if we take out 17:12–31, 41, 50, and 55–58. In fact, the Septuagint, a translation of the Old Testament into Greek made about 200 B.C. (this was the Bible used by early Christians), omits these very verses, and there is evidence that they may have been added later.

In some cases when we find evidence that an editor was using multiple sources, we can compare the edited version with an original source. Then we can look for patterns that reveal the purposes behind the editor's choices. The New Testament is an excellent place to attempt this type of analysis, since it often contains multiple accounts of the same event, as in the Gospels. Similarities in the original Greek wording and in the sequence of events make it virtually certain that at least some of the Gospel writers knew the work of others. The most accepted hypothesis is that Luke and Matthew both had read Mark and Q, a collection of Jesus' sayings that is now lost.

We see how this works in the story of Jesus walking on the water. Mark reported: "When they saw him walking upon the sea, they supposed it had been a spirit, and cried out: for they all saw him, and were troubled. And immediately he talked with them, and saith unto them, Be of good cheer: it is I; be not afraid. And he went up unto them into the ship; and the wind ceased: and they were sore amazed in themselves beyond measure, and wondered. For they considered not the miracle of the loaves: for their heart was hardened" (Mark 6:49–52).

Matthew, however, added the episode of Peter walking on the water and changed the ending: "When the disciples saw him walking on the sea, they were troubled, saying, It is a spirit; and they cried out for fear. But straightway Jesus spake unto them, saying, Be of good cheer; it is I; be not afraid. [Here follows the story of Peter]. And when they were come into the ship, the wind ceased. Then they that were in the ship came and worshipped him, saying, Of a truth thou art the Son of God" (Matthew 14:26–27, 32–33).

Why would Matthew make these changes? We can surmise that he might have felt that Mark's account omitted some important features and that it put the apostles in a bad light. Thus Matthew concluded his version with the apostles' recognition of Jesus' divinity rather than with their lack of understanding. This type of editorial change occurs throughout Matthew's gospel. He consistently changed verses where Mark had left the apostles misunderstanding or doubting to show that the apostles really did have faith (compare Mark 8:17–21 with Matthew 16:8–12; Mark 9:30–32 with Matthew 17:22–23). This editorial pattern is an important clue to understanding the purpose of Matthew's gospel. It may even be evidence that he wrote his book at a time when the apostles' authority was being questioned.

This approach to reading scripture—looking for contradictions and passages that do not fit together smoothly—may be unfamiliar to many Latter-day Saints. But it is important if we wish to know the relationship between the text and the events it relates and the men who wrote and edited it. Understanding their purposes in editing may be as important as understanding the events they described and the teachings they recorded.

I believe that the Book of Mormon is capable of being studied as a historical record. This necessarily involves looking at its more human aspects—including the personal and sometimes awkward choices of its human editor. (This kind of analysis, though, does provide evidence that Mormon was indeed a historical figure and a primary author of the Book of Mormon, which is, after all, Mormon's book.) Understanding the book as a historical record can help us in understanding its divine messages and inspiration.

Mormon's Editing

Unlike most of the biblical text, the Book of Mormon text readily acknowledges editing, and we are told quite a bit about the sources used. We can often see where primary sources are worked into Mormon's abridgment. We can also assume that, for nearly any passage, Mormon had much more information than he included. On the other hand, distinguishing Mormon's paraphrases from the original words of authors like Mosiah or Alma is virtually impossible. Perhaps the greatest difficulty is that we have Mormon's record only in translation. Important patterns are often clear only in the original languages. Nevertheless, careful reading and thinking can still give us some idea of how the Book of Mormon was put together. Like biblical scholars, we must rely on the observation of subtle contradictions and details that do not quite fit.

In looking at editing in the Book of Mormon, we will be primarily concerned with trying to determine the biases and purposes behind Mormon's editorial choices. I believe that two major tendencies are evident: he interpreted political events in spiritual terms, and he highlighted the distinction between the obedient and the disobedient. We see both of these in Mosiah 25.

After complex plot twists in which one group after another was lost in the wilderness, the peoples of Alma, Limhi, and Mosiah were finally all reunited in Zarahemla. Mormon reported: "Alma did speak unto them, when they were assembled together in large bodies, and he went from one body to another, preaching unto the people repentance and faith on the Lord. And he did exhort the people of Limhi and his brethren, all those that had been delivered out of bondage, that they should remember that it was the Lord that did deliver them" (Mosiah 25:15–16).

Two assumptions about this passage seem reasonable: Limhi and his brethren made up one of these large bodies of people, and Mormon had access to records of Alma's words to each of these groups. Mormon mentioned general preachings of repentance and faith, but the only specific instruction he recounted was the exhortation to Limhi's people to remember that the Lord was responsible for their deliverance. Why is this detail so important that it alone received attention when so much else was left out?

This editorial choice is especially puzzling when we recall that Limhi's people had freed themselves by getting their Lamanite guards drunk (see Mosiah 22). We even know the name of the man who concocted the scheme—Gideon. We also remember the conference in which Ammon and Limhi "began to consult with the people how they should deliver themselves out of bondage" (22:1). Their liberation seemed to be the result of sheer cunning—chapter twenty-two does not mention God once. And yet in chapter twenty-five, Mormon's editing stressed that, despite appearances, God delivered Limhi's people just as much as he did Alma's people (who had made a miraculous escape, recorded in Mosiah 24:16–25).

Of course this is precisely the point behind Mormon's editing—no matter what we may think about our own resource-fulness, decisiveness, and timing, God is still in charge. Mormon tended to interpret political and historical events in spiritual terms, and this inclination is evident in his editing as well as in his direct "thus we see" comments.

But there is more to Mosiah 25. A few verses earlier Mormon explained how the people had gathered together to hear readings of the records of Zeniff and Alma. He describes their reaction as follows:

> [7] Now, when Mosiah had made an end of reading the records, his people who tarried in the land were struck with wonder and amazement. [8] For they knew not what to think; for when they beheld those that had been delivered out of bondage they were filled with ex-ceedingly great joy. [9] And again, when they thought of their brethren who had been slain by the Lamanites they were filled with sorrow, and even shed many tears of sorrow. [10] And again, when they thought of the immediate goodness of God, and his power in delivering Alma and his brethren out of the hands of the Lamanites and of bondage, they did raise their voices and give thanks to God. [11] And again, when they thought upon the Lamanites, who were their brethren, of their sinful and polluted state, they were filled with pain and anguish for the welfare of their souls.

If one tries to imagine this scene, the importance of Mor-mon's editing becomes obvious. The people were undoubtedly moved by what they had heard. Yet are we to suppose that the people in unison thought of each of these things in turn, with one voice weeping and then praising as if on cue? (Remember that this behavior was described as occurring after the reading had finished.) Or is it more probable that some shed tears while others rejoiced, each reflecting individually on the great events that had been recounted?

The reactions of crowds are difficult to describe. Here, though Mormon apparently took a few liberties with the actual event, he established a vivid sense of the emotions that the people must have felt. Perhaps more importantly, Mormon's account is itself moving. Note how it shifts back and forth from joy in verse eight to sorrow in verse nine, to praise in verse ten, and back to pain and anguish in verse eleven. In each case, the pains of the disobedient contrast sharply and immediately with the joys of the obedient. The exposition of God's justice is clear, simple, and concise, and it owes its striking form to Mormon's editorial hand.

This type of editing is characteristic of the entire Book of Mormon. For example, Jacob described his editorial technique as follows: "Now the people which were not Lamanites were Nephites; nevertheless, they were called Nephites, Jacobites, Josephites, Zoramites, Lamanites, Lemuelites, and Ishmaelites. But I, Jacob, shall not hereafter distinguish them by these names, but I shall call them Lamanites that seek to destroy the people of Nephi, and those who are friendly to Nephi I shall call Nephites, or the people of Nephi, according to the reigns of the kings" (Jacob 1:13–14). Jacob informed us that his society was actually much more complex than it might appear. For the purposes of this record, however, he would drastically simplify the situation. Mormon continued this editorial style (see Alma 47:35, Mormon 1:8–9). But why? Why not give us the whole story?

The answer in part lies in Mormon's purpose, which was not to give an exact historical account of ancient Nephite culture, but rather to turn our hearts to God. One of the ways the Book of Mormon does this is by emphasizing that those who follow God are blessed, while those who reject him suffer. This theme was introduced in the book's second chapter when the Lord said to Nephi, "Inasmuch as ye shall keep my commandments, ye shall prosper, and shall be led to a land of promise. . . . Inasmuch as thy brethren shall rebel against thee, they shall be cut off from the presence of the Lord" (1 Nephi 2:20–21). The idea is repeated frequently throughout the Book of Mormon, and Nephi, Mormon, and others gave concrete examples to reinforce this theme.

22

The problem, however, is that life is more complicated than this. We all know of instances in which good people suffer while the evil go unpunished. And most people are neither entirely righteous nor wholly wicked. Yet because the principle of God's justice is ultimately true, Mormon helped us out in the Book of Mormon by simplifying stories so that we can clearly see the results of good and bad behavior. Thanks to Mormon's careful editing, there is no question as to who is righteous and who is wicked, and that the bad things that happen are truly terrible, while the good things are wondrous indeed.

We seem to have clear evidence in Mosiah 25 of Mormon's editing and the intentions that lay behind it, but the analysis of one chapter does not constitute conclusive proof. As we found in biblical scholarship, if we can identify clear patterns of editing, our arguments will be much stronger. Therefore, let us turn to another chapter—Alma 16, which tells of the destruction of Ammonihah, is another instance. Again, Mormon simplified to make moral lessons easier to identify and offered spiritual interpretations for political events.

The preceding chapters of Alma (8–15) recorded the story of Alma and Amulek's mission to Ammonihah, recounting their sermons and telling how, despite limited success, they were eventually rejected and thrown into prison. Then, in an act of terrible brutality, the people of Ammonihah drove Alma's male converts from the city and burned to death their wives and children. Finally Alma and Amulek were miraculously delivered from prison. Alma 16 begins as follows:

> [1] And it came to pass in the eleventh year of the reign of the judges over the people of Nephi, on the fifth day of the second month, there having been much peace in the land of Zarahemla, there having been no wars nor contentions for a certain number of years, even until the fifth day of the second month in the eleventh year, there was a cry of war heard throughout the land. [2] For behold, the armies of the Lamanites had come in upon the wilderness side, into the borders of the land, even

into the city of Ammonihah, and began to slay the people
and destroy the city. [3] And now it came to pass, before
the Nephites could raise a sufficient army to drive them
out of the land, they had destroyed the people who were
in the city of Ammonihah, and also some around the
borders of Noah, and taken others captive into the wilderness.

Mormon continued his tale by telling how the Nephite armies, with the help of the prophetic high priest Alma, defeated
the Lamanites and rescued the captives. Then Mormon made
the moral of his story absolutely clear. His editorial summary
stressed that "there was not one soul of them had been lost that
were taken captive," while "the people of Ammonihah were
destroyed; yea, every living soul of the Ammonihahites was
destroyed . . . and the carcases were mangled by dogs and wild
beasts of the wilderness" (16:8–10 — remember, the bad things
that happen are truly terrible, while the good things are wondrous indeed). Thus this chapter offers a striking illustration of
God's justice, by which the righteous are saved while the wicked
are punished.

But something is wrong with this picture. The innocent by-
standers are all rescued, and the wicked Ammonihahites are all
destroyed, but there is a third group not mentioned at all in
Mormon's summary. These are the people "around the borders
of Noah," some of whom were also killed in the Lamanite raid.
What exactly had happened to them? Why did some die and
some escape? We do not know, for they dropped entirely out
of Mormon's account and were never referred to again.

Mormon obviously had some information about them (thus
he mentioned them in verse three), but he chose not to elaborate
upon their fate. He edited them out. Why? I believe the answer
is that these people did not fit into the pattern of "the righteous
prosper, the wicked suffer." They complicated the moral message of his history. This is not to say that Mormon's message is
false. The principle of God's justice is, in an ultimate sense, true,

but the facts of day-to-day history do not always illustrate this principle adequately.

The purpose of the Book of Mormon makes the spiritual meaning of history much more important than any specific set of facts. Mormon was willing to simplify or streamline the facts to emphasize transcendent spiritual realities. He did not want too many complicated details to distract us from simple, vitally important truths. This type of editorial bias is complicated, for it involves the careful balancing of moral interpretation and historical accuracy. It was important to Mormon that his spiritual principles were manifested in actual events—the Book of Mormon is not a work of abstract theology, and Mormon did not make up stories to illustrate his principles. This editorial bias seems to be a constant in Mormon's editing. And it is all the more impressive for not being explicit.

Alma 16 also provides an example of interpreting a political event in spiritual terms. The first verse is remarkable for Mormon's insistence that this Lamanite raid was absolutely unexpected and unprovoked, "there having been much peace in the land of Zarahemla, there having been no wars nor contentions for a certain number of years." Given the juxtaposition of this event with the gross wickedness of the people of Ammonihah in the preceding chapters, the meaning is clear. An act of God destroyed the Ammonihahites in retribution for their arrogance, brutality, and rejection of his prophets.

Mormon reinforced this reading by framing the destruction within a prophecy. His editorial summary included the observation, "Their great city [was destroyed], which they said God could not destroy, because of its greatness. But behold, in one day it was left desolate" (16:9–10). Here Mormon was referring to an exchange that took place at the story's beginning. There the people of Ammonihah had rejected Alma's message with the words, "We will not believe thy words if thou shouldst prophesy that this great city should be destroyed in one day." Mormon there commented, "Now they knew not that God could do such marvelous works, for they were a hard-hearted and a stiffnecked people" (Alma 9:4–5; see also the predictions at Alma 9:18; 10:23). Clearly, Ammonihah's destruction was a marvelous work of God manifesting his divine power and justice.

However, Alma 25:2 alerts us to another possibility. Just as multiple versions of the same story make it difficult to miss the editing in Matthew and Mark, so also Mormon's editorial biases become obvious when we consider a second account of the city's destruction. It turns out that the city of Ammonihah was not destroyed as if by lightning from heaven. There was a natural series of causes and effects that led to the Lamanite raid. This series of events was begun by Ammon and his brethren, the great Nephite missionaries to the Lamanites.

Alma 17 begins a flashback that takes us back some fourteen years by relating the missionary adventures of the sons of Mosiah (Ammon and his brethren). These men, after years of afflictions and miracles, eventually enjoyed great success. They converted thousands of the Lamanites, who took the name Anti-Nephi-Lehies and entered into a close relationship with the Nephites. Other Lamanites, incited by Nephite dissenters, were furious and took up arms against their former comrades. The pacifist Anti-Nephi-Lehies chose to die rather than fight, and more than one thousand were killed.

Now Alma 25:

> [1] Those Lamanites were more angry because they had slain their brethren; therefore they swore vengeance upon the Nephites; and they did no more attempt to slay the people of Anti-Nephi-Lehi at that time. [2] But they took their armies and went over into the borders of the land of Zarahemla, and fell upon the people who were in the land of Ammonihah and destroyed them. [3] And after that, they had many battles with the Nephites, in the which they were driven and slain.

Here the flashback parallels the main narrative, but it does not entirely catch up until Alma 27:16, which continues the story from 17:5 and unites the two narratives. Such flashbacks and multiple accounts are complex editorial maneuvers, but Mormon

26

handled them fairly smoothly. Nevertheless, there are still evidences of extensive editing. For example, the "many battles" of 25:3 and 27:1 do not quite correspond to the account in 16:6–9, where the Lamanites were driven back after one great battle. Again I believe that Mormon was intent in chapter sixteen on not unduly complicating his narrative with unnecessary details that might distract the reader from more important spiritual truths.

Mormon included in the Book of Mormon two separate narrative strands that both included an account of Ammonihah's destruction. However, the explanation given in each version is quite different. One is spiritual (due to God's justice) and one political (due to Lamanite aggressions in the aftermath of Anti-Nephi-Lehi troubles). Yet significantly, Mormon did not see any contradiction between the two; it was simply a matter of different perspectives. Apparently God's will is sometimes manifest through ordinary historical means.

One last reference will complete our discussion of Alma 16. In Alma 49, Mormon returned to the destruction of Ammonihah once more when several years later the Lamanites came again to attack Ammonihah, now rebuilt. Mormon resumed his spiritual mode of interpretation when he reported their motives: "Because the Lamanites had destroyed it once because of the iniquity of the people, they supposed that it would again become an easy prey for them" (v. 3). Yet the venture was unsuccessful, and the disappointed Lamanite armies moved on to the city of Noah (home of our edited-out unfortunates). However, in this passage Mormon offered a military explanation of the Nephites' earlier losses there: "The city of Noah had hitherto been the weakest part of the land" (v. 15). Apparently Mormon did know more about the slaughtered people of Noah, but what he knew he did not mention in chapter sixteen because it did not fit in with the moral theme of that account.

Conclusions

Mormon was, as he himself stated, a purposeful editor. His hand can be seen throughout the Book of Mormon. He wove together complex narratives full of multiple strands, flashbacks, and interpretive comments. But perhaps even more impressive are the many places where he covertly interpreted his history through his choices of what to include, what to omit, and how to arrange his account so that it best fulfilled its objective of bringing souls to God. I have identified two aspects of his editing—simplification to highlight moral themes, and spiritual interpretation of political events. There are undoubtedly many more to be found, but these two techniques are significant in the Book of Mormon, and also in our larger Latter-day Saint culture.

Our lives are often complicated jumbles of good and bad, fortune and failure; and religion helps us make sense of them. We have adopted not only the doctrines taught directly in the Book of Mormon, but also Mormon's narrative style. In any testimony meeting, we encounter highly edited stories that pick out significant events and find spiritual meaning in situations that outsiders might regard as coincidental or commonplace. We tell stories of overcoming adversity, of gaining understanding, and of serving others.

Through these narratives, we affirm that those who follow God are blessed, while those who reject him suffer. Thoughtful members may struggle with the contradictions between actual and ideal history, but Mormon has provided a model for making greater spiritual truths discernable. A close reading of the Book of Mormon should include a careful analysis of Mormon's editing, for editing was the way he shaped his history to make it the bearer of God's word.

Chapter 3

MORMON'S EDITORIAL PROMISES

John A. Tvedtnes

An author may promise in the course of writing to return to a subject later to supply further details. Actually keeping such a promise can prove difficult. Even with modern writing aids, memory can betray a person into failing to tuck in the corners of plot or information. Mormon, the editor of much of the Book of Mormon as we have it, made these types of promises at least seven times. In each case, he or his son Moroni followed through perfectly.

The seven cases where Mormon promised to elaborate on some point are as follows:

○ Mormon spoke in Mosiah 21:35 of Limhi's people, saying that "an account of their baptism shall be given hereafter." Almost a hundred verses followed before he told in Mosiah 25:17–18 about that ordinance being performed.

○ The preaching mission of the sons of Mosiah was related in Alma 17–25, eighteen chapters after Mormon had said in Mosiah 28:9 and 19–20 that he would later tell about it.

○ In Alma 35:13, Mormon promised to describe the Nephite-Lamanite war that began in the eighteenth year. But, since he proposed first to copy Alma's teachings to his sons, he postponed the story of the war until Alma 43, where in verse three he introduced the topic with the words, "And now I return to an account of the wars."

○ Writing in Mosiah 28:11–19, Mormon said that he would later give the story of the Jaredites. He made this statement at the point where he mentioned that King Mosiah had translated the record of that people. Apparently the problems he faced in his role as commander of the Nephite armies in his people's battles against the Lamanites kept him from abridging the Jaredite record. But his son, Moroni, fulfilled the promise by giving us the Book of Ether. So Moroni preserved the Book of Mormon editorial pattern of not failing to cover what was promised, even though it took a generation.

o Third Nephi 18:36–37 contains Mormon's statement that Jesus had given his twelve disciples "power to give the Holy Ghost." He added, "I will show unto you hereafter that this record is true." In the next chapter, verse thirteen, he described how the Holy Ghost fell on the twelve after their baptism. Then at 4 Nephi 1:1, he wrote that those baptized by the twelve "did also receive the Holy Ghost." Further consistency was shown in Moroni's later quotation of Christ's words to the twelve, which Mormon had left out in 3 Nephi 18 where they logically might have been given: "Ye shall have power that to him upon whom ye shall lay your hands, ye shall give the Holy Ghost" (Moroni 2:2). He then added, "On as many as they laid their hands, fell the Holy Ghost" (v. 3). The reporting of the matter involved two prophets and four distinct passages of scripture, but eventually nothing was left out of the story.

o What is in our present scripture under the title the Words of Mormon serves as an editorial bridge between the book of Omni on the small plates and the book of Mosiah in Mormon's abridgment of the large plates. In verse two of Words of Mormon, Mormon said he hoped that his son Moroni would write "concerning Christ." That hope was realized about 350 pages later when Moroni told important matters concerning the Savior in Ether 3:17–20 and in 12:7, 16–22, and 38–41. At the very end of the whole volume (Mormon 9 and Moroni 2, 6, 7, 10), the son included his own testimony of Christ.

o In Helaman 2:12–14, Mormon said that he would speak more of Gadianton and his secret band "hereafter." Indeed he did. The problems caused by the robbers and much about their characteristics were detailed in Helaman 6; 3 Nephi 1:27–29; 2:11–

18; 3:1–4:29; and beyond in 4 Nephi and Mormon. The editorial comments in Helaman 2:12–14 are particularly interesting, for they show how Mormon thought and worked in carrying out his task of preparing the Nephite record.

In 2:4 we read of the "secret work of murder and of robbery." If these acts were secret, how is it that the record told so much about them? That there were murderers was of course obvious to the people of the time, but they could have known nothing about any plan or society that was indeed secret. Only later, in the period reported in Helaman 6, was the Gadianton band discovered and some of them were arrested. Perhaps their confessions revealed the secret. We can see that Mormon, the historian writing years later, would have been aware of those later events when he edited what we see as Helaman 2, so he could refer to "secret work."

If following through on editorial promises to return to a subject is difficult in writing, it is even harder done in haste with no written record to serve as a reminder of the promises made. In 1829 Joseph Smith dictated to Oliver Cowdery most of the scripture attributed to Mormon within the period of a few weeks, and without proofreading or revising. Under these circumstances, if Joseph were the original author, then leaving no gaps in the promised materials would have been a remarkable achievement. This makes it much more likely that Joseph was translating rather than creating, and that the editorial consistency is Mormon's work.

Chapter 4

COLOPHONS IN THE BOOK
OF MORMON

John A. Tvedtnes

In the heading before chapter 1 of 1 Nephi, we find
Nephi's outline of his record. It begins, "An account
of Lehi and his wife Sariah, and his four sons," and ends, "This
is according to the account of Nephi; or in other words, I, Nephi,
wrote this record." Sometimes these signposts appear before a
section to tell us what is to come. Other times, they appear at
the end to explain, recap, or mark the end of what has been
said. For lack of a better word, I call them colophons, though
technically colophons are notes or guidelines after a text.

Nephi set the pattern. He wrote his own titles, prefaces,
summaries, and conclusions. All of 1 Nephi 9 consists of Nephi's
statement about what he had been recording in the previous
eight chapters and what he intended yet to write. Note too the
subtle signal of his editorial guiding hand in the "amen" ending
the chapter. In 1 Nephi 14 he summarized the preceding chapters
and again concluded with "Amen." Other clear-cut examples
are in 15:36 and in 22:31, which ends the book of 1 Nephi.

We understand from 2 Nephi 5:28–33 that Nephi began writing the small plates account—what was to become 1 Nephi
through Omni—some thirty years after Lehi and Nephi left Jerusalem. Having a clear plan in mind when he began as to what
to include on the small plates, Nephi could begin his book with
the colophon that sounds like a table of contents.

In his editorial labors, Mormon followed Nephi's lead,[1] providing prefaces for the books he abridged. In addition, he wrote
introductions to pieces of original material he put into the on-

going abridgment he was making of the Nephite story. Mormon's statements are helpful in seeing how he went about preparing his materials.

The Words of Mormon

The Words of Mormon, though only about two pages, comprises a distinct book. It is chiefly — at least verses one through nine — a long editorial comment on how Mormon handled the records. The remaining nine verses simply provide a word bridge needed to carry the history down to the time of King Benjamin. From Mormon's account in that book, we know that he made it after abridging the history on the large plates to King Benjamin's reign. The book itself in its entirety thus acts as a colophon.

Mosiah

The lack of a preface for the book of Mosiah in the present Book of Mormon is probably because the text takes up the Mosiah account some time after its original beginning. The original manuscript of the Book of Mormon, written in Oliver Cowdery's hand, has no title for the Book of Mosiah. It was inked in later, prior to sending it to the printer for typesetting. The first part of Mormon's abridgment of Mosiah's record, including the colophon, was evidently on the 116 pages lost by Martin Harris.

After the Nephite colonies of Alma and Limhi came to the land of Zarahemla, King Mosiah II put directly into his record the writings of these two small groups (see Mosiah 25:5). He started in 9:1 with a first-person account by Zeniff. But before chapter 9, there is a preface, presumably Mormon's, beginning, "The Record of Zeniff — An account of his people. . . . " At Mosiah 10:22, Zeniff marked the end of his words with an editorial comment and the typical "Amen."

Mosiah 23 and 24 tell about Alma's colony. Mormon introduced them with this preface: "An account of Alma and the people of the Lord, who were driven into the wilderness by the people of king Noah." Finally Mormon signaled us at Mosiah 29:47 that all of what he calls the book of Mosiah had come to an end.

Alma

The book of Alma begins with a preface and ends with a summary statement in the last verse. In between there are a number of subdivisions set off by editorial statements. Mormon divided his abridgment of the book of Alma into (1) the record of Alma, which ends at 44:24 with "And thus ended the record of Alma"; (2) the record of Helaman, which is introduced by a preface between chapters 44 and 45 and which ends with an editorial statement in the last verse of chapter 62; and (3) the record of Shiblon, which is marked by statements at its beginning in 63:1 and its end at 63:11.

Mormon further subdivided his abridgment of Alma's own record in the book of Alma. A preface at the beginning of Alma 5 informs us that what follows consists of "The words which Alma . . . delivered." At 6:8, Mormon closed this extract from Alma's record with an editorial statement complete with "Amen." Alma 7 is a similar extract marked with colophons at its beginning and end. Note that current LDS editions of the Book of Mormon place the beginning prefaces for chapters 5 and 7 before the chapter numbers, as at Mosiah 23. Note also that, though the type is the same, Mormon's editorial words are distinct from those of the chapter summaries, which Orson Pratt first added in 1879.

The story of the mission of Alma and Amulek in the city of Ammonihah in Alma 9–15 also begins with a preface. Much, though not all, of the record is in the first person, as in the case of Zeniff's story. Inside this section, a preface that appears in 10:1 also introduces Amulek's speech and his dialogue with Ze-ezrom. The end of Amulek's contribution, Mormon marked by a statement at 11:46: "And thus ended the words of Amulek, or this is all that I [Mormon] have written." The next two chapters consist of Alma's words, after which Mormon noted, "And Alma spake many more words unto the people, which are not written in this book" (13:31). "This book" evidently refers to Mormon's own abridgment. The editorial summary for the tenth year, at

15:19, seems to end the entry begun by the preface to chapter nine.

A preface before the start of Alma 17 introduces the missionary record of the sons of Mosiah. This part seems to me to extend only to chapter twenty (although the editors of the 1920 LDS edition supposed that the record referred to in the preface went all the way to the end of chapter twenty-eight). Note another preface before chapter twenty-one, which tells of "the preaching of Aaron, and Muloki, and their brethren, to the Lamanites." Chapter twenty-six begins with still another preface, this one contained within the first verse. Notice also the editorial words in Alma 28:8-9, which speaks of two accounts in the previous eleven chapters.

Finally, Mormon put in parts of Alma's teachings to his sons. Each of the three segments has its own preface (see text immediately before chapters thirty-six, thirty-eight, and thirty-nine). The first two end with the words, "My son, farewell," while the last, which concludes the set, ends with the word "Amen."

We see from the number of these colophons that the book of Alma demanded a great amount of editorial judgement from Mormon. He gave us what he considered gems and highlights when he might have included much more from the supply of material handed down to him from Alma's time.

Helaman

The book of Helaman begins with a lengthy preface stating that it is a record of Helaman (II), who was son of Helaman (I), and of the sons of Helaman (II). The same statement is found in Helaman 16:25. In 3:37, Mormon noted the passing of Helaman II, whom his son Nephi succeeded as judge.

A preface before chapter seven tells us that Nephi wrote the chapters of the book of Helaman after that point. Helaman 7–12 has a formal title, "The prophecy of Nephi, the son of Helaman," as well as a preface mentioning the prophecy of Samuel, which begins with chapter thirteen. The preface leads me to think that this material was an extract from a separate record in Mormon's possession. Clearly a number of men had a significant hand in producing the book of Helaman. What is not clear is why the "books" were not divided up and labeled some other way, for example, turning the single book we know as Helaman into "Helaman II," "Nephi, son of Helaman," and "Lehi, son of Helaman."

3 and 4 Nephi

A preface at the beginning of the "Book of Nephi" (i.e., 3 Nephi) provides a brief genealogical sketch going back to Lehi and including information nowhere else mentioned. Mormon also inserted some editorial comments in 3 Nephi 6:8–26, apparently triggered by his inability to include much of what had transpired in the past twenty-five years. He commented on the nature of his record-keeping and identified himself. The insert ends with the characteristic "Amen." Chapters eight through eleven, detailing the days of darkness, are also set off by colophons. Mormon began in 8:1–2 by commenting on calendar dating and the author of the material he was abridging. He ended in 10:19 with the words "Therefore for this time I make an end of my sayings."

Chapters eleven through twenty-six cover Jesus' two public visits to the New World (Mormon also recorded a private visit to the twelve disciples in chapters twenty-seven and twenty-eight). A preface before chapter eleven reports, "Jesus Christ did show himself unto the people of Nephi." Mormon ended the section with the lengthy passage in 26:6–21, where he commented on his records, summarized Christ's visits, and described the results of those visits.

Fourth Nephi begins with a long title "An account of the people of Nephi, according to his record." Mormon concluded it with the words "And thus is the end of the record of Ammaron," signaling that the book had come to its end.

Prefaces and Summaries

Knowing the details of all these editorial comments is not necessary for readers primarily concerned with reading the text for its spiritual value. They do have value, however, in a number of other ways. For students of historical documents and ancient literary forms, they provide valuable clues to the process of writing and compiling the record. Furthermore, the large number of these statements in such intricate relations both with each other and in the overall structure of the book teach us something else. They make it obvious that they came from ancient writers, not from Joseph Smith.

Considering the way Joseph dictated the book to scribes, for the most part in a matter of weeks without revising what he had dictated, we should realize that he could not himself have come up with this complicated set of prefaces and summaries. It is unlikely that he would go to the trouble to insert anything like them (they are not required to move the story along). It is also most unlikely that, while dictating, he could keep in mind what he had promised in the prefaces and then remember to close off so many sections neatly with summaries. Much more believable are the claims in the Book of Mormon itself that the record was done by ancient writers working with written materials over long periods of time.

Note

1. Mormon did not, of course, pick up this idea from the small plates, of whose existence he was ignorant when he began his abridgment. He perhaps followed the pattern set by Nephi in his large plates.

Chapter 5

NEPHI AND THE EXODUS

Terrence L. Szink

One of best-known sections of the Book of Mormon tells the story of the journey of Lehi and his family from Jerusalem to the new promised land in the American continent. Yet, since the small plates were intended to contain the "things of God" (1 Nephi 6:4), why was this account included on the small plates while other things that seem to be more the "things of God" (such as the "many things which [Lehi] saw in visions and in dreams"–1 Nephi 1:16) were left out?

Quite probably, Nephi, the author of this section, consciously wrote his account of the wilderness journey in a way that would remind the reader of the Exodus of the children of Israel from Egypt. He did this to prove that God loved and cared for the Nephites, just as the Exodus from Egypt was proof of God's favor for the children of Israel. Therefore, this story of the journey truly is about the things of God and does belong on the small plates.

The Exodus as a Background

It is important to understand that Nephi wrote this record of his family's journey at least thirty years after they had left Jerusalem (see 2 Nephi 5:28–31). In his writing, he most likely referred to what had been put down on the larger, "historical" plates or on perishable materials. He could pick and choose information from those earlier sources and shape it any way he saw fit. The result was not a day-to-day or even a year-to-year account of what had happened. Rather, it was a record that highlighted certain events and put special emphasis on "the things of God."

One of the most important "things of God" for the children of Israel was the Exodus from Egypt. That event more than any other defined them as a people. Their journey to the promised land in Canaan is recalled time and again throughout the Old Testament. Not surprisingly, then, Nephi would be reminded of the Exodus while his group made their own wilderness journey through Arabia. He was familiar with the Exodus both in story form as he might have heard it from his father and through annual Israelite rituals such as the Passover as they were acted out. He also knew about it from reading the brass plates, which included "the five book of Moses" (1 Nephi 5:10–12). He taught his brothers from those writings "that they might know concerning the doings of the Lord in other lands, among people of old" (1 Nephi 19:22–23). He might even have referred to the account of the Exodus written on the brass plates as he wrote on the small plates.

With this in mind, let us examine the account of the wilderness journey of Lehi's party and see how often it is similar to the account of the Exodus in the Bible.

The Voice of Murmuring in the Wilderness

The wilderness of Sinai and the wilderness of the Arabian peninsula were both harsh environments. Both the Israelites and the people of Lehi suffered hunger during their journeys, and they complained about it:

We did return without food to our families, and being much fatigued, because of their journeying, **they did suffer much for the want of food.** And it came to pass that **Laman and Lemuel and the sons of Ishmael did begin to murmur exceedingly,** because of their sufferings and afflictions in the wilderness; and also my father began to

The whole congregation of the children of Israel murmured against Moses and Aaron in the wilderness: and the children of Israel said unto them, . . . Ye have brought us forth into this wilderness, to kill this whole assembly with **hunger.** And Moses said, . . . The Lord heareth your murmurings which ye murmur against him: and

murmur against the Lord his God; yea, and they were all exceedingly sorrowful, even that **they did murmur against the Lord** (1 Nephi 16:19–20).	what are we? **your murmurings are not against us, but against the Lord** (Exodus 16:2–3, 8).

In both cases the uncommon word *murmur* is used. In both the Old Testament and the Book of Mormon, *murmur* is used primarily for the exoduses. Forms of the Hebrew root *lwn* (translated "to murmur" in the King James version) occur eighteen times in the Old Testament. All but one of them are connected with the Exodus. How is the English word *murmur* used in the Book of Mormon? It appears thirty-three times; of these, nineteen describe events in the Old World wilderness.

Of course we do not know exactly what word Nephi used since we do not have the original text. But this peculiar term is used with unusual frequency to describe the Book of Mormon wilderness experience in the same way that it is used almost exclusively to describe a similar experience in the Old Testament. There are two possible explanations: (1) Joseph Smith consciously copied the King James version, or (2) Nephi used the wording from the brass plates (essentially like our Bible) to remind his audience of the previous Exodus, and Joseph Smith's translation of this material was literal enough to preserve the similarity. In view of the complicated nature of the parallels between the two stories, the second explanation is far more likely.

Both the Old Testament and the Book of Mormon mention that this murmuring about the lack of food was directed against the Lord himself rather than against his prophet-leaders. The similarity continues in that the problem of food was solved miraculously. For Israel, manna from heaven was the solution. For the group in the Book of Mormon, the answer was no less wonderful. They were instructed by the Lord to look at the Liahona, their miraculous "compass." When they looked, they saw written directions that led Nephi to a place where he was able to kill game. When the family saw that he had obtained food for them, "how great was their joy! And it came to pass that they did humble themselves before the Lord, and did give thanks unto him" (1 Nephi 16:32; see also verse 39). In both cases, the Lord provided for his people in a miraculous way.

Reasonable Fears and Foolish Desires

The tough life in the two wildernesses led to fear of death, expressed several times in both the Book of Mormon and Exodus:

This he spake because of the stiffneckedness of Laman and Lemuel; for behold they did murmur in many things against their father, because he was a visionary man, and had **led them out of the land of Jerusalem,** to leave the land of their inheritance, and their gold, and their silver, and their precious things, **to perish in the wilderness.** And this they said he had done because of the foolish imaginations of his heart (1 Nephi 2:11; see also 1 Nephi 5:2; 16:35).

They said unto Moses, Because there were no graves in Egypt, **hast thou taken us away to die in the wilderness?** wherefore hast thou dealt thus with us, to **carry us forth out of Egypt?** (Exodus 14:11; see also Numbers 21:5).

This fear of death was perhaps justified given the circumstances. It was expressed as the statement that it would have been better to have died before they had gone into the wilderness:

Thou art like unto our father, led away by the foolish imaginations of his heart; yea, he hath led us out of the land of Jerusalem, and we have wandered in the wilderness for these many years; and our women have toiled, being big with child; and they have borne children in the wilder-

The children of Israel said unto them, **Would to God we had died by the hand of the Lord in the land of Egypt,** when we sat by the flesh pots, and when we did eat bread to the full; **for ye have brought us forth into this wilderness, to kill this whole assembly with hunger** (Exodus 16:3).

41

ness and suffered all things, save it were death; and **it would have been better that they had died before they came out of Jerusalem than to have suffered these afflictions** (1 Nephi 17:20).

All the children of Israel murmured against Moses and against Aaron: and the whole congregation said unto them, **Would God that we had died in the land of Egypt!** (Numbers 14:2).

At particularly stressful moments (for example, in the Book of Mormon at the death of Ishmael or in the Bible upon hearing the spies report the risks of attacking the Canaanites in the promised land), an unwise desire was expressed to return to the place they had left:

The daughters of Ishmael **did mourn exceedingly,** because of the loss of their father, and because of their afflictions in the wilderness; and **they did murmur against my father,** because he had brought them out of the land of Jerusalem, saying: Our father is dead; yea, and we have wandered much in the wilderness, and we have suffered much affliction, hunger, thirst, and fatigue; and after all these sufferings we must perish in the wilderness with hunger. And thus they did murmur against my father, and also against me; **and they were desirous to return again to Jerusalem** (1 Nephi 16:35–36).

All the congregation **lifted up their voice, and cried; and the people wept that night.** And all the children of Israel **murmured against Moses and against Aaron:** and the whole congregation said unto them, Would God that we had died in the land of Egypt! or would God we had died in this wilderness! And wherefore hath the Lord brought us unto this land, to fall by the sword, that our wives and our children should be a prey? **were it not better for us to return into Egypt? And they said one to another, Let us make a captain, and let us return into Egypt** (Numbers 14:1–4).

Note the striking similarity between the two occasions: there was crying and mourning, followed by murmuring, which finally culminated in the desire to return. This desire was irrational because, in both cases, to return could have meant death. The children of Israel likely would have been punished for the death of Pharaoh's host in the Red Sea, while Nephi, Laman, Lemuel, and Sam could well have been punished for the killing of Laban in Jerusalem.

That such fears and desires would be felt during such a difficult journey need not surprise us, but Nephi described these fears and desires in terms that remind us of the experiences of the children of Israel during their flight from Egypt. His purpose was to highlight the spiritual aspects of the events he experienced, and, from the way he highlighted them, it appears as though he was influenced by the wording of the Exodus account.

The Liahona and the Serpent

Perhaps the object that more than any other represents the wilderness journey of Lehi and his family in the minds of modern readers is the Liahona. This "round ball of curious workmanship" (1 Nephi 16:10) showed them which way to go in the wilderness, led Nephi to a source of life-saving food, and gave the group other special instructions when needed. Nephi commented concerning it, "Thus we see that by small means the Lord can bring about great things" (1 Nephi 16:29).

Much later the prophet Alma turned the Liahona over to his son Helaman, along with other sacred relics. While explaining the history of this object, Alma referred to the story of another brass object, the image of a serpent that the Lord commanded Moses to make in order to save the children of Israel from the bites of "fiery serpents":

O my son, do not let us be slothful because of the easiness of the way; for so was it with our fathers; for so was it prepared for them, that **if they would look they might live**; even so it is with us. The way is prepared, and if we	The Lord said unto Moses, Make thee a fiery serpent, and set it upon a pole: and it shall come to pass, that every one that is bitten, **when he looketh upon it, shall live.** And Moses made a serpent of brass, and put it upon a pole,

43

REDISCOVERING THE BOOK OF MORMON

will look we may live forever (Alma 37:46).	and it came to pass, that if a serpent had bitten any man, when he beheld the serpent of brass, he lived (Numbers 21:8–9).

The similarity in these cases is in the relationship between the people and the objects. To be healed, they had to act on simple faith. Obviously, both the Liahona and the serpent served as symbols of Christ. In Alma 37:38–47, the Liahona is compared to the words of Christ, which can guide us through our own trials. People must seek, pay attention, and obey to get the benefits. Regarding the serpent image, Christ himself referred to it as a symbol of both his being lifted up on the cross and his being slain. Again, the benefit could be had only by a person's acting from faith—by obedient "looking" at the object (see John 3:14–15). With both objects, the way was too easy for some to convince them to act. Referring to the metal serpent, Nephi says, "The labor which they had to perform was to look; and because of the simpleness of the way, or the easiness of it, there were many who perished" (1 Nephi 17:41).

Alma makes a similar statement regarding the Liahona: "Because those miracles were worked by small means it did show unto them marvelous works. They were slothful, and forgot to exercise their faith and diligence and then those marvelous works ceased, and they did not progress in their journey; therefore, they tarried in the wilderness, or did not travel a direct course, and were afflicted with hunger and thirst, because of their transgressions" (Alma 37:41–42).

Lead, Kindly Light

The Liahona was not the only help Lehi and his family received from the Lord. In describing this help, Nephi once again drew on the images, and apparently also the language, of Exodus:

I will also be your light in the wilderness; and I will prepare the way before you,	The Lord went before them by day in a pillar of a cloud, to lead them the way;

44

if it so be that ye shall keep my commandments; wherefore, inasmuch as ye shall keep my commandments **ye shall be led towards the promised land; and ye shall know that it is by me that ye are led.** Yea, and the Lord said also that: After ye have arrived in the promised land, **ye shall know that I, the Lord, am God; and that I, the Lord, did deliver you from destruction; yea, and I did bring you out of the land of Jerusalem** (1 Nephi 17:13–14).

and by night in a pillar of fire, to give them light; to go by day and night (Exodus 13:21).

I will take you to me for a people, and I will be to you a God: **and ye shall know that I am the Lord your God, which bringeth you out from under the burdens of the Egyptians** (Exodus 6:7–8).

The similarity of the texts is interesting, but a difference is enlightening as well. In Exodus the concept of a people chosen by God is emphasized, while in the Book of Mormon the idea is reversed—a people choose God through obedience to his commandments. This idea is also a major theme in Nephi's sermon to his brothers (see 1 Nephi 17:23–43).

Clearly Nephi did not just copy the Exodus story; rather, he adapted it to his purpose, no doubt by inspiration. Perhaps he had seen how the perversion of the idea of being the "chosen people" had contributed to the Israelites' downfall by making them proud. He may also have worried that his brothers' belief that "the people who were in the land of Jerusalem were a righteous people" (1 Nephi 17:22) was a sign that they were falling into the same error.

High on a Mountain Top

After the Lehi group had crossed the desert, Nephi received a summons from the Lord to ascend a mountain. Moses faced the same call at Sinai once they had left Egypt:

The voice of the Lord came unto me, saying: Arise, and

The Lord came down upon mount Sinai, on the top of the

get thee into the mountain. And it came to pass that I arose and went into the mountain, and cried unto the Lord (1 Nephi 17:7).

mount: and the Lord called Moses up to the top of the mount; and Moses went up (Exodus 19:20).

The Lord said unto Moses, Come up to me into the mount, and be there: . . . and Moses went up into the mount of God (Exodus 24:12–13).

While on the mountain, Nephi received detailed instructions concerning the ship he was to build, just as Moses received orders regarding the building of the tabernacle:

The Lord spake unto me, saying: Thou shalt construct a ship, **after the manner which I shall show thee,** that I may carry thy people across these waters (1 Nephi 17:8).

The Lord spake unto Moses saying, . . . Let [the children of Israel] make me a sanctuary. . . . **According to all that I shew thee, after the pattern of the tabernacle,** and the pattern of all the instruments thereof, even so shall ye make it (Exodus 25:1, 8–9).

In both cases a pattern was shown to the prophet, after which he was to build the structure. In both cases the purpose is mentioned.

While the two structures were very distinct, yet some of the words used to describe the craftsmanship involved in the building of each are similar:

We did work timbers of **curious workmanship.** And the Lord did show me from time to time after what manner I should work the timbers of the ship. Now I, Nephi did not work the timbers after the manner which was learned by

Moses said unto the children of Israel, See, the Lord hath called by name Bezaleel. . . . **He hath filled him with the spirit of God, in wisdom, in understanding, and in knowledge, and in all manner of workmanship;** and men, neither did I build the ship after the manner of men; but **I did build it after the manner which the Lord had shown unto me;** wherefore, it was not after the manner of men (1 Nephi 18:1–2).

to devise **curious works,** to work in gold, and in silver, and in brass, and in the cutting of stones, to set them, and in carving of wood, to make any manner of cunning work (Exodus 35:30–33).

In both cases the workmanship was described as "curious." In Nephi's case it was not "after the manner of men," while in Exodus the workmen were uniquely filled "with the spirit of God" in order to do their work.

Nephi's Powerful Sermon

When Nephi's brothers saw that he had begun to build a ship, they began to mock him and complain, refusing to help him. Nephi responded by retelling the history of the Exodus, touching on many of the ideas he would later use in writing the story of their own wilderness journey. Near the end, Nephi draws a clear parallel between the two wilderness experiences, directly comparing his brothers to the murmuring children of Israel: "[The Lord] did bring them out of the land of Egypt. And he did straiten them [gave them hardships] in the wilderness with his rod; for they hardened their hearts, even as ye have; and the Lord straitened them because of their iniquity" (1 Nephi 17:40–41).

If his brothers were so much like the children of Israel, then do we not see Nephi in a similar position as Moses? For example, Nephi proclaimed the power that the Lord had given him in a way that brings to mind Moses' power over the Red Sea:

I said unto them: If God had commanded me to do all things I could do them. If he should command me that I should **say unto this water, be thou earth, it should be earth:** and if I should say it, it would be done (1 Nephi 17:50).

But lift thou up thy rod, and stretch out thine hand over the sea, and divide it: and the children of Israel **shall go on dry ground through the midst of the sea** (Exodus 14:16).

This sermon, with its references to Moses and the Exodus, is the most direct evidence we have that Nephi was conscious of the similarity of the two situations. At the conclusion of this sermon, Nephi reported that his brothers were so humbled by his speech and fearful that they "durst [not] . . . lay their hands upon [him] nor touch [him] with their fingers, even for the space of many days" (1 Nephi 17:52). This situation recalls the return of Moses from speaking to the Lord on Sinai: "When Aaron and all the children of Israel saw Moses, behold, the skin of his face shone; and they were afraid to come nigh him" (Exodus 34:29–30).

Two Parties, Too Wild

Once the ship was completed, Lehi's family boarded it and set sail for the promised land. After a while, Laman, Lemuel, and the sons of Ishmael began "to make themselves merry." Nephi's description of this partying suggests a comparison to the incident with the golden calf during the Exodus:

After we had been driven forth before the wind for the space of many days, behold, my brethren and the sons of Ishmael and also their wives began to **make themselves merry,** insomuch that they **began to dance, and to sing,** and to speak with much rudeness, yea, even **that they did forget by what power they had been brought thither;** yea, they were lifted up unto **exceeding rudeness** (1 Nephi 18:9).

He had made it a molten calf: and they said, **These be thy gods, O Israel, which brought thee up out of the land of Egypt.** . . . The people sat down to eat and to drink, and **rose up to play** (Exodus 32:4–6).

When Joshua heard the noise of the people as they shouted, he said unto Moses, There is a noise of war in the camp. And he said it is not the voice of them that shout for mastery, neither is it the voice of them that cry for being overcome: but **the noise of them that sing do I hear.** And it came to pass, as soon

> as he came nigh unto the camp, that he saw the calf, and **the dancing. . . .** Moses saw that **the people were naked** (Exodus 32:18–19, 25).

The singing, dancing, and nakedness before the golden calf were apparently part of a ritual connected with this idol. Is Nephi's mention of "much rudeness" and "exceeding rudeness" comparable to Moses' seeing that "the people were naked"? I suggest a connection. Also interesting is Nephi's statement that "they did forget by what power they had been brought thither." Compare this to the statement in Exodus about the molten calf: "These be thy gods, O Israel, which brought thee up out of the land of Egypt." The children of Israel had also forgotten that God's direct power had saved them to that point. Finally, note that in both cases the prayer of an individual was what saved the people, who were almost destroyed by a justifiably angry God.

A New Credo

Israel followed the custom of retelling the Exodus experience to remind them of their dependence on God. The transplanted Israelites in the New World continued the same kind of memory, but with a twist. They not only remembered the acts of God among the Israelites fleeing Egypt, they also retold the story of the journey of Lehi and his family through the desert and to the new promised land. Eight times in the Book of Mormon, the Exodus was recalled. Lehi's journey from Jerusalem is referred to at least ten times. Even the Lamanites may have followed this custom to an extent (see Alma 22:9).

In two places in the Book of Mormon, the two exoduses are retold together. The first is from a speech by King Limhi to his people; the second is from Alma's instructions to his son Helaman:

> Lift up your heads, and rejoice, and put your trust in God, in that God who was the God of Abraham, and

49

Isaac, and Jacob; and also, that God who brought the children of Israel out of the land of Egypt, and caused that they should walk through the Red Sea on dry ground, and fed them with manna that they might not perish in the wilderness; and many more things did he do for them. And again, that same God has brought our fathers out of the land of Jerusalem, and has kept and preserved his people even until now (Mosiah 7:19–20).

For he has brought our fathers out of Egypt, and he has swallowed up the Egyptians in the Red Sea; and he led them by his power into the promised land; yea, and he has delivered them out of bondage and captivity from time to time. Yea, and he has also brought our fathers out of the land of Jerusalem; and he has also, by his everlasting power, delivered them out of bondage and captivity, from time to time even down to the present day (Alma 36:28–29).

In the second pair of verses, note that Alma describes the two situations in identical terms. These two passages indicate that, in the minds of at least some of the Nephite writers, the wilderness journey experienced by Lehi, Ishmael, and their families had become equivalent in importance to the Exodus of Israel from Egypt.

Conclusions

There are a number of parallels between the stories of these two groups of people, both led by God's hand through trials in a desert wilderness to a new land. Some are general, and others are specific and very clear. It seems to me that such a large body of parallels cannot be accounted for by coincidence. It appears that Nephi purposefully wrote his account in a way that would reflect the Exodus. His intention was to prove that God loved and cared for the Nephites just as he did the children of Israel during the Exodus from Egypt.

Certainly this connection could not have been a product of Joseph Smith's writing. The parallels to Exodus occur at dozens of places throughout the Book of Mormon record. No hasty

50

copying of the Bible could have produced such complex similarities, not to mention the differences that remain. In fact, because they are so quiet and underlying, no Latter-day Saint until our day has even noticed these comparisons. Nephi clearly composed a masterpiece full of subtle literary touches that we are only now beginning to appreciate.

Chapter 6

JACOB AND HIS
DESCENDANTS AS AUTHORS

John S. Tanner

As a church, we tend to emphasize the universal, timeless doctrines of the scriptures and forget how our favorite verses relate to the speaker and to the circumstances in which he spoke. This is especially true of Jacob and his descendants. We don't sufficiently appreciate how distinctive Jacob is as an author or how unusual the books of Enos through Omni are as a history of Jacob's family. Just recently, for example, a colleague of mine made reference to *Nephi's* teaching that "to be learned is good if they hearken unto the counsels of God" (2 Nephi 9:29). This quote is Jacob's, of course; it comes from a magnificent two-day sermon recorded in 2 Nephi. My colleague had remembered the doctrine but forgotten both the speaker (Jacob) and the context (a sermon).

The Writings of Jacob and His Descendants in Context

The writings of Jacob and his descendants form part of the small plates, a section of the Book of Mormon that Mormon included intact, presumably without editing. Only on the small plates may Joseph Smith have found someone's "handwriting" other than that of Mormon or Moroni. Speaking in the first person, Jacob and his descendants seem more individual, even in translation, than other writers whose words were more obviously edited by Mormon and Moroni. From Jacob through Omni, the record displays the complex variety one expects of a text written by many hands. The stylistic diversity of Jacob and his descendants is a powerful witness that we are dealing with

52

material written by several ancient authors rather than by one person in early nineteenth-century New York.

Consider, for example, the transition between Omni and the Words of Mormon. It has the rough edges we would expect to find in a bridge between an unedited text and an edited abridgment. At this point in the book, Mormon explains for his readers a number of puzzling pieces that would make up his record. He discusses two different civilizations (the Nephites and Mulekites), two separate time frames (Mosiah's and Mormon's), and three groups of records (the small plates, the large plates, and his abridgment of the large plates). Mormon also mentions a fourth set of records (the brass plates) as he introduces the Book of Mosiah (see 1:3).

To make matters more confusing, just before Mormon's bridge, Amaleki in the Book of Omni records two dramatic episodes of cultural contact involving several major Book of Mormon civilizations. Amaleki first tells of an encounter between Nephites from the land of Nephi and Mulekites in the land of Zarahemla. This is our first introduction to a group that left Jerusalem at roughly the same time as did the Lehite group, about 586 B.C. (see Omni 1:13–19). Amaleki then recounts the Mulekites' prior contact with Coriantumr, the last survivor of yet another, even more ancient civilization about whom we've also heard nothing till this reference, but whose history will be given later (see Ether).

Thus in a few pages, the text refers to events happening across 2500 years of history and relating to every major Book of Mormon group. It does so, moreover, in a way that requires specific knowledge of how each civilization began and how it would end. No wonder that, despite Mormon's best efforts to smooth the transition, readers often find it difficult to understand how the parts fit together. In order to make full sense of these few pages from Omni to Mosiah, the reader (and writer) has to know Book of Mormon history from the coming of the Jaredites to the demise of the Nephites (not to mention the story of the lost 116 pages).

Yet Mormon makes the transition flawlessly—at least with respect to historical details. The transition is rougher with respect to style. The style of the small plates (Omni and before) is different from the style of Mormon's bridge (Words of Mormon) and of his abridgment of the large plates (Mosiah and after). These rough edges provide strong evidence that this part of the Book of Mormon is precisely what it claims to be: namely, a first-person document that is being spliced into a larger history by someone who knows the full story to come.

As a literary critic, I am naturally drawn to first-person documents. I listen for echoes of a human voice in every sort of writing or speech, however impersonal it is supposed to be—even in prophetic speeches. For example, I occasionally have my wife read conference talks aloud while I try to guess, from their style alone, who gave them. I am usually right. So, too, with the scriptures. I try to glimpse the man behind the message—not out of desire to discredit divine inspiration, but from professional habit and out of love for the spokesmen through whom God speaks. I will indulge in this sort of speculation here.

Of course, my guesses about the human characteristics of Jacob and his descendants may be wrong, just as I have sometimes guessed wrong about the author of a conference address. Nevertheless, I'm convinced that we can better appreciate scripture by asking questions about its human authors and by trying to put ourselves in their places. As Brigham Young told the saints: "Do you read the Scriptures, my brothers and sisters, as though you were writing them a thousand, two thousand, or five thousand years ago? Do you read them as though you stood in the place of the men who wrote them? If you do not feel thus, it is your privilege to do so" (*Journal of Discourses*, 7:333).

Before looking at Jacob, let me share one example of how understanding context can enrich our appreciation of content. The example is drawn from Nephi's psalm (see 2 Nephi 4:15–35), in which he sorrows over his weaknesses and afflictions, rejoices in his blessings from God, and pleads for divine help and mercy. Although Nephi's lament never mentions Lehi, it occurs just after Nephi records the death of his father. Is this merely coincidence? I think not. Consider what the death of Lehi meant to Nephi. Father Lehi had held the family together, with great difficulty. He and Nephi had shared the same vision, literally (of the Tree of Life) and figuratively (of commitment to God). When Lehi died, Nephi lost a friend as well as a father and prophet; he lost his confidant, advisor, and shield against the hatred of his brothers. Thus Nephi had ample reason to reflect on his distress, as he does in his psalm.

Before Lehi's death, Nephi had foreseen in revelation the tragic division between Lamanites and Nephites (see 1 Nephi 12:22–23). When Lehi died, Nephi must have known that the long-dreaded crisis was now both inevitable and near. With no father to turn to but his Heavenly Father, Nephi cries for strength: so lonely is his new burden of leadership, so dangerous his enemies, and so strong the temptation to be angry "because of [his] enemies" (2 Nephi 4:29) — meaning, I suppose, his brothers. I like to read his psalm, then, by remembering its human context, recorded in a verse that immediately precedes it: "And it came to pass that he [Lehi] died, and was buried" (2 Nephi 4:12).

The Plates as Jacob's Family History

Now let us turn to Jacob and his descendants. After passing into Jacob's hands, the small plates became increasingly focused on the history of Jacob's family rather than on the history of the whole Nephite group. Understanding this is critical. Many distinctive features of the text can be explained by the fact that the record became primarily genealogical. From Jacob on, the plates were no longer kept by the rulers (see Jacob 1:9). Jacob and his descendants were not kings. From all we can tell, they did not play a leading role in political or military matters. This has major consequences for the record they left. After Nephi, never again do the authors of the small plates occupy a central position in the government. Of course, the small plates were always set aside for spiritual things rather than secular matters (see 1 Nephi

19:1-6; Jacob 1:2), but, from Jacob on, the small plates were written increasingly from a perspective outside the community's official life (see, for example, Enos 1:24).

Jacob's family eventually passed out of the prophetic line as well. Only Jacob himself clearly held a position of religious authority equivalent to that of high priest (see Jacob 1:17-19). His son Enos and grandson Jarom described themselves as only one among many prophets (see Enos 1:19, 22; Jarom 1:4). Jarom may not have done any public teaching or preaching at all. Although he referred to "my prophesying" and "my revelations," he spoke in the third person of "the prophets, and the priests, and the teachers [who] labor diligently, exhorting . . . the people to diligence; teaching the law of Moses" (Jarom 1:11) — as if he were not one of them. Also he wrote, "Our kings and our leaders were mighty men in the faith of the Lord; and they taught the people the ways of the Lord" (1:7), sounding like a bystander outside the loop of government power and official church responsibility.

On the other hand, Jarom referred to Nephite warfare and trade in the first person: "We withstood the Lamanites. . . . And we . . . became exceedingly rich in gold . . . in buildings, and in machinery, and also in iron and copper, and brass and steel, making all manner of tools of every kind to till the ground, and weapons of war" (Jarom 1:7-8). Jarom sounds as if he was a soldier and artisan. Likewise, Jarom's son Omni fought for the Nephites, but there is no evidence that he did so as a military leader or that he had any religious calling. Far from it, he confessed he was a "wicked man" (Omni 1:2). The same is true of Jacob's other descendants who contributed to the Book of Omni. Abinadom admitted that he knew "of no revelation save that which has been written" (Omni 1:11). Amaleki said that the people "were led by many preachings and prophesyings" (Omni 1:13). The impersonal, passive phrasing implies that he did not himself act as one of the prophets or preachers.

This lack of either government or religious authority among Jacob's descendants does not mean that the Nephites had fallen into a complete dark age. Although they were not prophets themselves, these writers tell us prophets still lived among them. Enos even spoke of "exceedingly many" unnamed prophets (Enos 1:22). Jarom told of men "who [had] many revelations, . . . mighty men in faith of the Lord" (Jarom 1:4, 7). Amaron spoke of the Lord's sparing the righteous portion of the Nephites during his day, proving there was a righteous remnant (see Omni 1:7). And Amaleki wrote of "many preachings and prophesyings" (Omni 1:13).

If we remember that this is a family record, we'll be less likely to overgeneralize about the apostasy of the whole Nephite civilization. Perhaps there were great prophets mentioned in Mormon's lost abridgment. We do not know, since the record comes from Jacob's descendants who fell from prominence and perhaps from grace. Precisely because the plates are a family chronicle, their spiritual quality varies sharply with that of the family. This is the only place I know where a self-professed "wicked man" (Omni) wrote scripture. Later descendants of Jacob were merely ordinary men who happened to belong to an extraordinary lineage. They became scriptural authors only because the plates became mainly a family record—and none of us can choose our relatives, not even Jacob.

Beginning with Jarom, Jacob's descendants kept the record so "that our genealogy may be kept" (Jarom 1:1; compare Omni 1:1). This purpose had not been mentioned by Nephi or Jacob. For many of Jacob's later descendants, a genealogical entry is about all they would write. Yet even this is something. However pale their own lives must have seemed compared to those of the heroic first generation, however embarrassing it must have been, each man obediently fulfilled his charge, adding his own name to the end of the sacred record. We can learn something about duty from this.

Further, many of Jacob's descendants (especially Omni and Abinadom) were refreshingly frank about their weaknesses. Perhaps we could learn from their humility and unblinking self-honesty as well. Moreover, all Jacob's descendants—even "wicked" Omni—treated the sacred record with respect. They appear to have felt the plates' power. The very inadequacy they expressed implies that they had read the record and been moved, even intimidated, by its majesty. So it's not entirely fair to dismiss these men as apostate. Perhaps we shouldn't even assume that the self-confessed are completely reprobate. All Jacob's posterity manifested humility, honesty, reverence for the sacred, and a common commitment to duty. This suggests that Jacob's legacy of righteousness was not utterly lost in his posterity. His righteous blood still flowed in their veins, his sensitivity still circulated in their souls.

Jacob's Literary Style

This brings me to Jacob himself. Jacob's style is unique among Book of Mormon authors. He simply sounds different. He used a more personal vocabulary than most and took a more intimate approach to his audience. Consider the contrast with his brother Nephi. Nephi "delights," even "glories" in plainness (2 Nephi 31:3; 33:6). He frankly rebuked and frankly forgave his brothers (see 1 Nephi 7:21). He plunged into difficult tasks—getting the brass plates, facing down starvation, building a ship. Jacob, by contrast, seemed more anxious and withdrawn. He was openly pained that he had to use "much boldness of speech" to his brethren, especially in the presence of their women and children, "whose feelings are exceedingly tender and chaste and delicate before God" (Jacob 2:7).

He prefaced his temple discourse by admitting that he felt "weighed down with much . . . anxiety for the welfare of [their] souls": "It grieveth my soul and causeth me to shrink with shame before the presence of my Maker. . . . Wherefore, it burdeneth my soul that I should be constrained . . . to admonish you according to your crimes, to enlarge the wounds of those who are already wounded. . . . And those who have not been wounded, instead of feasting upon the pleasing word of God have daggers placed to pierce their souls and wound their delicate minds" (Jacob 2:3, 6, 9).

This is vintage Jacob: intimate, vivid, vulnerable. He used words about feelings—like *anxiety, grieve,* and *tender*—more frequently than any other Book of Mormon writer. For example, half the book's references to *anxiety* occur in Jacob, and over two-thirds of the references to *grieve* and *tender* (or their derivatives), as well as *shame,* are Jacob's. He is the only person to have used *delicate, contempt,* and *lonesome.* Likewise, he is the only Book of Mormon author to have employed *wound* in reference to emotions; and he never used it, as everyone else did, to describe a physical injury. Similarly, Jacob used *pierce* or its variants frequently (four of the ten instances in the Book of Mormon), and he used it exclusively in a spiritual sense. Such evidence suggests an author who lived close to his emotions and who knew how to express those emotions.

Like many sensitive people, Jacob did not preach harsh messages easily. Many times he openly shared his anxiety with his audience, as in the preface to his temple discourse discussed above. The structure of that sermon may also reflect his reluctance to speak harshly. He first addressed the relatively easy issue (pride) and then, reluctantly, moved to the "grosser crime," whoredoms (see Jacob 2:22–23).

When Jacob did speak, however, he spoke vividly and even eloquently. Notice the concrete words in the phrase: "Instead of *feasting* upon the pleasing word of God [they] have *daggers* placed to *pierce* their souls and *wound* their *delicate* minds" (Jacob 2:9; italics added). Or consider, "The *sobbings* of their hearts ascend up to God. . . . Many hearts *died, pierced* with *deep wounds*" (2:35; italics added). Here are strong words welded to strong feelings.

Jacob's ability to find concrete words for abstract spiritual experience is the hallmark of his style. Perhaps he learned it by feasting upon the "tender" words of his "trembling" father (see 1 Nephi 8:37; 2 Nephi 1:14), and then passed his style on to his son Enos. At any rate, when Enos recounted the spiritual *wrestle* and *hunger* that led to his guilt being *swept* away, it appears that Jacob's words had *sunk deep* into the boy's style as well as his soul (see Enos 1:2–6). Like Jacob, Enos also described the intangible through language drawn from the tangible.

Jacob's style is evident wherever his words appear. Even his sermon recorded in 2 Nephi, separated from the Book of Jacob by many chapters and many years, bears clear resemblance to his later temple discourse. Both sermons contain vivid, emotion-laden language. Both call upon the people to "awake" lest they become "angels of the devil"—a phrase unique to Jacob (2 Nephi 9:9, 47; Jacob 3:11). Both mention Jacob's desire to rid his garments of the people's blood and his consciousness of the Lord's "all-searching eye" (2 Nephi 9:44; Jacob 1:19; 2:2, 10). Likewise, Jacob prefaced two long scriptural quotations (one from Isaiah, the other from Zenos) by expressing his "anxiety" and his "over anxiety" for his audience (2 Nephi 6:3; Jacob 4:18). It is inconceivable to me that Joseph Smith could have invented such a subtle difference of style for Jacob and then remembered to use it so many chapters later as he rapidly dictated the translation.

Jacob's Themes

Jacob's writing is also consistently focused on several favorite themes. One of his favorites, probably because of his own experience living in exile, was scattered Israel's preservation. He seemed to take special comfort in the promises made to scattered Israel, identifying the Lehite colony with Israel on the isles of the sea: "My beloved brethren, . . . let us . . . not hang down our heads, for we are not cast off; nevertheless, we have been driven out of the land of our inheritance; but we have been led to a better land, for the Lord has made the sea our path, and we are upon an isle of the sea" (2 Nephi 10:20).

Note Jacob's typically poetic phrasing that translates the idea of sadness into something concrete ("hang down our heads") and that describes the sea voyage as "made the sea our path." Beyond the style, note the message of comfort and hope—the same message Jacob quoted from Isaiah (see 2 Nephi 7:1–2; 8:3–12). Few descriptions of God's love in all scripture rival Isaiah's in chapters 40–66. To these chapters was Jacob drawn, for he delighted in scriptural assurances that God would not abandon exiled Israel.

This, I believe, ought to provide us with a clue as to how Jacob read Zenos, an ancient prophet on the brass plates. We often pay so much attention to what Zenos has told us about the history of Israel that we miss the powerful message that likely drew Jacob to the allegory: namely, that God loves and looks after the house of Israel, no matter where its people are scattered. The allegory is more than a complex puzzle whose solution unlocks world history, as some of us read it. The allegory also dramatizes God's steadfast love and active concern. Zenos's allegory ought to take its place beside the parable of the prodigal son. Both stories make the Lord's mercy so movingly memorable.

A key phrase in the allegory is "it grieveth me that I should lose this tree," repeated eight times. By means of such repetition, the allegory celebrates the Lord's long-suffering love. The frequent repetition of the line describes the quality of that divine love – it is unfailing, persistent, tenacious. This message of the Lord's love matters as much as, if not more than, the historical details of his plan to redeem Israel. Yes, the allegory tells how the Lord of the vineyard will work out his grand design in history. But more than this, it shows that he weeps over the loss of his trees: "It came to pass that the Lord of the vineyard wept, and said unto the servant: What could I have done more for my vineyard" (Jacob 5:41; see also Moses 7:28–41). The Lord of the universe grieves that he should lose *any* tree of the vineyard. What a remarkable witness! I find this allegory one of the most eloquent scriptural testimonies of God's love anywhere. Surely Jacob did too.

But just so we don't miss the point, Jacob told us what matters most in the allegory: It is *not* figuring out history. Rather, it is feeling "how merciful is our God unto us, for he remembereth the house of Israel . . . and he stretches forth his hands unto them all the day long." This feeling should lead us to repent: "Wherefore, my beloved brethren, I beseech of you in words of soberness that ye would repent, and come with full purpose of heart, and cleave unto God as he cleaveth unto you" (Jacob 6:4–5). This is the neglected message of Zenos's allegory. By better understanding Jacob and the circumstances under which he taught and wrote, we understand better why he used Zenos's allegory. Seeing it through his eyes, we find in it the meaning he intended.

Jacob's Biography

When Jacob quoted scriptures by Zenos or Isaiah, we can easily sense a close link between the man and his message. He must have felt strongly about these prophets' promises to scattered Israel, for he himself was a displaced person. This close link between Jacob's life and his message also shows up elsewhere. Let me list five facts about Jacob's life and suggest how each might be connected to his themes and style.

(1) Jacob was born "in the days of [Lehi's] tribulation" (2 Nephi 2:1). He was raised on raw meat rather than milk and probably orphaned at a young age. Some people are hardened by hardship, but not Jacob. Lehi promised Jacob that God would "consecrate thine afflictions for thy gain" (2 Nephi 2:2), and Jacob's sensitive style provides evidence that this promise was fulfilled. Long afflictions seem to have softened Jacob's spirit, verifying the famous Book of Mormon teaching about the value of "opposition in all things." Significantly, that teaching occurs as part of Jacob's patriarchal blessing (2 Nephi 2:11). We should remember Jacob when we teach the principle that adversity can have sweet uses. The evidence shows that the boy took Lehi's lesson to heart.

(2) Jacob was a child of a house divided, suffering from abusive brothers. He saw a family feud evolve into a more or less permanent state of war. Think what it meant for Jacob to be Laman and Lemuel's brother. The Lamanites were not distant, faceless, nameless enemies; they were kinsmen—brothers, nephews, and cousins whose names and families he knew. This helps me read with more sympathy Jacob's sad parting observation: "Many means were devised to reclaim and restore the

Lamanites to the knowledge of the truth; but it all was vain, for they delighted in wars and bloodshed, and they had an eternal hatred against us, their brethren" (Jacob 7:24).

"Against us, their brethren" — Jacob used the word *brethren* often in his discourses to the Nephites too. It seems to have been his favorite way of addressing his people: he used it some fifty times, while he almost never addressed his audience directly as "my people," the term Nephi preferred. Jacob's choice of what to call his audience suggests an intimate family relationship with them and also shows his humility. At the same time, it reminds us that Jacob's audience — including those he criticized so severely for whoredoms — were his kinsmen. No wonder Jacob felt anxious and pained. The erring Lamanites and Nephites were his relatives.

(3) Jacob was the younger brother of a prophet-colonizer. Nephi must have cast a large shadow, and Jacob's writing suggests he was very aware of this shadow. The people decided to adopt Nephi's name as a royal title (see Jacob 1:11), but Jacob himself chose to group all righteous family lines (including his own) under the title Nephites (Jacob 1:13–14). This may reveal his respect for his older brother (and perhaps his detachment from governmental matters) and serve to symbolize his humble deference to Nephi. Jacob presented himself as less prominent than his brother, the founder.

In addition, neither Jacob nor his descendants appear to have added new plates to the ones Nephi made. This may simply mean that they lacked the proper materials or skill to fashion plates, though both Jacob and Jarom mention an abundance of gold in the promised land (see Jacob 2:12; Jarom 1:8). More likely, it reveals something about the meaning of the plates in Jacob's and his family's minds: namely, that they saw the plates as primarily Nephi's record, a sacred legacy from an incomparable man and cultural hero, to be added to only sparingly by those who followed. Even Jacob, whose contribution to the small plates is sublime and considerable, still confessed that his "writing has been small" (Jacob 7:27). Evidently, he was comparing his authorship to the extensive writing of his illustrious older brother. All the later authors in Jacob's family seem to have suffered from similar feelings of inferiority.

Jacob also seems to have lived in Nephi's shadow for another reason. His writing is more limited in historical scope than that of his older brother. Of course in touching but lightly on history, he was following Nephi's instruction and example. After the death of Lehi, Nephi too said little more about history. He resolved, rather, to write on the small plates only the things of his soul and charged his brother Jacob to do the same (see 2 Nephi 4:15; Jacob 1:2–4). Jacob obediently confined himself almost wholly to the ministry, recording sermons, discussions of scripture, and one story about a conflict with Sherem. He said nothing about the move to the land of Nephi and little of the colonization. The result is that Jacob comes across more as a priest and less as a colonizer than Nephi.

(4) Jacob was visited by Christ. In this respect, he was not a bit inferior to his brother. Nephi's tribute to Jacob seems to acknowledge this: "Jacob also has seen him [the Christ] as I have seen him" (2 Nephi 11:3; compare 2 Nephi 2:4). Jacob knew the Master; his writing is full of the testimony of Christ. Indeed, he is the first Nephite prophet to whom Christ's name was revealed (see 2 Nephi 10:3). He wrote his record so that his posterity might know "that we knew of Christ, and we had a hope of his glory many hundred years before his coming" (Jacob 4:4).

(5) Finally, to end where I began, Jacob was a pilgrim, a wilderness writer. He was twice an outcast—first wandering with his family across the desert and great sea; then fleeing from the first settlements in America even deeper into the wilderness (see 2 Nephi 5:5–6). Like nomadic Abraham, the only security these New World exiles knew lay in their God and his law. Eternity was their covering, rock, and salvation (compare Abraham 2:16). Their experience in the wilderness may help explain why both Nephi and Jacob quoted from the brass plates more than any other Book of Mormon prophet. The brass plates were

tangible links to the world they had left behind, as well as a key to the civilization they hoped to build.

How hard forging a new civilization must have seemed to Jacob! He had never even known the old one personally. Nephite survival must have often seemed perilous and precarious to this early pioneer. Despairing would have been easy, especially for a sensitive man like Jacob. He surely realized that time, geographic isolation, and sin could easily destroy the sacred traditions he was trying to teach. Or, if these failed, the Lamanites might succeed, for they were determined, as Jacob wrote, to "destroy our records and us, and also all the traditions of our fathers" (Enos 1:14). No wonder Jacob's writing refers so often to anxiety.

Jacob's Farewell

The cost the wilderness exacted on Jacob is most evident in his final farewell. His parting words express the accumulated sorrows of a life of struggle: "I conclude this record . . . by saying that the time passed away with us, and also our lives passed away like as it were unto us a dream, we being a lonesome and a solemn people, wanderers, cast out from Jerusalem, born in tribulation, in a wilderness, and hated of our brethren, which caused wars and contentions; wherefore, we did mourn out our days" (Jacob 7:26). By now it should be clear how in substance and style this leave-taking could only be written by Jacob, of all Book of Mormon authors. It fits the facts of his life as a man, and it captures his sensitivity, vulnerability, and eloquence as a writer.

Jacob's tone here is very different from that of his brother's powerful farewell. Where Jacob ended quietly and on a minor key of distress, Nephi concluded with timpani rolls and cymbal clashes: "I glory in plainness; I glory in truth; I glory in my Jesus." Nephi was all confidence: "I shall meet many souls spotless at his judgment-seat"; his words challenge us to be righteous, as he had his older brothers: "You and I shall stand face to face before his bar." His last statement restated his lifelong commitment to absolute obedience; it could serve as an epitaph: "For thus hath the Lord commanded me, and I must obey" (2 Nephi 33:6–7, 11, 15). Nephi's farewell never fails to move me.

Jacob's words are no less moving but in a very different way. Jacob, too, felt assured of personal salvation. He looked forward to meeting the reader at the "pleasing" judgment bar of God (Jacob 6:13). But his farewell seems much less optimistic about the salvation of others: "O then, my beloved brethren, repent ye, and enter in at the strait gate, and continue in the way which is narrow, until ye shall obtain eternal life. O be wise; what can I say more? Finally, I bid you farewell, until I shall meet you before the pleasing bar of God, which bar striketh the wicked with awful dread and fear. Amen" (Jacob 6:11–13).

No other Book of Mormon author uses the term *dread*. No one else uses *lonesome,* nor can I imagine any other Book of Mormon author writing "our lives passed away like as it were unto us a dream," or "we did mourn out our days." None is so open about anxiety, none so poetic. No wonder Neal Maxwell called Jacob a prophet-poet. Jacob is a poet whose voice I've learned to love and whom someday I hope to meet.

Chapter 7

THE STEALING
OF THE DAUGHTERS
OF THE LAMANITES

Alan Goff

A minor story in the Book of Mormon provides an example of how complex the task of reading the book can be. It also illustrates how much richer our understanding can be when we remember that the Book of Mormon is an ancient record with connections to other ancient records, particularly the Old Testament. In the book of Mosiah, a band of wicked priests hid in the wilderness and kidnapped some young women to be their wives (see 20:1–5). This story can be read as an adventure tale. If looked at carefully, however, it shows the kind of connections between the Book of Mormon and the Old Testament that demonstrate that the Book of Mormon is an ancient book.

The story of kidnapping by the wicked priests is a minor part of the record of the people of Zeniff. When King Noah, ruler over the Zeniffites, rejected the prophet Abinadi's message and had him killed, the priest Alma and his followers separated from the rest of the people. Soon thereafter, the Lamanites attacked the people of Zeniff. As they fled from the Lamanites, King Noah commanded them to abandon their families. Instead, they executed Noah and attempted to kill his priests (see Mosiah 17–19). These priests escaped into the wilderness, led by Amulon, one of their number, and later kidnapped some daughters of the Lamanites to be their wives. Angered by the kidnapping and assuming the Zeniffites were guilty, the Lamanites attacked them. Peace was restored when the Lamanites learned who the real kidnappers were (see Mosiah 20).

A Biblical Parallel

This story of the abduction of young Lamanite women is similar to a story in the Bible in which men from the tribe of Benjamin kidnap daughters of Israel at Shiloh. The end of the book of Judges contains three stories about the tribe of Benjamin. In the first, Benjaminites abused and murdered a Levite concubine (see Judges 20). In the second, the other eleven tribes gathered to punish the offenders, and a civil war resulted (see Judges 19). The third story tells of the kidnapping (see Judges 21).

After destroying most of the tribe of Benjamin, the Israelites realized that this tribe was in danger of extinction. To preserve the tribe, the Benjaminites needed wives. But the Israelites had vowed not to allow their daughters to marry the Benjaminites. To get around their vow, they instructed the Benjaminites to kidnap the daughters of the Israelites who lived at Shiloh while the young women danced in the vineyards. As the daughters of Shiloh gathered, the Benjaminites lay hidden. The girls danced, and the Benjaminites stole them to be their wives.

The Stealing of the Daughters of the Lamanites

The similarities between the stories in Mosiah and Judges are complex and carefully stated:

Then they said, Behold, there is a feast of the Lord in Shiloh yearly in a place which is on the north side of Bethel, on the east side of the highway that goeth up from Bethel to Shechem, and on the south of Lebonah. Therefore they commanded the children of Benjamin, saying, Go and lie in wait in the vineyards; and see, and behold, if the

Now there was a place in Shemlon where the daughters of the Lamanites did gather themselves together to sing, and to dance, and to make themselves merry. And it came to pass that there was one day a small number of them gathered together to sing and to dance (Mosiah 20:1–2).

68

daughters of Shiloh come out
to dance in dances, then come
ye out of the vineyards, and
catch you every man his wife
of the daughters of Shiloh,
and go to the land of Benjamin
(Judges 21:19–21).

The Bible clearly mentions the incident as a yearly ritual. The Book of Mormon mentions it as a regular occurrence, not telling us how often ("one day"). In both stories the kidnapped virgins became the wives of the abductors. The record says that the priests of Noah, "being ashamed to return to the city of Nephi, yea, and also fearing that the people would slay them, therefore they durst not return to their wives and their children" (Mosiah 20:3), so they watched the dancers and kidnapped substitute wives. When the narrative returned to the story of Amulon and his fellow priests, the daughters of the Lamanites were then called "their wives" (Mosiah 23:33).

In both stories, the abductors, like peeping toms, waited and watched the spectacle. The Benjaminites lay in wait in the vineyards watching the dancing. The wicked priests also found the place where the girls danced, then "they laid and watched them" (Mosiah 20:4). We know that the priests hid because in the next verse they "came forth out of their secret places" and abducted twenty-four of the dancing maidens. Not only is the watching stressed in both stories, but also the lying in wait. These were not crimes of passion, but ones of premeditation.

The Meaning of Parallels

Some Book of Mormon critics have seen the parallels between the two stories and concluded that Joseph Smith merely copied the story from Judges. They conclude that any similarities in stories indicate plagiarism. Biblical scholars take a more sophisticated approach than do these critics to texts that may appear to borrow from other texts. Scholars often see similarities between stories as evidence of the writer's sophistication and of the richness of the text.

For example, the first of the stories about the Benjaminites, telling of the rape and death of a concubine, is similar to an earlier Bible story of Lot and his two visitors at Sodom. The story in Judges tells of a Levite and his concubine who were returning home from a visit to her father's house in Bethlehem. At a late hour they arrived at Gibeah, a Benjaminite city. Only one old man was willing to take the travelers in. As the host entertained, the men of the city gathered outside and demanded that the host bring the Levite outside so they could rape him. The host protested this violation of the law of hospitality and offered his own virgin daughter and the Levite's concubine as substitutes. The Levite instead pushed his concubine out to the mob, who "abused her all the night until the morning" (Judges 19:25). In the morning she was dead.

This story is obviously similar to the story of Lot's visitors in Genesis 19. In both stories the guests were taken in, the inhabitants of the cities threatened a homosexual rape, and the host offered two women as substitutes to spare the men. Obviously readers are meant to see a relationship between the two stories. Biblical scholars see this as an example of conscious borrowing intended both to enhance the meaning of the second story and to emphasize how wicked Gibeah had become. The story in Genesis 19 can easily be read and understood with no awareness of the story in Judges 19, but to understand Judges 19 in any complete way the reader must see the connection to Sodom. The Levite was portrayed unfavorably compared to Lot's divine visitors. The visitors to Sodom effected a divine rescue, while the Levite threw out his own concubine to save himself.[1]

I believe that, in a similar way, the story of the abduction in Mosiah means more when we see it light of the story in Judges. I feel that the author of the story in Mosiah borrowed consciously from the story in Judges, which he knew from the plates of brass, to help make his point.

The story of the abduction of the daughters of Shiloh is the final story in Judges. One of the main purposes of Judges was to justify the establishment of a king. Judges described the evil the Israelites did in the Lord's sight (see Judges 3:7; 4:1), explaining that they did evil because there was no king over the people (see Judges 17:6; 18:1). Judges ends with three stories about the tribe of Benjamin that illustrate this evil. The stories are preceded by a statement about the lack of a king over the land: "And it came to pass in those days, when there was no king in Israel . . . " (Judges 19:1). The third story ends with a similar statement: "In those days there was no king in Israel: every man did that which was right in his own eyes" (Judges 21:25). The topsy-turvy world described in Judges 17–21 demonstrates that doing what is right in one's own eyes is often the same thing as doing what is evil in the Lord's eyes.[2]

By emphasizing parallels to the kidnapping story in Judges, the author of the story in Mosiah seems to me to have strengthened the moral point. The wicked priests led by Amulon were also evil, doing what was right in their own eyes rather than following the Lord.

Other Parallels

Understandably, the text shows disapproval of all that Amulon and his fellow priests did. The parallel case from Judges of doing what is right in man's eyes is only one way the text shows this disapproval. There are other parallels that further discredit Amulon and his companions.

After the Lamanites captured Amulon and his people, the record states that "Amulon did gain favor in the eyes of the king of the Lamanites" (Mosiah 24:1). In gaining the favor of the Lamanites, these priests clearly lost favor with God. There is a note of disapproval in the narrator's words when he says that the people of Amulon not only found favor in the eyes of the Lamanite king, but also that the king appointed these men to be teachers over all his people (see Mosiah 24:1). As teachers, these priests taught the Lamanites the language of the Nephites (see Mosiah 24:4), "nevertheless they knew not God; neither did the brethren of Amulon teach them anything concerning the Lord their God, neither the law of Moses; nor did they teach them the words of Abinadi" (Mosiah 24:5).

71

On the other hand, Alma taught his people how God delivered both the followers of Limhi and Alma out of bondage (see Mosiah 25:10, 16). He also taught them "repentance and faith on the Lord" (Mosiah 25:15) as he organized them into congregations. The author emphasizes how different from Alma the priests of Noah were. He says directly that the priests of Noah didn't teach the Lamanites Abinadi's words. He also specifically mentions that Alma "went about privately among the people, and began to teach the words of Abinadi" (Mosiah 18:1). Both Alma and Amulon entered the narrative as priests of Noah. Upon hearing the words of Abinadi, Alma repented, but Amulon refused to repent. Alma taught the prophet's words in secret, while Amulon and his priests utterly refused to teach them to the Lamanites.

The reader is led to see the contrasting lives, not just of Alma and Amulon, but of the people of Limhi and Alma and the people of Amulon. Both Alma and Amulon led colonies into the wilderness: Alma and his people, when Noah's soldiers discovered their "movement," "took their tents and their families and departed into the wilderness" (Mosiah 18:32, 34). Amulon and his followers also fled into the wilderness, but at Noah's command they left their families behind (see Mosiah 19:11–23).

The wicked priests abandoned their wives when King Noah "commanded them that all the men should leave their wives and their children, and flee before the Lamanites" (Mosiah 19:11), then they went about trying to find substitute wives. The other Zeniffites would rather have perished than leave their wives and children behind (see Mosiah 19:12). Thus those who remained behind "caused that their fair daughters should stand forth and plead with the Lamanites that they would not slay them" (Mosiah 19:13). The daughters inspired "compassion" among the Lamanites, for they "were charmed with the beauty of their women" (Mosiah 19:14). Later, Amulon would do the same thing, sending out the Lamanite daughters he and the other priests had kidnapped to plead for mercy (see Mosiah 23:33–34).

The text has set up parallel examples for the reader to compare. The Zeniffites sent men out to find those who had fled their children and wives, "all save the king and his priests" (Mosiah 19:18), and had vowed that they would return to their wives and children or die seeking revenge if the Lamanites had killed them (Mosiah 19:19). The parallel stories of sending the two sets of daughters to beg for mercy from the Lamanites teach the reader that what appear to be the same actions actually differ when performed by the good-hearted on the one hand or the evil-hearted on the other.

When we compare the people as the text invites us to do, we contrast the care the men of Limhi showed for their wives and children with the abandonment by the priests of Noah. All of these events define the lack of moral character of the priests. The fact that the Lamanite king was willing to permit the stealing of the Lamanite daughters by welcoming Amulon and the priests into his kingdom speaks badly of this king, just as the Israelites' encouragement of the Benjaminites to kidnap their own daughters speaks badly of all Israel. The people of Limhi, on the other hand, "fought for their lives, and for their wives, and for their children" (Mosiah 20:11). These differences reveal not only the character of the priests of Noah, who abandoned their families rather than fall into Lamanite hands, but also of the Nephites, who decided to face death with their families rather than abandon them.

The text is clearly unsympathetic to the people of Amulon. The connection between the two stories of abduction is a hint from the author that their actions were reminiscent of a time, reported in Judges, when the Israelites didn't follow God's law but did what was right in their own eyes. The priests are portrayed as indifferent to God, in spite of their position, which should have made them more anxious to follow God.

The Book of Mormon story of the stealing of the Lamanite daughters cannot be accounted for by the simplistic claim that it was just copied from the Bible. The Book of Mormon makes sophisticated use of the story to make its own point. Critics of

73

the Book of Mormon believe that the author of the text used the earlier story from Judges, and I agree. But unlike them, I believe that the parallel enhances the book and reveals it to be an ancient document rather than a modern imitation.

Notes

1. Stuart Lasine, "Guest and Host in Judges 19: Lot's Hospitality in an Inverted World," *Journal for the Study of the Old Testament* 29 (June 1984): 40.

2. Lasine, 55.

LANGUAGE AND LITERATURE

Chapter 8

THE HEBREW BACKGROUND
OF THE BOOK OF MORMON

John A. Tvedtnes

The English translation of the Book of Mormon shows many characteristics of the Hebrew language. In many places the words that have been used and the ways in which the words have been put together are more typical of Hebrew than of English. These *Hebraisms,* as I will call them, are evidence of the authenticity of the Book of Mormon—evidence that Joseph Smith did not write a book in English but translated an ancient text and that his translation reflects the Hebrew words and word order of the original.

There can be no doubt that the Nephites spoke Hebrew. Not only did they come from Jerusalem, where Hebrew was commonly spoken at that time, but Moroni himself indicated that they knew Hebrew (see Mormon 9:32–34). Therefore, the English translation of the Book of Mormon not surprisingly contains characteristics of Hebrew.

We do not know exactly what language was used on the original plates of the Book of Mormon. Nephi described the writing system as a combination of "the learning of the Jews and the language of the Egyptians" (1 Nephi 1:2). Moroni, writing a thousand years later, called it "reformed Egyptian" (Mormon 9:32–34). This might mean that they used Egyptian symbols to represent Egyptian words, or that they used Egyptian symbols as a shorthand to represent Hebrew words, or even that they used both Egyptian and Hebrew symbols to represent Hebrew words. Whatever reformed Egyptian was, it must have been influenced by the language that the Nephites used in daily speech—Hebrew. That influence can be seen in the Hebraisms preserved in the English translation.

The Hebraisms in the Book of Mormon help persuade us that it is authentic. The following story will illustrate. During the years 1968–71, I taught Hebrew at the University of Utah. My practice was to ask new students to respond to a questionnaire, giving some idea of their interests and linguistic background. One student wrote that she wanted to study Hebrew in order to prove the Book of Mormon was a fraud. She approached me after class to explain.

When I inquired why she felt the Book of Mormon was fraudulent, she stated that it was full of errors. I asked for an example. She drew my attention to Alma 46:19, where we read, "When Moroni had said these words, he went forth among the people, waving the rent part of his garment in the air." She noted that in the 1830 edition (p. 351), this read simply "waving the rent of his garment." In English, the *rent* is the hole in the garment, not the piece torn out of the garment. Therefore, Moroni could not have waved it. This was an error, she contended, and adding the word *part* later was mere deception.

This was my first introduction to variations in different editions of the Book of Mormon. Without a Hebrew background, I might have been bothered by it. But the explanation was clear when I considered how Mormon would have written that sentence. Hebrew does not have to add the word *part* to a verbal substantive like *rent* as English requires. Thus, *broken* in Hebrew can refer to a *broken thing* or a *broken part,* while *new* can refer to a *new thing.* In the verse the student cited, *rent* would mean *rent thing* or *rent part.* Thus, the "error" she saw as evidence of fraud was really a Hebraism that was evidence for the authenticity of the Book of Mormon.

Significantly, the first (1830) edition of the Book of Mormon contains many more Hebraisms than later editions. Later editions, especially in 1837, 1840, and 1876, were edited to improve the English in areas where the text appeared to be awkward. Unfortunately, this destroyed some of the evidence for a Hebrew original. Therefore, I will occasionally refer to the reading of the 1830 edition to illustrate Hebraisms in the Book of Mormon.

Construct State

When English shows a possessive or descriptive relationship between two nouns, it usually puts the possessive or descriptive noun first: *the king's house* or *wood house*. Hebrew, however, uses the opposite order: *house the king* (which would usually be translated *house of the king*) or *house wood* (*house of wood*). If the Hebrew word order is kept in the English translation, the word *of* must be added, even though it does not exist in the Hebrew.

The Book of Mormon contains a large number of what appear to be translations from the Hebrew preserving the Hebrew word order:

> "plates of brass" instead of brass plates (1 Nephi 3:24)
> "works of righteousness" instead of righteous works (Alma 5:16)
> "words of plainness" instead of plain words (Jacob 4:14)
> "chains of hell" instead of hell's chains (Alma 5:7)
> "voice of the Spirit" instead of the Spirit's voice (1 Nephi 4:18)
> "skin of blackness" instead of black skin (2 Nephi 5:21)
> "night of darkness" instead of dark night (Alma 34:33)
> "rod of iron" instead of iron rod (1 Nephi 8:19)

The Hebrew-like expression *land of promise* appears twenty-two times in the Book of Mormon, while *promised land* (common in English) is found only ten times.

Adverbials

Hebrew has fewer adverbs than English. Instead, it often uses prepositional phrases with the preposition meaning *in* or *with*. The English translation of the Book of Mormon contains more of these prepositional phrases in place of adverbs than we would expect if the book had been written in English originally — another Hebraism. Here are some examples:

"with patience" instead of patiently (Mosiah 24:15)

"with much harshness" instead of very harshly (1 Nephi 18:11)

"with joy" instead of joyfully (Jacob 4:3)

"in spirit and in truth" instead of spiritually and truly (Alma 34:38)

"in righteousness" instead of righteously (1 Nephi 20:1)

"with gladness" instead of gladly (2 Nephi 28:28)

Cognates

Cognates are related words that come from the same root. For example, the English noun *student* is cognate to the verb *study* and the adjective *studious*. In Hebrew, a verb is sometimes followed by a noun that is a cognate, such as "**wrote** upon it a **writing**" (Exodus 39:30) and "she **vowed** a **vow**" (1 Samuel 1:11). In English, cognates are used much less often. Using such cognates is often considered an awkward or inelegant style in English. Someone writing in English would be more likely to use "she vowed" or "she made a vow." Even in translation from the Hebrew, the King James Bible sometimes avoids using cognates. In Genesis 1:11, a literal translation of the Hebrew would be "Let the earth **grass grass**," but the English translation reads "Let the earth bring forth grass."

The Book of Mormon uses cognates much more often than we would expect if the book had originally been written in English. These cognates show the Hebrew influence of the original. One of the best-known examples is "I have **dreamed** a **dream**" (1 Nephi 8:2). That is exactly the way that the same idea is expressed in literal translation of the Old Testament Hebrew (see Genesis 37:5; 41:11).

Here are some other examples of the use of cognates in the

Book of Mormon, each followed by the more normal expression for English:

> "**work** all manner of fine **work**" (Mosiah 11:10) instead of *work well*
>
> "and he did **judge** righteous **judgments**" (Mosiah 29:43) instead of *judge righteously* or *make righteous judgments*
>
> "**build buildings**" (2 Nephi 5:15; Mosiah 23:5) instead of *erect buildings* or simply *build*
>
> "this was the **desire** which I **desired** of him" (Enos 1:13) instead of *what I desired*
>
> "I will **work** a great and a marvelous **work**" (1 Nephi 14:7) instead of *perform a great and marvelous work*
>
> "**taxed** with a **tax**" (Mosiah 7:15) instead of *taxed*
>
> "**cursed** with a sore **cursing**" (2 Nephi 1:22; Jacob 3:3) instead of *cursed sorely*

Compound Prepositions

Hebrew often uses compound prepositions, made up of a preposition plus a noun, in places where English would normally use just a preposition. For example, Hebrew uses compound prepositions that would be translated literally as *by the hand of* and *by the mouth of*. English would normally use just *by*. The Book of Mormon contains many examples that appear to show the influence of this Hebrew use of compound prepositions:

> "ye shall be taken **by the hand of** your enemies" (Mosiah 17:18)
>
> "I have also acquired much riches **by the hand of** my industry" (Alma 10:4)
>
> "sold into Egypt **by the hands of** his brethren" (Alma 10:3)
>
> "the words which have been spoken **by the mouth of** all the holy prophets" (1 Nephi 3:20)
>
> "**by the mouth of** angels, doth he declare it" (Alma 13:22)

Hebrew uses another compound preposition that would be translated literally as *from before the presence of* or *from before the face of.* English would normally use simply *from.* The influence of the Hebrew can be seen in these Book of Mormon passages:

"they fled **from before my presence**" (1 Nephi
   4:28)

"he had gone **from before my presence**" (1 Nephi 11:12)

"they were carried away . . . **from before my face**" (1 Nephi 11:29)

The Conjunction

Hebrew uses conjunctions much more frequently than English does. One clear example of this can be found in lists of items. In English, the conjunction *and* is normally used only before the last item in a list, such as *wood, iron, copper, and brass.* But Hebrew usually uses a conjunction before each item. The Book of Mormon contains many examples of this Hebrew-like usage, such as this one found in 2 Nephi 5:15: "in all manner **of** wood, **and of** iron, **and of** copper, **and of** brass, **and of** steel, **and of** gold, **and of** silver, **and of** precious ores."

This kind of repetition is so prominent in the Book of Mormon that Professor Haim Rabin, President of the Hebrew Language Academy and a specialist in the history of the Hebrew language, once used a passage from the Book of Mormon in a lecture in English to illustrate this principle, because, he explained, it was a better illustration than passages from the English Bible.

In such lists, Hebrew also repeats related elements such as prepositions, articles, and possessive pronouns. Here are some examples from the Book of Mormon:

"**And** it came to pass that he departed into the wilderness. **And** he left **his** house, **and** the land of **his** inheritance, **and his** gold, **and his** silver, **and his** precious things, **and** took nothing with him, save it were **his** family **and** provisions, **and** tents,

and [he, 1830] departed into the wilderness" (1 Nephi 2:4).

"**And** it came to pass that we went down to the land of **our** inheritance, **and** we did gather together **our** gold, **and our** silver, **and our** precious things" (1 Nephi 3:22).

" . . . All mankind were **in a** lost **and in a** fallen state . . . " (1 Nephi 10:6).

" . . . **My** gospel . . . **and my** rock **and my** salvation . . . " (1 Nephi 13:36).

" . . . **The city of** Laman, **and the city of** Josh, **and the city of** Gad, **and the city of** Kishkumen, have I caused to be burned with fire" (3 Nephi 9:10).

" . . . **All their** men **and all their** women **and all their** children . . . " (Mosiah 24:22).

Such repetition seems to be a waste of precious space on the plates, except for the fact that it is required by the Hebrew language.

Another difference between Hebrew and English conjunctions is that in Hebrew the same conjunction can carry both the meaning *and* and also the opposite meaning *but*. Here are two well-known Bible passages in which the King James Version renders the conjunction *but:*

"Of every tree of the garden thou mayest freely eat: **but** of the tree of the knowledge of good and evil, thou shalt not eat of it" (Genesis 2:16–17).

"And as for Ishmael . . . I will make him a great nation. **But** my covenant will I establish with Isaac" (Genesis 17:20–21).

Evidence for Hebraism in the Book of Mormon lies in the fact that some passages use the conjunction *and* when *but* is expected. Here, for example, are two different versions of the Lord's promise to Lehi:

"Inasmuch as ye shall keep my commandments

ye shall prosper in the land; **but** inasmuch as ye
will not keep my commandments ye shall be cut
off from my presence" (2 Nephi 1:20; compare Alma
50:20).

"Inasmuch as ye shall keep my commandments
ye shall prosper in the land; **and** inasmuch as ye
will not keep my commandments ye shall be cut
off from my presence" (2 Nephi 4:4).

In one of the quotations of this promise, Joseph Smith rendered the conjunction *and,* while in another place, he rendered
it *but.* In other Book of Mormon passages, Joseph translated *and*
when in English we would expect *but* because a contrastive meaning is clearly called for:

"And when I speak the word of God with sharpness they tremble and anger against me; **and (= but)**
when I use no sharpness they harden their hearts
against it" (Moroni 9:4).

"He commanded the multitude that they should
cease to pray, and also his disciples. **And (= but)**
he commanded them that they should not cease to
pray in their hearts" (3 Nephi 20:1).

Another difference in the use of conjunctions is that in biblical Hebrew, a language with no punctuation, the conjunction
also serves as a marker of parenthesis. The words we would put
inside parentheses in English are preceded by the conjunction
in Hebrew, and, at the conclusion, the next phrase is introduced
by the conjunction. In the following biblical example, the same
conjunction has been variously rendered *and, for,* and *that* by
the King James translators to fit the requirements of the English
language: "As they that bare the ark were come unto Jordan,
and the feet of the priests that bare the ark were dipped in the
brim of the water, **(for** Jordan overfloweth all his banks all the
time of harvest,) **that** the waters . . . stood and rose up" (Joshua
3:15–16). We see that *for* and *that,* two English renditions of the

same Hebrew conjunction, served to set off what the English translators chose to mark with the parentheses.

The Book of Mormon also uses conjunctions to mark parenthetical phrases. In the Book of Mormon examples listed below, I have added parentheses to illustrate:

> "After I, Nephi, having heard all the words of my father, concerning the things which he saw in a vision, and also the things which he spake by the power of the Holy Ghost, which power he received by faith on the Son of God (**and** the Son of God was the Messiah which should come) **and** it came to pass that I, Nephi, was desirous also that I might see, and hear, and know of these things" (1 Nephi 10:17, reading of 1830 edition).

> "When Jesus had spoken these words unto Nephi, and to those who had been called, (**now** the number of them who had been called, and received power and authority to baptize, was twelve) **and** behold, he stretched forth his hand . . . " (3 Nephi 12:1).

A special use in Hebrew of this kind of parenthetical phrase is the introduction of a name. In English, we usually say something like, "there was a man named X," or "there was a man whose name was X." While the Book of Mormon has many such examples, it often reflects the Hebrew usage, which is, "there was a man (**and** his name was X.)" In the examples which follow, I have added parentheses where necessary:

> "Zoram did take courage at the words which I spake (**now** Zoram was the name of the servant) **and** he promised . . . " (1 Nephi 4:35).

> "They took him (**and** his name was Nehor) **and** they carried him . . . " (Alma 1:15).

Another Hebrew-like use of the conjunction in the Book of Mormon is the expression *and also*. In Hebrew, it is used to emphasize the close links between two things, as in this biblical passage: "**Both** drink thou, **and** I will **also** draw for thy camels" (Genesis 24:44). Here are some examples from the Book of Mormon that seem to reflect the Hebrew usage:

> "They . . . worshiped the Father in his name, **and also** we worship the Father in his name" (Jacob 4:5).
>
> "The Lord hath heard the prayers of his people, **and also** the prayers of his servant, Alma" (Mosiah 27:14).
>
> " . . . What the Lord had done for his son, **and also** for those that were with him . . . " (Mosiah 27:21).
>
> "**Now** the sons of Mosiah were numbered among the unbelievers; **and also** one of the sons of Alma was numbered among them" (Mosiah 27:8).

Subordinate Clauses

Biblical Hebrew begins subordinate clauses with prepositions plus a word that translates as *that*, such as in Ezekiel 40:1: "**after that** the city was smitten." Such a use of *that* in English is awkward and therefore rare. Yet it appears frequently in the Book of Mormon, another evidence of Hebrew influence. It was even more frequent in the 1830 edition, but many of the *that*s were dropped from later editions to read more smoothly (noted in the following examples by brackets).

> "And **because that** they are redeemed from the
> fall" (2 Nephi 2:26)
> "**because that** my heart is broken" (2 Nephi 4:32)
> "**because that** ye shall receive more of my word"
> (2 Nephi 29:8)
> "**because [that]** they had hardened their hearts"
> (1 Nephi 16:22)
> "**because [that]** ye are of the house of Israel" (2
> Nephi 6:5)
> "**before [that]** they were slain" (1 Nephi 13:15)

"**before [that]** he shall manifest himself in the
flesh" (Enos 1:8)
"and **after that** I had been lifted up upon the
cross" (3 Nephi 27:14)
"**after that** I am gone to the Father" (3 Nephi
28:1)
"**after [that]** I have abridged" (1 Nephi 1:17)
"**after [that]** he hath been commanded to flee" (1
Nephi 3:18)

The Relative Clause

In Hebrew, the word that marks the beginning of a relative
clause (generally translated *which* or *who* in English) does not
always closely follow the word it refers back to, as it usually
does in English. Some Book of Mormon passages give the impres-
sion of having been translated from such Hebrew sentences:

"Our brother Nephi . . . has taken it upon him
to be our ruler and our teacher, **who** are his elder
brethren" (1 Nephi 16:37) instead of *to be a ruler
and teacher to us, who are his elder brethren.*

"The Egyptians were drowned in the Red Sea,
who were the armies of Pharaoh" (1 Nephi 17:27)
instead of *the Egyptians, who were the armies of Pharaoh, were drowned in the Red Sea.*

"Then shall they confess, **who** live without God
in the world" (Mosiah 27:31) instead of *then shall
they who live without God in the world confess.*

Extrapositional Nouns and Pronouns

Hebrew often uses a noun or pronoun as the direct object
of the verb in one clause and a pronoun referring to the same
person or thing in the following clause in a way that seems
unnecessary or redundant in English. For example in Genesis
1:4, we read, "God saw the **light,** that **it** was good." In this case,
the King James Bible reflects the Hebrew wording, despite the
fact that in English the normal way of saying this would be,

"God saw that the light was good." This Hebraic usage is also found in the Book of Mormon:

> "I beheld, and saw **the people of the seed of my brethren** that **they** had overcome my seed" (1 Nephi 12:20).
>
> "I beheld **the wrath of God,** that **it** was upon the seed of my brethren" (1 Nephi 13:14).
>
> "And I beheld **the Spirit of the Lord,** that **it** was upon the Gentiles" (1 Nephi 13:15).
>
> "I . . . beheld **the power of the Lamb of God,** that **it** descended" (1 Nephi 14:14).

Interchangeable Prepositions

In biblical Hebrew, the prepositions that are translated *in* and *to* in English are often interchangeable. This would not usually work in English. In at least two Book of Mormon passages, the 1830 edition used *to* and *in* in ways that reflect the Hebrew usage, although later editions were changed to reflect the normal English use.

In 1 Nephi 7:12, the 1830 edition read "let us be faithful **in** him." Both *in* and *to* are possible in biblical Hebrew, but, when speaking of God, *faithful in* is usual. *Faithful to* is more normal in English, and *in* was changed to *to* in later editions of the Book of Mormon.

In 1 Nephi 17:14, the 1830 edition read "after ye have arrived **to** the promised land." Both *in* and *to* are possible in biblical Hebrew, but *arrive to* is much more common. English prefers *arrive at*.

Comparison

Comparison in English is usually expressed in this way: a certain thing is more X than a second thing, or a certain thing is Xer than a second thing. The words *more* and *than* or the suffix *-er* express the comparison. In Hebrew, comparison is expressed by a word that is translated as *from* in this way: a certain thing is X *from* a second thing. The Book of Mormon frequently uses the word *above* in comparisons in a way that is more like the Hebrew use of *from* than the English use of *more* or *-er,* apparently reflecting a Hebrew influence.

"a land which is **choice above** all other lands" (1
   Nephi 2:20; see 13:30)
"the tree which is **precious above** all" (1 Nephi
   11:9; see 15:36)
"most **abominable above** all sins" (Alma 39:5)
"the fruit . . . which is **sweet above** all that is
   sweet, and which is **white above** all that
   is white, yea, and **pure above** all that is
   pure" (Alma 32:42)

Naming Conventions

When a child is born, we say in English that his father and mother "called him X" or "named him X." The same is true in naming places, for example, "He called his ranch Pleasant Valley." But Hebrew expresses it quite differently: "He called the name of his son X." In Hebrew, it is the *name* that is "called," not the child or the place. Perhaps the best-known example from the Bible is the one found in Isaiah 7:14: "Behold, a virgin shall conceive, and bear a son, and shall **call his name** Immanuel." This idiom is found in a number of places in the Book of Mormon:

"we did call the **name** of the place Shazer" (1
   Nephi 16:13)
"and they called the **name** of the city Moroni"
   (Alma 50:13–14)
"he had three sons; and he called their **names**
   Mosiah, and Helorum, and Helaman"
   (Mosiah 1:2)
"they called their **names** Anti-Nephi-Lehies"
   (Alma 23:17)

Possessive Pronouns

In Hebrew, a possessive pronoun is added to the end of the noun. Thus *my book* would be *the book of me.* This Hebraic usage is reflected in several examples from the Book of Mormon:

> "hear **the words of me**" (Jacob 5:2)
>
> "the Gentiles shall be great in **the eyes of me**" (2 Nephi 10:8)
>
> "how unsearchable are the depths of **the mysteries of him**" (Jacob 4:8)
>
> "they are delivered by **the power of him**" (2 Nephi 9:25)
>
> "setteth at naught **the atonement of him** and the power of his redemption" (Moroni 8:20)

Words Used in Unusual Ways

At several points in the Book of Mormon, we encounter English words used in ways that are unknown or unexpected in our language. King Mosiah said, "I shall give this people a name, that thereby they may be distinguished **above** all the people" (Mosiah 1:11). In English we would expect *distinguished from.* But the Book of Mormon passage reflects the normal Hebrew expression, which uses the compound preposition that means *from above.*

Jacob wrote that Nephi instructed him regarding Nephite sacred preaching, revelations, and prophecies that "I should engraven the **heads** of them upon these plates" (Jacob 1:4). The term *head* seems out of place. We would expect something like *most important* to be used. But the expression is readily explainable in terms of Hebrew. The Hebrew word for the head of the body is sometimes used to describe things as *chief* (see Deuteronomy 33:15; Psalm 137:6; and Proverbs 1:21) or *precious* (see Amos 6:1; Song of Solomon 4:14; Ezekiel 27:22). This is probably the sense in which Jacob used the word.

Nephi wrote, "We are upon an **isle** of the sea" (2 Nephi 10:20). It seems strange to have Nephi call the American continent an island. But the Hebrew word generally translated *isle* in the Bible has a wider range of meaning than just *island.* It most often refers to coastal lands.

Alma 13:18, speaking of Melchizedek, notes that "he was the king of Salem; and he did reign **under** his father." This may reflect the normal biblical Hebrew use of the preposition *under* for the meaning *instead of*. The same preposition is rendered *instead of* in some passages of the King James Bible. For example, after King Amaziah had been murdered, "all the people of Judah took Azariah . . . and made him king **instead of** his father Amaziah" (2 Kings 14:21).

In Ether 8:11 we read "he desired her **to** wife." English would prefer *for a wife*. There is a Hebrew preposition that means both *to* and *for*. Furthermore, the Hebrew word used for *wife* really means *woman*. In three Book of Mormon passages, the word *women* appears to mean *wives:*

> "Our **women** did bear children" (1 Nephi 17:1).
> "Our **women** have toiled, being big with child; and they have borne children" (1 Nephi 17:20).
> "For behold, he hath blessed mine house, he hath blessed me, and my **women,** and my children, and my father and my kinsfolk; yea, even all my kindred hath he blessed" (Alma 10:11).

There is much more linguistic evidence for the influence of Hebrew on the Book of Mormon, but the examples of Hebraisms that I have cited should be enough to demonstrate that the Book of Mormon is an authentic ancient text influenced by Hebrew. Many expressions used in the Book of Mormon are awkward or unexpected in English, even in Joseph Smith's time. Yet they make good sense when viewed as translations, perhaps as too literal translations, from an ancient text written in a Hebrew-like language.

Chapter 9

MOURNING, CONSOLATION, AND REPENTANCE AT NAHOM

Alan Goff

The death and burial of Ishmael at Nahom (see 1 Nephi 16:34–39) can puzzle readers who are uncertain about how the story fits into Nephi's overall account or uncertain about why the incident is included at all. This section, however, is one of those parts of the Book of Mormon that contain hints of a deeper meaning than what appears on the surface. At least one important meaning of the Nahom episode is connected with the word *Nahom* itself.

The journey of Lehi's party in the wilderness of Arabia is marked by the mention of this place-name, which Joseph Smith did not translate into English. It turns out that the word connects earlier biblical traditions with the rebellion of Laman and other members of the party against Lehi and Nephi. In order to see these connections, let's break down the narrative verse by verse and compare these links with older Hebrew traditions:

34. *"Ishmael died, and was buried in the place which was called Nahom."*

A connection with the Hebrew verb *naham* is suggested in a footnote to this verse in the 1981 edition of the Book of Mormon. The Hebrew word means "to mourn or to be consoled." But a much stronger connection with biblical tradition unfolds in the account that follows the verse. The scholar Damrosch says this about the word:

> It [the root for *naham*] appears twenty-five times in

the narrative books of the Bible, and in every case it is associated with death. In family settings, it is applied in instances involving the death of an immediate family member (parent, sibling, or child); in national settings, it has to do with the survival or impending extermination of an entire people. At heart, *naham* means "to mourn," to come to terms with a death; these usages are usually translated . . . by the verb "to comfort," as when Jacob's children try to comfort their father after the reported death of Joseph.[1]

The idea of mourning is obvious in the events that occur at Nahom. But Nephi goes beyond the obvious at this point. In the following verses, he uses connotations of the word *naham/ nahom* in the story of the rebellion by members of the party. Those subtle references deepen the meaning of the whole incident.

35. *"The daughters of Ishmael did mourn exceedingly, because of the loss of their father, and because of their afflictions in the wilderness; and they did murmur against my father, because he had brought them out of the land of Jerusalem, saying: Our father is dead; yea, and we have wandered much in the wilderness, and we have suffered much affliction, hunger, thirst, and fatigue; and after all these sufferings we must perish in the wilderness with hunger."*

Thus we learn that at Nahom Ishmael's daughters mourned, not only because of their father's death, but also because of the difficulty of life in the wilderness. We find a parallel in the use of the word *murmur* in the story of the children of Israel rebelling against Moses. Every time (except once) the Old Testament used the Hebrew root *lwn*, translated as some form of *murmur*, it was in stories of wilderness trials (see, for example, Exodus 15:24; 16:7; Numbers 14:2; Deuteronomy 1:27). They rebelled against their prophet's leadership and complained about their hard life in the wilderness in the same way that Lehi's party both rebelled and complained at Nahom. So Nephi used this technical term accurately to describe their particular case of trouble and rebellion in the wilderness.

From this parallel, we understand that Nephi saw their journey as following a type or model. He considered their flight from dangerous Jerusalem through harsh wilderness to be similar to the Exodus of the Israelites from oppression in Egypt. He constantly described the flight of Lehi's party in terms used hundreds of years earlier to describe Israel's forty-year journey from Egypt to their promised land. *Nahom/naham* is one of those words that reminds us of the connection Nephi saw.

Mircea Eliade has spent a lifetime analyzing myths and religions around the world. He concluded that "archaic man" (ancient peoples) felt that life was most significant at moments when the people were repeating ancient types or symbolic patterns. In contrast, they considered mere day-to-day happenings as much less important. Further, they felt a need to reenact the events that they thought had occurred at the foundation of their nation. Eliade believes that they repeated in their ceremonies those foundational events because these were thought of as pivotal.[2]

Latter-day Saint youths who occasionally pull handcarts across a part of a pioneer trail for even a few days may realize the powerful hold such reenactment can exercise even on us. In light of this human tendency to recall and act out history, I would be surprised if Nephi had not chosen to use the language of the Exodus to express what was happening to his own group, for the parallels were obvious.

Note that the plight of the children of Israel had been to "wander in the wilderness" (Numbers 14:33; 32:13) for forty years. In Nephi's record the daughters of Ishmael complained that they have had to "wander much in the wilderness." The brief, pointed language is very appropriate, for with this little phrase Nephi not only described their situation, but also recalled a basic idea or theme in Israelite life—the Exodus.

Later generations frequently recalled that image of flight into the wilderness and applied it to their own circumstances. For example, the book of Job proclaims that all people are in God's hands, for "he taketh away the heart of the chief of the people

94

of the earth, and causeth them to wander in a wilderness where there is no way" (Job 12:24). The Psalmist also recalls God's power over all the earth by saying that God "poureth contempt upon the princes, and causeth them to wander in the wilderness, where there is no way" (Psalm 107:40). The entire Seventy-eighth Psalm dwells on the great deeds God performed for the children of Israel while they wandered in the wilderness, although "how oft did they provoke him in the wilderness, and grieve him in the desert!" (verse 40). The daughters of Ishmael couldn't speak of wandering in the wilderness without recalling this ancient pattern or type.

At Nahom the complaint against Lehi and Nephi was that they had led the daughters of Ishmael and their families into the wilderness "[to suffer] much affliction, hunger, thirst, and fatigue" and probably to "perish in the wilderness with hunger." This murmuring reminds us again of an incident involving Moses and his people: "The whole congregation of the children of Israel murmured against Moses and Aaron in the wilderness: and the children of Israel said unto them, Would to God that we had died by the hand of the Lord in the land of Egypt, when we sat by the flesh pots, and when we did eat bread to the full; for ye have brought us forth into this wilderness, to kill this whole assembly with hunger" (Exodus 16:2–3).

The rebellion was not limited just to murmuring, however. It expressed itself in another way also evident in the Exodus account:

36. "They did murmur against my father, and also against me; and they were desirous to return again to Jerusalem."

The daughters of Ishmael's murmuring was accompanied by a desire to return to the land they had left. Again, that mirrors a similar aspect of the Exodus centuries earlier. After some Israelite spies had scouted the land of promise, they returned to the camp in the wilderness. There they described the power of the inhabitants.

When the children of Israel heard that, they "murmured against Moses and against Aaron: and the whole congregation

95

said unto them, . . . Wherefore hath the Lord brought us unto this land, to fall by the sword, that our wives and our children should be a prey? were it not better for us to return into Egypt? And they said one to another, Let us make a captain, and let us return into Egypt" (Numbers 14:2–4). In seeing in the pattern of his family's wanderings the pattern of the Exodus, Nephi not surprisingly mentioned this parallel, the desire to return that accompanied murmuring.

But Laman and Lemuel had a different complaint and a distinct idea of what would pay them back for the injuries they had supposedly suffered:

37. *"Laman said unto Lemuel and also unto the sons of Ishmael: Behold, let us slay our father, and also our brother Nephi, who has taken it upon him to be our ruler and our teacher, who are his elder brethren."*

The Israelites had rebelled against Moses in the wilderness under the leadership of three men, Korah, Dathan, and Abiram. These men complained that Moses had taken too much of the leadership for himself: "Is it a small thing that thou hast brought us up out of a land that floweth with milk and honey, to kill us in the wilderness, except thou make thyself altogether a prince over us?" (Numbers 16:13). This charge recalls the still earlier moment, in Egypt, when a Hebrew slave accused Moses, "Who made thee a prince and a judge over us?" (Exodus 2:14). The elder brothers' charge against Nephi was the same—he had usurped power. Laman and Lemuel found consolation at Nahom in the thought that they could get even by killing both Lehi and their younger brother.

Damrosch tells us some interesting things about the connection of "consolation" and killing:

> From this basic meaning of regret following the death of a family member, the term [*naham*] becomes applied to other cases of regret or change of heart, . . . almost always when the repenter is meditating murder. "Repentance" [or change of heart] then involves either the decision to kill, or conversely, the decision to stop killing.

96

> The term can be used in quite ignoble circumstances, as
> when Esau comforts himself for the loss of his birthright
> by deciding to kill Jacob (Gen. 27:42), but usually it is
> God who repents, either negatively or positively; neg-
> atively, by deciding to destroy his people; positively, by
> commuting a sentence of destruction.[3]

Verse thirty-seven identifies an additional theme found in
Israelite history: the theme of the younger brother surpassing
the elder. It is a recurring thread that unifies the stories of the
Old Testament patriarchs. As early as Cain and Abel, and down
to Ephraim and Manasseh, the younger brother found favor not
only in the father's eyes (or sometimes the mother's), but also
in God's. Abraham favored his son Isaac over his older half-
brother (see Genesis 21:9–14), while Isaac's younger son, Jacob,
took the birthright and blessing from his brother Esau (Genesis
27:22–35). Further, Joseph ended up being honored by his elder
brothers when he saved them in Egypt, and Jacob crossed his
arms to give the chief blessing to Joseph's youngest son,
Ephraim. The same theme continues in the story of Samuel
choosing David to be king instead of his older brothers (see 1
Samuel 16:10). In the Book of Mormon the pattern is repeated,
for Laman claimed that Nephi wanted to usurp the rightful authority of the elder brothers:

*38. "Now, he says that the Lord has talked with him, and also that
angels have ministered unto him. But behold, we know that he lies unto
us; and he tells us these things, and he worketh many things by his
cunning arts, that he may deceive our eyes, thinking, perhaps, that he
may lead us away into some strange wilderness; and after he has led
us away, he has thought to make himself a king and a ruler over us,
that he may do with us according to his will and pleasure. And after
this manner did my brother Laman stir up their hearts to anger."*

In spite of the fact that Laman had seen an angel and heard
him proclaim Nephi's eventual rule (1 Nephi 3:29), he claimed
that Nephi was unrighteously trying to rule over them. A parallel
with the Bible again comes to mind. Joseph, whom the Nephites
looked to as their forefather, had dreams and visions. His broth-

ers complained to him, "Shalt thou indeed reign over us? or shalt thou indeed have dominion over us? And they hated him yet the more for his dreams, and for his words" (Genesis 37:8). "When they saw him afar off, even before he came near unto them, they conspired against him to slay him. And they said one to another, Behold, this dreamer cometh" (Genesis 37:18–19). The term *dreamer* in particular is derogatory—the "master of dreams," the "baal of dreams."

In the Book of Mormon, Laman and the others conspire to kill both dreamers in their family, for Nephi is "like unto our father, led away by the foolish imaginations of his heart" (1 Nephi 17:20). Earlier they "did murmur in many things against their father, because he was a visionary man, and had led them out of the land of Jerusalem" (1 Nephi 2:11).

Chapter seventeen begins with the group departing Nahom. A reader sensitive to Hebrew narrative recognizes that a change of scene also signals the end of one story and the beginning of another. Just as Esau repented of (that is, regretted) his murderous desire, and just as Joseph's brothers eventually repented of their conspiracy to kill him, at Nahom "they" (the complainers) "did repent" and "were chastened." They "did turn away their anger." The word *naham* is used in the Hebrew Bible even to describe Yahweh's "changing his mind" or "repenting," as when he was sorry in Noah's day for having created mankind.

We see that the biblical parallels to Nephi and his family are many and pointed. It seems impossible that Nephi was not aware of them and did not intend that we see them in the story as he wrote it for us to read. We are just beginning to understand the complexity of Book of Mormon narratives. What Nephi wrote for us about his life and his relations with his family is a complex account. Merely reading the text may not be enough to allow us to understand it fully. If the Book of Mormon was written as a sophisticated text, then we must be sophisticated readers to understand it.

This situation in trying to understand Nephi may be similar to the Nephites' situation as they tried to understand Hebrew prophets. The Nephites had difficulty understanding Isaiah, so Nephi gave them two rules: (1) be filled with the spirit of prophecy as they read and (2) try to understand the symbolic meanings of the text "after the manner of the things of the Jews" (2 Nephi 25:4–5).

Nephi said that he had "not taught [the Nephites] many things concerning the manner of the Jews" (2 Nephi 25:2). This lack of knowledge of the way Jews prophesied and phrased the revelations did have the advantage of keeping the Nephites free of the Jews' "works of darkness, and their doings" (2 Nephi 25:2). But it also made more difficult the Nephites' task of understanding Isaiah and the other Hebrew prophets because "there is none other people that understand the things which were spoken unto the Jews like unto them" (2 Nephi 25:5).

Nephi's writings, though "plain," still rely on his knowledge of the manner of Jewish prophecy and the meanings of the Hebrew expressions he used. The brief narrative of what happened at Nahom turns out to be deeper in meaning than we might have thought. The narrative is far richer if we take into account Nephi's background when he wrote his record. At the same time, it points to a great many more complexities that await our probings as we continue to focus on this keystone scripture.

Notes

1. David Damrosch, *The Narrative Covenant* (San Francisco: Harper and Row, 1987), 128–29.

2. See Mircea Eliade, *Patterns in Comparative Religion,* tr. Rosemary Scheed (New York: New American Library, 1958).

3. Damrosch, 129.

Chapter 10

POETRY IN THE
BOOK OF MORMON

Richard Dilworth Rust

A dam fell that men might be;
and men are, that they might have joy.

Arranging this memorable thought from the Book of Mormon into two lines reveals its poetic character. Arranged in four lines, its neat structure is even more apparent.

> Adam fell
>   that men might be;
>   and men are,
> that they might have joy.
>   (2 Nephi 2:25)

In this case, understanding the structure enhances our understanding of the meaning: the fall of Adam allows mankind to exist, and the potential destiny of mankind can bring ultimate joy.

Rather than being an isolated example, this brief piece is just one of numerous poetic passages throughout the Book of Mormon, which are usually unrecognized as poetry because they are printed as prose. When arranged as verse, however, the poetic parts of the Book of Mormon are unveiled as having great beauty and power.

Poetic Features of the Psalm of Nephi

A fine example of strength and lyricism in Book of Mormon poetry may be found in the following segment of what has been called the Psalm of Nephi (see 2 Nephi 4:15–35). (In this and subsequent poems, the line arrangement is mine.)

Awake, my soul! No longer droop in sin.
Rejoice, O my heart, and give place no more for the
enemy of my soul.

Do not anger again because of mine enemies.
Do not slacken my strength because of mine
afflictions.
Rejoice, O my heart, and cry unto the Lord, and say:
O Lord, I will praise thee forever;
yea, my soul will rejoice in thee, my God, and the
rock of my salvation.

O Lord, wilt thou redeem my soul?
Wilt thou deliver me out of the hands of mine
enemies?
Wilt thou make me that I may shake at the
appearance of sin?
May the gates of hell be shut continually before me,
because that my heart is broken and my spirit is
contrite!

O Lord, wilt thou not shut the gates of thy
righteousness before me,
that I may walk in the path of the low valley,
that I may be strict in the plain road!
O Lord, wilt thou encircle me around in the robe of
thy righteousness!
(vv. 28–33a)

The dominant poetic feature of the Psalm of Nephi is parallelism. An idea expressed in one line is completed, amplified,
contrasted, or reversed in the subsequent line or lines. Both
completion and contrast are evident in these lines:

He hath filled me with his love,
even unto the consuming of my flesh.
He hath confounded mine enemies,
unto the causing of them to quake before me.
(vv. 21–22)

The second line completes the thought begun in the first line;

similarly, the fourth line completes the third. Taken together, the third and fourth lines contrast with the first two lines.

Contrast with intensification is found in the next verse:

> Behold, he hath heard my cry by day,
> and he hath given me knowledge by visions in
>   the nighttime.
> (v. 23)

"Nighttime" contrasts with "day." The intensification comes in the greater detail communicated in the second line where the Lord's response to Nephi's cry is identified.

Both opposition and repetition of an idea in reverse order are found in these lines. (Here and in all subsequent passages, italics are mine, to clarify the parallels.)

> Wilt thou *make my path straight* before me!
> Wilt thou not place a *stumbling block* in my way—
> but that thou wouldst *clear my way* before me,
> and *hedge not up my way*, but the ways of mine
>   enemy.
> (v. 33)

Intensification of thought and feeling are especially evident in the following lines. Here two kinds of movement (travel through the wilderness and then over the ocean) are expressed. These are joined with increasing divine aid—from "support," through "leading," to "preservation":

> My God hath been my support;
> he hath led me through mine afflictions in the
>   wilderness;
> and he hath preserved me upon the waters of the
>   great deep.
> (v. 20)

The next passage illustrates inverted parallelism or chiasmus (literally, a crossing). The subjects of the phrases in chiasmus are basically reversed in order in the second half. The impact of line 1 is amplified in line 3; the words "soul" and "heart" are returned to in reverse order in lines 7 and 9. "Sin" (l. 2), which is the "enemy of my soul" (l. 4), is replaced with their opposites, the "Lord" (l. 8) and "God" (l. 10). While in lines 1 through 4 Nephi's appeals to the soul and heart are accompanied by advice on what not to do—"no longer droop," "give place no more"— the mirror use of *heart* and *soul* in lines 7 through 10 tells what should be done—"rejoice," "praise." These sandwich the center two lines (5 and 6) of commanding oneself not to falter.

1 Awake, my *soul!*
2 No longer droop in *sin.*

3 Rejoice, O my *heart,*
4 and give place no more for the enemy of my
     soul.

5 Do not anger again because of mine enemies.
6 Do not slacken my strength because of mine
     afflictions.

7 Rejoice, O my *heart,*
8 and cry unto the Lord, and say: O Lord, I will
     praise thee forever;

9 yea, my *soul* will rejoice in thee,
10 my God, and the rock of my salvation.
(vv. 28–30)

The Poetry of Isaiah and the Book of Mormon

Each of the features we have seen is characteristic of poetry found in the Old Testament. Especially in the books of First and Second Nephi, this resemblance is what we would expect when we consider that Nephi delighted in the words of Isaiah (see 2 Nephi 25:5) and that Nephi and his brother Jacob quoted much from Isaiah—one of the greatest poets of the Old Testament. When they present poetry of their own, it sounds much like Isaiah. Arranged in poetic lines, the following example of a passage that Jacob quoted from Isaiah reveals the rhythm of ideas and the great poetic power of Isaiah:

My righteousness is near;
my salvation is gone forth,
and mine arm shall judge the people.

> The isles shall wait upon me,
> and on mine arm shall they trust.
> Lift up your eyes to the heavens,
> and look upon the earth beneath;
> for the heavens shall vanish away like smoke,
> and the earth shall wax old like a garment;
> and they that dwell therein shall die in like manner.
> But my salvation shall be forever,
> and my righteousness shall not be abolished.
> > (2 Nephi 8:5–6;
> > cf. Isaiah 51:5–6)

In its rhythm, this passage begins with "righteousness" and "salvation" and ends with "salvation" and "righteousness" — which are, of course, closely related to each other. In the middle are two contrasts of the heavens and the earth.

Having just quoted this passage and others from Isaiah, Jacob employed poetry himself to help sustain the high level of what he had just been teaching the people. While his poetry is not as vivid as Isaiah's, it contains some of the same elevated expression and rich comparison.

> O the greatness and the justice of our God!
> For he executeth all his words,
> and they have gone forth out of his mouth,
> and his law must be fulfilled.
> But, behold, the righteous,
> the saints of the Holy One of Israel,
> they who have believed in the Holy One of Israel,
> they who have endured the crosses of the world,
> and despised the shame of it,
> they shall inherit the kingdom of God,
> which was prepared for them from the foundation of
>   the world,
> and their joy shall be full forever. . . .
>
> O then, my beloved brethren,
> come unto the Lord, the Holy One.
> Remember that his paths are righteous.
> Behold, the way for man is narrow,

but it lieth in a straight course before him,
and the keeper of the gate is the Holy One of Israel;
and he employeth no servant there;
and there is none other way save it be by the gate;
for he cannot be deceived,
for the Lord God is his name.

(2 Nephi 9:17–18, 41)

Poetry and Prophecy

As with the poetry of the Old Testament, Book of Mormon poetry was used to make the passage more unified and memorable. Because of its effects, poetry was not used in the Book of Mormon to report common events. Instead, it was used for more formal speech, such as sermons, instructions, and especially prophecy. When a Book of Mormon prophet said or implied, "Thus saith the Lord," what followed likely was poetic. Since *prophesy* means "to utter by divine interpretation," we would expect the prophetic message to be of an elevated nature, rather than simply phrased in everyday language. Poetry helps the prophetic message to reach beneath surface meanings by adding rhythmic repetitions intended to focus our attention and touch our souls.

Scholars who have analyzed Biblical poetry have emphasized the correlation between prophecy and the use of poetry. David Noel Freedman wrote that, for "communication or action between heaven and earth, the appropriate language is that of poetry. Prose may be adequate to describe setting and circumstances and to sketch historical effects and residues; [but] only poetry can convey the mystery of the miraculous and its meaning for those present."[1] Robert Alter agreed: "Since poetry is our best human model of intricately rich communication, not only solemn, weighty, and forceful but also densely woven with complex internal connections, meanings, and implications, it makes sense that divine speech should be represented as poetry."[2]

Through poetry, according to T. R. Henn, prophecies exalt the heart of man: words and imagery acquire depth by repetition, and there is a peculiar exaltation proper to the chant.[3] As Edgar

105

Allan Poe put it in another context: "Without a certain continuity of effort—without a certain duration or repetition of purpose—the soul is never deeply moved. There must be the dropping of the water upon the rock."[4] This noble effect is the intent of Book of Mormon poetry as much as that of the Bible.

Early in the Book of Mormon, in the second chapter, we can detect a shift from Nephi's prose to the Lord's poetry. Nephi's prose is a straightforward description of events. But when the Lord speaks, we see a number of poetic elements that give force to his words, make them more memorable, and increase the levels of meaning: There is a rhythm resulting from a structure of cause-and-effect relationships (following the pattern "inasmuch as ye or they do x, ye or they shall receive y"). There is repetition with an rising order of significance ("land of promise," "land which I have prepared for you," and "land which is choice above all other lands"). And the concluding two patterns in the last four lines show contrast between punishment and blessing.

> Laman and Lemuel would not hearken unto my
> words; and being grieved because of the hardness
> of their hearts I cried unto the Lord for them. And
> it came to pass that the Lord spake unto me, saying:
>> Blessed art thou, Nephi, because of thy faith,
>> for thou hast sought me diligently, with lowliness
>>   of heart.
>> And inasmuch as ye shall keep my commandments,
>> ye shall prosper,
>> and shall be led to a land of promise;
>> yea, even a land which I have prepared for you;
>> yea, a land which is choice above all other lands.
>> And inasmuch as thy brethren shall rebel against
>>   thee,
>> they shall be cut off from the presence of the Lord.
>> And inasmuch as thou shalt keep my
>>   commandments,
>> thou shalt be made a ruler and a teacher over thy
>>   brethren.
>
> (1 Nephi 2:18–22)

106

We find a similar shift in Alma 7:8–9:

> Now as to this thing I do not know; but this much
> I do know, that the Lord God hath power to do all
> things which are according to his word. But behold,
> the Spirit hath said this much unto me, saying: Cry
> unto this people, saying—
>
>> Repent ye, and prepare the way of the Lord,
>> And walk in his paths, which are straight;
>> For behold, the kingdom of heaven is at hand,
>> And the Son of God cometh upon the face of the
>> earth.

In Alma's excerpt, one idea builds on another. Personal repentance is the foundation for preparing the way of the Lord, then preparing leads to action ("walk in his paths"). Personal actions then become the basis for the universal—the general expectation of first the coming of the kingdom of heaven and second the more specific coming of the Lord.

The next poem is about God's power promised to Nephi the son of Helaman. The idea is first expressed as increasing levels of physical power (famine, to pestilence, to destruction). Then it is given spiritual significance (sealed/loosed in heaven). Destructive power builds in intensity from rending the temple, to leveling a mountain, to the climax of divine power that will smite the people. With the confidence that comes from having seen this vision of God's power, Nephi was ready to declare the simple but meaningful message: "Except ye repent ye shall be smitten, even unto destruction."

> As he was thus pondering . . . the wickedness of
> the people of the Nephites, . . . a voice came unto
> him saying: . . .
>
>> Behold, thou art Nephi, and I am God.
>> Behold, I declare it unto thee in the presence of mine
>> angels,
>> that ye shall have power over this people,
>> and shall smite the earth with famine,

and with pestilence,
and destruction,
according to the wickedness of this people.
Behold, I give unto you power,
that whatsoever ye shall seal on earth shall be sealed
    in heaven;
and whatsoever ye shall loose on earth shall be
    loosed in heaven;
and thus shall ye have power among this people.
And thus, if ye shall say unto this temple
it shall be rent in twain,
it shall be done.
And if ye shall say unto this mountain,
Be thou cast down and become smooth,
it shall be done.
And behold, if ye shall say
that God shall smite this people,
it shall come to pass.
And now behold, I command you,
that ye shall go and declare unto this people,
that thus saith the Lord God, who is the Almighty:
Except ye repent ye shall be smitten,
even unto destruction.

And behold, now it came to pass that when the Lord had spoken these words unto Nephi, he did stop and did not go unto his own house, but did return unto the multitudes who were scattered about upon the face of the land, and began to declare unto them the word of the Lord which had been spoken unto him, concerning their destruction if they did not repent (Helaman 10:3, 6–12).

Three Other Book of Mormon Poems

Finally, a close look at three more poems from the Book of Mormon will show how they are carefully designed to reach the heart as well as the mind. First, the prayer of worship and praise by Zenos in Alma 33 is marked by simplicity and clarity. Its power is developed by repetition that varies slightly but meaningfully:

1 Thou art merciful, O God,
    for thou hast heard my prayer,
        even when I was in the wilderness;
    yea, thou wast merciful
        when I prayed concerning those who were
            mine enemies,
        and thou didst turn them to me.
   Yea, O God, and thou wast merciful unto me
        when I did cry unto thee in my field;
        when I did cry unto thee in my prayer,
        and thou didst hear me.
   And again, O God, when I did turn to my house
        thou didst hear me in my prayer.
   And when I did turn unto my closet,
   O Lord, and prayed unto thee,
        thou didst hear me.

2 Yea, thou art merciful unto thy children
        when they cry unto thee,
            to be heard of thee and not of men,
            and thou wilt hear them.

3 Yea, O God, thou hast been merciful unto me,
        and heard my cries in the midst of thy
            congregations.
   Yea, and thou hast also heard me when I have
            been cast out
        and have been despised by mine enemies;
   yea, thou didst hear my cries,
        and wast angry with mine enemies,
        and thou didst visit them in thine anger with
            speedy destruction.

4 And thou didst hear me
        because of mine afflictions and my sincerity;
     and it is because of thy Son
        that thou hast been thus merciful unto me,

>therefore I will cry unto thee in all mine
>   afflictions,
>for in thee is my joy;
>for thou hast turned thy judgments away
>   from me,
>because of thy Son.
>(Alma 33:4–11)

In the first stanza there is a movement from the dangerous exterior ("wilderness"—a place where one encounters enemies) to the cultivated exterior ("field") to the safe interior ("house") to the even more secure interior ("closet"). The second stanza serves as a transition, moving the focus from place (stanza 1) to human or social environment (stanza 3). In either case, however, whether with fellow saints ("thy congregations") or with foes ("mine enemies"), Zenos was confident in the integrity of his direct relationship with God ("to be heard of thee and not of men").

The third stanza contains a striking variation from the first. In the first stanza, Zenos expressed gratitude that his enemies were turned to him (that is, their hearts were softened toward him). But in the third, when they renewed their unkindness to him (casting him out and despising him), the prophet cried to God over his afflictions, until God chose to punish Zenos's enemies.

The concluding stanza links Christ with the mercy referred to earlier—bringing to a climactic close the intensified power created throughout the poem by the repetition of "merciful." This stanza moves from past ("thou didst hear me") to future ("I will cry unto thee") to present ("thou hast turned thy judgments away"), closing with the powerful and final repeated phrase: "Because of thy Son."

The poem builds intensity with variations on "hear," "cry," and "merciful." These three words are developed in the first stanza, with "thou didst hear me" working as a repeating climax. They are interlinked in the second stanza, with the principle of prayer being applied to all of God's prayerful children. Then in

110

the third stanza, when we come to "thou didst hear my cries," we feel the emotional shrillness of "cries" in the context of Zenos's being "despised by mine enemies"; here the tension has increased as well. The fourth and last stanza resolves the problem and has a calming effect. The preceding stanza repeats the expressions "enemies," "angry/anger," and "destruction"; in contrast, the last stanza emphasizes "sincerity," "joy," and especially the repeated "because of thy Son."

In this second example, Alma's instruction to his son Helaman contains this elevated poetic exhortation:

1   O, remember, my son, and *learn* wisdom in thy
    youth;
2   yea, *learn* in thy youth to keep the
    commandments of God.
3   Yea, and *cry unto God* for all thy support;
4   yea, let all thy *doings* be *unto the Lord,*
5   and whithersoever thou *goest* let it be *in the
    Lord;*
6   yea, let all thy *thoughts* be directed *unto the
    Lord;*
7   yea, let the *affections* of thy heart be placed *upon
    the Lord forever.*
8   Counsel with the Lord in all thy doings,
9   and he will direct thee for good;
10 yea, when thou liest down at *night* lie down
    unto the Lord,
11 that he may watch over you in your sleep;
12 and when thou risest in the *morning*
13 let thy heart be full of thanks unto God;
14 and if ye do these things,
15 ye shall be lifted up at the *last day.*
                        (Alma 37:35–37)

The second line adds to the kind of learning found in the first. Line three sets up a relationship with God that in the next four lines receives greater importance and emphasis, moving from crying, to doing, to going, and, in lines six and seven, from thoughts to affections. The relationship advocated between

Helaman and the Lord in the second half of the poem is more intimate, starting with "counsel with the Lord" (contrast with the more distant "cry unto God" in the first half). The paired opposites of times of day are used in the climax of the poem. The actions of lying down at night unto the Lord and rising in the morning with thanks unto God are followed by being lifted up at the last day.

In the third example, notice the poetic repetitions in Moroni's account of the song of the Jaredites and then in his narrative "hymn" describing their preservation. (Italics here emphasize repetitions, synonyms, and opposites.)

> They did *sing praises unto the Lord;*
> yea, the brother of Jared did *sing praises unto the Lord,*
> and he did thank and *praise the Lord*
> all the *day* long;
> and when the *night* came,
> they did not cease to *praise the Lord*.
>
> *And thus they were driven forth;*
> and no *monster* of the sea could break them,
> neither *whale* that could mar them;
> and they did have light continually,
> whether it was *above the water* or *under the water*.
> *And thus they were driven forth,*
> three hundred and forty and four days *upon the water*.
>
> And they did *land upon the shore of the promised land*.
> And when they had *set their feet upon the shores of the promised land*
> they *bowed themselves* down upon the face of the *land,*
> and did *humble themselves before the Lord,*
> and did *shed tears of joy before the Lord,*
> because of the multitude of his tender mercies over them.

(Ether 6:9–12)

These and other poetic passages show how much more the Book of Mormon can open up with more extensive and thorough

112

poetic analysis. Evidence of the abundant poetry in the book should also encourage us to listen to exalted Book of Mormon passages, especially the words of the Lord. Read out loud, the poetic elements of the Book of Mormon will resonate, touching us as beautiful music does. Feeling the Christ-centered poetry of the book, one may well be stirred to cry with Nephi:

> I glory in plainness;
> I glory in truth;
> I glory in my Jesus,
> > for he hath redeemed my soul from hell.
> > > (2 Nephi 33:6)

Or we may be led to feel the poetic force of Abinadi's testimony of Christ:

> He is the *light* and the *life* of the world;
> yea, a *light* that is endless,
> that can never be darkened;
> yea, and also a *life* which is endless,
> that there can be no more death.
> > (Mosiah 16:9)

Notes

1. "Pottery, Poetry, and Prophecy: An Essay on Biblical Poetry," in *The Bible in Its Literary Milieu,* ed. John Maier and Vincent Toller (Grand Rapids, Michigan: Wm. B. Eerdmans Publishing Co., 1979), 92.

2. *The Art of Biblical Poetry* (New York: Basic Books, 1985), 141.

3. See "The Bible as Literature," in *Peake's Commentary on the Bible,* ed. Matthew Black and H. H. Rowley (Surrey, England: Thomas Nelson & Sons, 1962), 12–13.

4. *"Twice-told Tales,* by Nathaniel Hawthorne; a Review," *Graham's Magazine,* May 1842, p. 298.

Chapter 11

A MASTERPIECE: ALMA 36

John W. Welch

Chiasmus is a style of writing known in antiquity and used by many ancient and some modern writers. It consists of arranging a series of words or ideas in one order, and then repeating it in reverse order. In the hands of a skillful writer, this literary form can serve several purposes. The repeating of key words in the two halves underlines the importance of the concepts they present. Furthermore, the main idea of the passage is placed at the turning point where the second half begins, which emphasizes it. The repeating form also enhances clarity and speeds memorizing. Readers (or listeners) gain a pleasing sense of completeness as the passage returns at the end to the idea that began it. Identifying the presence of chiasmus in a composition can reveal many complex and subtle features of the text.

As early as the first century B.C., Greek readers of Homer's *Odyssey* noted a fine example. In a conversation between Odysseus and his mother Anticleia in the underworld, Odysseus asks his mother's ghost:

a How she had died,
 b Was it by a disease,
  c Or by the gentle shafts of Artemis.
   d About his father,
    e About his son Telemachus,
     f Whether another had assumed his royal power,
      g And about his wife, where does she stay.

Anticleia responds in exactly the reverse order:

g' She stays in thy halls,
 f' No man has taken thy honor,
  e' Telemachus is a peaceful lord,
 d' Your father remains in the fields,
  c' Artemis did not slay me,
 b' Nor did a disease,
a' But I died of grief for thee.
                    (*Odyssey*, 11.170)

Many examples of chiasmus have been identified in the Hebrew Bible. A prime case is Leviticus 24:13–23. (Here and in other examples, I have added italics to emphasize correspondences.) Reporting the execution of a blasphemer, this text reads:

a And *the Lord spake unto Moses,* saying,
 b Bring forth him that hath *cursed without the camp;* and let all that heard him . . . *stone him.*
  c And thou shalt *speak unto the children of Israel,* saying,
   d Whosoever curseth his God shall bear his sin . . . : as well the *stranger,* as he that is *born in the land.*
    e And he that killeth *any man* shall surely be put to death.
     f And he that killeth *a beast* shall make it good; beast for beast.
      g And if a man cause *a blemish* in his neighbour . . . , *so shall it be done to him;*
       h breach for breach,
             eye for eye,
             tooth for tooth:
      g' as he hath caused *a blemish* in a man, *so shall it be done to him* again.
     f' And he that killeth *a beast,* he shall restore it:
    e' and he that killeth *a man,* he shall be put to death.
   d' Ye shall have one manner of law . . . for the *stranger,* as for *one of your own country.* . . .
  c' And Moses *spake to the children of Israel,*
 b' that they should bring forth him that had *cursed out of the camp,* and *stone him* with stones.
a' And the children of Israel did as *the Lord commanded Moses.*

The symmetrical structure of this passage is obvious, long, and pleasing. It is unlikely that this elaborate, precise pattern was formed by accident.

Not all chiasms, however, are created equal. They differ in purpose, precision, and artistic achievement. Some are very clear; others are not. Some are very long; others are short. We must learn to look carefully to know whether a passage may be an actual chiasm and whether it is significant. After evaluating hundreds of proposed chiasms in a wide variety of lengthy texts, I have found that only a few texts unmistakably rate as planned, successful chiasms. Alma 36 is one of the best.

Alma 36 was one of the first chiasms I discovered within the Book of Mormon in 1967. Many years later, it still remains one of my favorites. It is a masterpiece of composition, as good as any other use of chiasmus in world literature, and it deserves wide recognition and appreciation. I cannot imagine that its complex and purposeful structure happened unintentionally. Its sophistication as a piece of literature definitely shows Alma's skill as a writer.

Here, we are going to look at the overall structure of Alma 36 and then analyze many of its details. It will quickly become evident that this text shows a very high degree of chiasm at several levels of complexity.

Level 1: The Overall Structure of Alma 36

We begin by finding the main girders in its structure or framework. The following summary of the chapter, in which Alma tells his son Helaman about his dramatic conversion, shows the basic elements. There are seventeen key elements, each repeated twice (verse numbers are indicated in parentheses):

a My son give ear to my *words* (1)
 b *Keep the commandments* and ye shall *prosper in the land* (1)
  c Do *as I* have done (2)
   d *Remember the captivity* of our fathers (2)
    e They were in *bondage* (2)
     f He surely did *deliver* them (2)
      g *Trust* in God (3)
       h Supported in *trials, troubles, and afflictions* (3)
        i Lifted up at the *last day* (3)
         j *I know* this not of myself but *of God* (4)
          k *Born of God* (5)
           l I sought to destroy the church (6–9)
            m My *limbs* were paralyzed (10)
             n Fear of being in the *presence of God* (14–15)
              o *Pains* of a damned soul (16)
               p *Harrowed up by the memory of sins* (17)
                q I remembered *Jesus Christ, a son of God* (17)
                q' I cried, *Jesus, son of God* (18)
               p' *Harrowed up by the memory of sins* no more (19)
              o' Joy as exceeding as was the *pain* (20)
             n' Long to be in the *presence of God* (22)
            m' My *limbs* received strength again (23)
           l' I labored to bring souls to repentance (24)
          k' *Born of God* (26)
         j' Therefore *my knowledge* is *of God* (26)
        h' Supported under *trials, troubles, and afflictions* (27)
       g' *Trust* in him (27)
      f' He will *deliver* me (27)
       i' and *raise me up at the last day* (28)
     e' As God brought our fathers out of *bondage* and captivity (28–29)
    d' Retain in *remembrance their captivity* (28–29)
   c' Know *as I* do know (30)
  b' *Keep the commandments* and ye shall *prosper in the land* (30)
 a' This according to his *word* (30).

The design of this text is amazing. I am especially impressed with the repetition of the name "Jesus Christ, Son of God" at the very center of the chapter. This unquestionably had deep significance for Alma. It is one of the best examples of any ancient author succeeding in placing the most important concept at the central or turning point of his passage. By this, the structure of the chapter powerfully communicates Alma's personal experience, for the central turning point of his conversion came precisely when he called upon the name of Jesus Christ and asked for mercy. Nothing was more important than this in Alma's conversion — neither the appearance of the angel, nor the prayers of his father and the priests. Just as this was the turning point of Alma's life, he makes it the center of this magnificent composition.

Level 2: The Full Text of Alma 36

We have seen the main girders of the structure. Now, at a more detailed level, we are able to detect panels of text filling in the gaps. There is no simple way to display these segments except to set forth every word in the chapter. The following arrangement is largely self-explanatory. I have grouped the text into segments, each having corresponding counterparts in the two halves.

I encourage readers to take time to read the text several times. The lettering of key parts (**A, B, C,** etc.) is the same as in the preceding discussion (Level 1). Lowercase a, b, c, etc., indicate matching phrases within shorter sections. As will be discussed below, some of these words serve in more than one way. Sometimes the repeated (italicized) phrases function in the overall structure of the chapter, sometimes they stand within substructures or single sections. At other times they bridge from one section to the next. All these elements work together in masterful harmony to create a composition that flows smoothly from one part to the next. The movement of concepts and phrasings from one section to another is never awkward or abrupt.

verse

A *My son,* give ear to *my words;* [1]

B for I swear unto you *that*
inasmuch as ye shall keep the commandments of God
ye shall prosper in the land.

C I would that ye should do *as I have done,* [2]
in remembering the *captivity of our fathers;*

D **a** for they were *in bondage,*
   b and none could *deliver them*
      c except it was the God of Abraham,
      c and the God of Isaac,
      c and the God of Jacob;
   b' and he surely did *deliver them*
a' *in* their *afflictions.*

A And now, O *my son* Helaman, behold, thou art in [3]
      thy youth,
and therefore, I beseech of thee that
thou wilt *hear my words* and learn of me;

E for I do know that whosoever shall put their *trust in God*
shall be *supported* in their *trials,*
      and their *troubles,*
      and their *afflictions,*

and *shall be lifted up at the last day.*

F And I would not that ye think that I *know of myself* — [4]
   a not of the temporal
   b but of the spiritual,
   a' not of the carnal mind
   b' but *of God.*

G Now, behold, I say unto you, [5]
if I had not been *born of God*
I should not have known these things;
but God has, by the mouth of his holy angel,
made these things known *unto me,*
not of any worthiness *of myself;*

119

verse

H   For I went about with the sons of Mosiah,   [6]
seeking to destroy the church of God;
but behold, God sent his holy angel to stop us by the way.
And behold, he *spake unto us,* as it were the   [7]
   voice of thunder,
and the whole *earth* did tremble beneath our *feet;*
and we all *fell to the earth,*
for the *fear* of the Lord came upon us.

But behold, the voice said unto me: Arise.   [8]
And I arose and *stood* up, and beheld the angel.
And he said unto me: [9]
If thou wilt of thyself be destroyed,
seek no more to destroy the church of God.
And it came to pass that I *fell to the earth;*   [10]
and it was for the space of three days and three nights
that I could not open my mouth,
neither had I the use of *my limbs.*

And the angel *spake* more things *unto me,*   [11]
which were heard by my brethren, but I did not hear them;
for when I heard the words—
If thou wilt be destroyed of thyself,
seek no more to destroy the church of God—
I was struck with such great *fear* and amazement
lest perhaps I should be destroyed,
that *I fell to the earth* and I did hear no more.

I   But I was *racked* with eternal *torment,*   [12]
for my soul was *harrowed up* to the greatest degree and
   racked with *all my sins.*

Yea, I did remember *all my sins* and *iniquities,*   [13]
for which I was *tormented* with the *pains of* hell;

Yea, I saw that I had rebelled against my God,
and that I had not kept his holy commandments.

Yea, and I had murdered many of his children,   [14]
or rather led them away unto destruction;

verse

Yea, and in fine so great had been my *iniquities,*
that the very thought of coming into *the presence of my God*
   did *rack* my soul with inexpressible horror.

Oh, thought I, that I could be banished and become   [15]
   extinct
both soul and body,

That I might not be brought to stand in *the presence of my*
   God,
to be judged of my deeds.

And now, for three days and for three nights was   [16]
   I *racked,*
even with the *pains of* a damned soul.

J   And it came to pass that as I was thus *racked* with   [17]
   torment,
while I was *harrowed up by the memory of my many sins,*

K   behold, I *remembered* also to have heard my father prophesy
   unto the people concerning the coming of one
Jesus Christ, a Son of God,
to atone for the sins of the world.

K'   Now, as my mind caught hold upon this thought,   [18]
   I cried within my heart:
O Jesus, thou Son of God,
have mercy on me, who am in the gall of bitterness,
and am encircled about by the everlasting chains of death.

J'   And now, behold, when I thought this, I could   [19]
   remember my *pains no more;*
yea, I was *harrowed up by the memory of my sins no more.*

I'   And oh, what *joy,* and what marvelous light I did   [20]
   behold;
yea, my soul was filled with *joy* as exceeding as was my
   pain!

121

verse

a   Yea, *I say unto you, my son,*   [21]
  b   that there could be *nothing so exquisite* and so bitter
   c   as were *my pains.*
a'   Yea, and again *I say unto you, my son,*
  b'   that on the other hand, there can be *nothing so*
        exquisite and sweet
   c'   as was *my* joy.

Yea, methought I saw, even as our father Lehi saw,   [22]
"God sitting upon his throne,
surrounded with numberless concourses of angels,
in the attitude of singing and praising their God;"
yea, and my soul did long to be there.

H'   But behold, *my limbs* did receive their strength again,   [23]
and I *stood* upon my *feet,*
and did manifest unto the people
that I had been *born of God.*

Yea, and from that time even until now,   [24]
I have labored without ceasing,
that I might bring souls unto repentance;

G'   that I might bring them to taste of the *exceeding joy*
        of which I did *taste;*
that they might also be *born of God,*
        and be filled with the Holy Ghost.

Yea, and now behold, *O my son,*   [25]
the Lord doth give me *exceedingly great joy*
   in the fruit of my labors;
For because of the word which he has imparted   [26]
   unto me,
behold, many have been *born of God,*

F' and have *tasted*
    as I have *tasted,*
and have *seen* eye to eye
    as I have *seen;*
therefore they do *know* of these things of which I have
      spoken,
    as I do *know;*
and the *knowledge* which I have is *of God.*

E' And I have been *supported*   [27]
    under *trials*
    and *troubles* of every kind,
    yea, and in all manner of *afflictions;*

    yea, God has *delivered* me
      from prison,
      and from bonds,
      and from death;

    Yea, and I do put my *trust in him,*
    and he will still *deliver* me.

    And I know that he *will raise me up at the last day,*   [28]
    to dwell with him in glory.

D' Yea, and I will praise him *forever,*
    for he has *brought our fathers out* of *Egypt,*
    and he has swallowed up the *Egyptians* in the Red Sea;

    a and he led them by his *power* into the promised *land;*
    b yea, and he has *delivered them out of bondage and*
        captivity
      c *from time to time;*
    a' yea, and he has also *brought our fathers*   [29]
      out of the *land* of Jerusalem;
      b' and he has also by his everlasting *power, delivered*
        them out of bondage and captivity,
        c' *from time to time* even down to the *present day;*

verse

C'   And I have always retained *in remembrance their captivity;*
         yea, and ye also ought to retain *in remembrance, as I have*
         done, their captivity.

B'   But behold, *my son,* this is not all;   [30]
         a   for *ye ought to know as I* do know,
           b   *that inasmuch as ye shall keep the commandments of God*
           c   *ye shall prosper in the land;*
         a' and *ye ought to know* also,
           b' that inasmuch as ye will not *keep the commandments*
                  of God
           c' ye shall be cut off from his presence.

A'   Now this is according to his *word.*

Level 3: Detailed Relations between the Paired Sections

The impressive overall structure of the full text of this complex passage becomes even more evident as pairs of sections are examined. Refer back to the full text to see the following detailed relationships:

Sections A and A' introduce and conclude the chapter by referring to Alma's "words" and the "word" of God.

Sections B and B' both state that prosperity comes from keeping the commandments of God. B states the principle once; B' repeats it twice, once positively and once negatively.

Sections C and C' exhort Helaman to remember, as Alma has done, the captivity of the fathers. C says that Helaman should do as Alma has done; on the other hand, C' states what Alma has done, and then moves, in the opposite order, to the obligation this imposes upon Helaman.

Sections D and D' both speak of bondage and deliverance. Section D itself is a small chiasm, composed of the following elements:

a for they were *in bondage,*
 b and none could *deliver them*
  c except it was the God of Abraham,
  c and the God of Isaac,
  c and the God of Jacob;
 b' and he surely did *deliver them*
a' *in their afflictions.*

The expression "did deliver them *in* their afflictions" (instead of *from* their afflictions) seems odd, except when it is understood as a chiastic link to the phrase "in bondage." At the center of D is the triplet, "the God of Abraham, and the God of Isaac, and the God of Jacob," while D' speaks of three deliverances of the fathers by God—from Egypt, of the Israelites in the land of promise, and of Lehi and his descendants from time to time. D' also contains several interesting pairings: two references to "Egypt," two uses of the phrase "brought our fathers out," two occurrences of the phrase "delivered them out of bondage and captivity from time to time," and a minor chiasm in the two phrases "by his *power* into the promised *land*" and "the *land* of Jerusalem by his everlasting *power.*"

E and E' are both marked by the triplet, "supported under trials, troubles, and afflictions." In E' the third member of this triplet is stressed, "yea, and in all manner of afflictions," to make the repetition clear. Both E and E' speak of putting one's "trust in God" and of being "lifted up at the last day." In E, the idea of trusting in God is presented as it applies collectively to all people; in E' the point is personalized, telling how Alma had been individually supported and thus had personally trusted in God to be raised up at the last day. The triplet "trials, troubles, and afflictions" appears at the center of E. A new triplet ("prison, bonds, death"), speaking of Alma's personal deliverance while at Ammonihah (Alma 14), stands at the center of E', flanked by words drawn from E.

F and F' both affirm that Alma speaks of his own knowledge. In F, Alma first asserts that he personally does not know "of himself," but only knows "of God." F' extends this theme collectively to Alma's converts, that they also know as he knows. This sequence from the personal to the collective reverses the sequence from the collective to the personal that was found in E and E'.

The clear theme in both G and G' is being "born of God." The phrase appears once in G and emphatically twice in G'. The "mouth" of God's angel is mentioned in G, and the "taste" of Alma's exceeding joy is doubled in G'.

H and H' speak of the contrast between Alma's persecution of the church and being stricken by the angel of the Lord on the one hand, and his recovery and work to bring souls to repentance on the other hand. Both sections speak of "limbs," "feet," "earth," and of falling down or standing up. H itself is an interesting composition. Three times it intones the phrase "seek no more to destroy the church of God," which is the language of the angel. This three-fold repetition has a powerful dramatic effect.

I and I' contrast the agony of Alma's suffering (in I) with the joy of his conversion (in I'). Indeed, the contrast is made explicit in I': "Yea, my soul was filled with joy as exceeding as was my pain" (Alma 36:20). This statement strongly supports the idea that Alma consciously created the chiastic structure of this chapter. (Faint traces of an original eight-part poem seem to be found in section I.)

Another remarkable thing about Alma 36:22 is the fact that Lehi's words are not just summarized, but are precisely quoted. These twenty-one words are a verbatim quote of 1 Nephi 1:8. Such exactness cannot be explained by thinking that Joseph turned to 1 Nephi and copied the words of Lehi from what Oliver Cowdery had already recorded from Joseph's dictation, for 1 Nephi may not yet even have been translated at the time when Joseph and Oliver were translating Alma 36.[1] Evidently, Alma was very meticulous in quoting Lehi's words from the small plates of Nephi when he composed Alma 36, and Joseph Smith's dictated translation preserved that exactitude.

The paired sections J and J' are distinguished by their unique use of the nearly identical phrases "harrowed up by the memory of my many sins," and "harrowed up by the memory of my sins no more."

Sections K and K' stand at the center of the composition, naming "Jesus Christ, a son of God," and "Jesus, thou son of God." Only when Alma remembered that his father had spoken of the atonement of Christ and then called upon Jesus Christ did his tormented condition change. At the absolute center stand the words "atone," "mind," and "heart," bordered by the name of Jesus Christ. The message is clear: Christ's atonement and man's responding sacrifice of a broken heart and willing mind are central to receiving forgiveness from God.

Level 4: Weaving Factors

In addition to the close relationships that exist between each pair of sections, the fact that each segment flows smoothly into the next adds another dimension to the textual complexity of this chapter. No awkwardness, no sharp breaks are found here. Bridges connect each section to the one that follows it. These linkages are accomplished largely by introducing a minor item in one section that anticipates ideas in the next.

For example, the phrase "my words" at the end of A blends into the beginning of B, "for I swear."

"Captivity" at the end of C blends directly into "bondage" at the beginning of D.

"Afflictions" at the end of D, from which the fathers were delivered, later appears more significantly at the center of E, promising further support and salvation.

The introductory phrase "for I do know" in E anticipates all of Alma's knowledge in F, and F ends with the words "of God," which is where G begins, being born "of God."

G ends with Alma acknowledging his unworthiness, which leads naturally into H, the section where he tells about Alma's wickedness in "seeking to destroy the church of God."

H first introduces the ideas of "fear" and being "destroyed," which intensify in I as "torment" and "inexpressible horror."

J starts with a single use of a key word that was mentioned four times in I, "racked." The memory of "sins" in J and J' surround the centrally stated purpose of Christ's coming, "to atone for the *sins* of the world."

Moving from the center now back out to the end, similarly subtle steps of transition and weaving again occur. J' states twice that Alma remembered his pains "no more," and this leads directly to the contrast between the former pain and the joy that replaced that agony in I'.

Alma's longing to go into the presence of God at the end of I' evokes the idea of physical movement, which flows into H' as Alma's limbs recover their strength.

H' ends with the phrase "that I might bring," and G' begins with the same phrase "that I might bring."

The idea of Alma's joy in I' looks forward to the joy of Alma's converts two segments later in G'; the joy in I' is called "exquisite," whereas in G' it is both times called "exceeding."

As G' ("taste," "born of God") blends into F', the phrases "as I have tasted" and "as I have seen" grow into the phrase "as I do know," so that by the end F' returns to the theme of F, namely the divine source of Alma's knowledge.

E' ends with a unique phrase "to dwell with him in glory," which seems to have been introduced as a transition to D', which begins with the idea of "praising" (glorifying) God forever. Alma will praise God forever because of his deliverance from bondage and captivity, which is the theme taken up in C' in remembering the captivity of the fathers.

C' ends with the exhortation "ye also ought to," a connecting phrase that is repeated twice in B'.

These weaving links are subtle but effective. They make the transitions from section to section smooth and flowing. This reflects a highly polished literary product. If an author uses chiasmus mechanically, it can produce rigid, stilted writing (a poor result from an author misusing or poorly implementing any artistic device). Alma, however, does not simply stick a list of ideas together in one order and then awkwardly and slavishly retrace his steps through that list in the opposite order. His work has the markings of a skillful, painstaking writer, one completely comfortable with using this difficult mode of expression well.

Level 5: Degree of Chiasticity

We now are in a position to see how complex the chiasm of Alma 36 really is. Chiasmus can occur in any literature, but it only becomes meaningful when its degree of chiasticity is high. Only when the chiastic format is truly complex and concise are we justified in supposing that the author intentionally followed the pattern. Judged by the following criteria, the degree of chiasmus in Alma 36 is extremely high and can best be explained by concluding that Alma learned it as part of a long literary tradition extending back to Old Testament prophets.

Objectivity. The chiastic pattern of Alma 36 is objectively verifiable. It is not based on loose connections, imaginative synonyms, or conceptual relationships. Few texts contain such overt evidence as this.

Purpose, climax, and centrality. Chiasmus is an excellent literary device to convey the sense of conversion. The turning point of Alma's chapter communicates both in form and substance the turning point of Alma's life. Thus, the placement of the name of Jesus Christ at the center of Alma 36 is highly purposeful. The central elements of this passage are its focus.

Boundaries. Chiasm is strongest if it operates upon a whole literary unit. Alma 36 is a literary unit.

Length. The longer and clearer the chiasm, the higher its degree of chiasticity. Alma 36 is among the longest clear chiasms found anywhere.

Density and dominance. Alma 36 contains 1230 total words. Around 175 figure directly in the chiasm. And these 175 are substantial, not minor, words in the text.

Mavericks and random repetition. A chiasm is less convincing if important words in the structure appear elsewhere in the text outside the suggested arrangement. Alma 36 meets this rule very well. For example, of the thirty key structural words, only three ("word," "commandments," and "know") ever appear outside their respective sections. There is very little random repetition of these thirty key words or of any other words in Alma 36.

Balance. Alma 36 exhibits a strong degree of balance. The first half of the structure contains 52.4% of the words, and the second half, 47.6%. Even minor words like "behold" (six times in each half) and "my" (eighteen times in the first half and seventeen in the second) occur equally in the two halves.

Return. Alma 36 conveys a powerful sense of completeness. It clearly returns to the ideas with which it began.

Stylistic Compatibility. Alma wrote other passages that are strongly chiastic. For example, there is Alma 41:13–15, which was apparently given by Alma to Corianton on the same day he gave Alma 36 to Helaman. Obviously chiasmus was distinctly part of Alma's literary style and not a one-time fluke.

Aesthetics. Alma 36 is fluent and harmonious. Chiasmus is a rather rigid pattern, yet here it does not draw undue attention to itself, and it does not detract from the warmth we would expect in such a personal account.

Setting. Perhaps Alma gave Helaman a kind of double blessing such as was customary for Israelites to give their firstborn son (see Deuteronomy 21:17). At least this blessing was double-structured. In contrast, Alma's blessing to his second son, Shiblon (in Alma 38), consists of only the first half of Helaman's blessing. This is not likely to have occurred by chance.

Intentionality. Short of an actual statement by Alma certifying that he used this pattern on purpose, it is difficult to imagine a clearer case than Alma 36. This conclusion is further supported by comparing Alma 36 with Mosiah 27 and Alma 38.

Level 6: Comparison of Mosiah 27 and Alma 36

Mosiah 27:10–32 gives an account of the actual, spontaneous words that Alma used when he spoke to the people right after his conversion. That was the original statement of what Alma retells in Alma 36. Twenty or so years separated the events of Mosiah 27 and Alma 36; still it is obvious that the same person made both statements. For instance, certain distinctive phrases in Mosiah 27 reappear in Alma 36, such as "destroy the church of God," "with the sons of Mosiah seeking to destroy the church," "lead astray," "rebelling against God," "he spake as it were with a voice of thunder," "earth to shake upon which they stood," "fell to the earth," and so on through several more. So the story as reported in Mosiah 27 has close verbal connections with Alma 36, even though one hundred pages of text separate the two versions.

In terms of form, however, the two accounts are quite different. The sentences in Mosiah 27 are short, contrasting statements, such as, "I was in the darkest abyss; but now I behold the marvelous light of God" (v. 29). After Alma had reflected on his experience for over twenty years, he regrouped all the elements from the dark side of his conversion and placed them in the first half of Alma 36. Then he took all the joyous factors and concentrated them into the second half of Alma 36. In short, he reorganized his earlier words into a masterful single statement of his conversion.

Anyone who claims that a passage is chiastic should be able to prove it. In my opinion, the case with respect to Alma 36 is established. It fits all the rules, from the objective to the aesthetic. This text ranks as one of the best uses of chiasmus one can imagine. It merits high acclaim and recognition. Despite its complexity, the meaning of the chapter is both simple and profound. Alma's words are both inspired and inspiring, religious and literary, historical and timeless, clear yet complex — a text that deserves to be pondered for years to come.

Notes

1. See "How Long Did It Take Joseph Smith to Translate the Book of Mormon?" *Ensign,* January 1988, pp. 46–47.

Chapter 12

BOOK OF MORMON
IMAGERY

Richard Dilworth Rust

They were many times buried in the depths of the sea, because of the mountain waves which broke upon them" (Ether 6:6).

"[Wicked King Noah] shalt be as a stalk, even as a dry stalk of the field, which is run over by the beasts and trodden under foot" (Mosiah 12:11).

Each of these Book of Mormon passages is given life by the pictures or images they awake in our minds. In Ether the power comes from referring directly to "mountain waves." The memorable picture of King Noah is not so direct, being formed from a figure of speech: the ruler is like a "dry stalk" crushed under foot. Without their imagery, these verses would lose beauty and vitality.

Imagine if the statements had only been something like, "The Jaredites faced great difficulty in crossing the ocean," or, "The life of King Noah shall become of little value." Imagery helps make the Book of Mormon appeal to all our senses (our sight, hearing, touch, smell, taste, and even our spiritual sense). We should be grateful for this, because some of our deepest responses to truth are through our senses and emotions. But many of us are not as aware as we might be of how scripture affects us. By stepping back and looking at imagery in the Book of Mormon as a whole, we can discover patterns hidden beneath the surface of our usual reading that increase the book's meaning and impact.

132

Let us begin by looking at a phrase and concept that we read over and over: "It must needs be, that there is an opposition in all things" (2 Nephi 2:11). Writers and speakers in the Book of Mormon use image-stimulating language to support and explain this teaching. Mental pictures raised within us thus deepen our understanding and anchor in our memories the principle that opposition can benefit the righteous. This spiritual truth is presented to us in vivid images, the most prominent of which are (1) fire, (2) light and darkness, (3) captivity and deliverance, (4) wilderness or wandering, (5) water or fruitfulness, and (6) dust.

With some of these images, the opposition is obvious, as in the contrast between light and darkness or between captivity and deliverance. But even the single images, like fire, are used to emphasize opposition. Fire accompanied Lehi's call to be a prophet (remember how Moses received his call at the burning bush). And the righteous will be saved by fire. Yet the wicked will be destroyed by it (see 1 Nephi 22:17), so there are two opposing sides to the one symbol.

The same is true of the image of the wilderness. For some of Lehi's family, departing into the wilderness proved to be a means to salvation, yet the rebellious sons disliked where they went. From their perspective, Lehi had led them out to "perish in the wilderness" (1 Nephi 2:11). Thus, as with essentially all of the Book of Mormon images, while there is a risk of loss or death associated with an image, such as fire or water, there are also great rewards that come from going through or over water, being enveloped in flames, coming out of dust, breaking the chains of bondage, wandering through the wilderness, and the like. This two-sidedness will become clearer as we look briefly at each major group of images.

1. Fire

Lehi's dream showed that the justice of God that divides the wicked from the righteous is like a flaming fire (see 1 Nephi 15:30). From that point on to the end of the Book of Mormon, fire is viewed in contradictory ways.

Fire played an unexpected role in the experience of the brothers Nephi and Lehi when the Lamanites imprisoned them (see Helaman 5:21–49). When they were about to be put to death, these prophets were encircled about by fire. Instead of destroying them, it freed them from prison. At the same time, their Lamanite captors, who had been imprisoned within walls of their hatred and error toward the Nephites, were set free when they repented and a pillar of protecting fire encircled them about. At that point, they all were "filled as if with fire" by the Holy Ghost (v. 45).

Again, the people who saw the resurrected Christ at Bountiful saw their children encircled by fire (see 3 Nephi 17:24). This stands in contrast to the terribly destructive fires from which they had recently escaped at the time of Christ's crucifixion. The same contrast is visible when Mormon said that the righteous are to be baptized "with fire and with the Holy Ghost" (Mormon 7:10), while the holiness of Jesus Christ "will kindle a flame of unquenchable fire" within the wicked (Mormon 9:5). Thus, while the source of the fire — God — is the same, punishing or glorifying depends on the spiritual condition of the recipient.

2. Light and Darkness

As Christ is called a fire, so he is a light in the wilderness (see 1 Nephi 17:13). In vision, Lehi saw the Son of God as glowing brighter than the sun (see 1 Nephi 1:9). He also saw Christ's apostles dressed in startlingly white garments (see 1 Nephi 1:10; 12:10; cf. 3 Nephi 19:25). Both physically and figuratively, light and whiteness are associated with truth, purity, and divine guidance, just as darkness is associated with unbelief and error (for example, see Alma 40:14). To move from darkness to light gives concrete meaning to the process of redemption. This is apparent in Lamoni's experience when he entered unconsciousness into a dark condition but arose from it enlightened — the "dark veil of unbelief was being cast away from his mind, and the light . . . of everlasting life was lit up in his soul" (Alma 19:6).

The most dramatic opposition of light and dark is connected with the appearance of Jesus Christ. Samuel the Lamanite had

134

predicted that there would be great lights in heaven at the Savior's birth, but he prophesied that darkness would attend the Savior's death (see Helaman 14:3, 20). In the first part of Samuel's prophecy, light and order were associated with the Creator and creation (a new star). On the other hand, the chaos of things splitting apart as well as intense darkness—the opposites of creation—were associated with the creator's death.

The Savior's coming to the Nephites out of darkness and great destruction was to them a miracle of light. A "Man" descended out of heaven dressed in a white robe, and he declared, "I am the light and the life of the world" (3 Nephi 11:11). In a series of unforgettable instructions, the Savior taught those who stood before him at Bountiful to be "the light of this people," to realize that "the light of the body is the eye," and that "I am the law, and the light." They were also to hold up their light "that it may shine unto the world." Later he caused the "light of his countenance" to shine upon his disciples, "and behold they were as white as the countenance and also the garments of Jesus" (3 Nephi 12:14; 13:22; 15:9; 18:24; 19:25).

We are able to feel the power of this light imagery, and we can join with Moroni in expressing through language about light our gratitude for the Book of Mormon and the Lord's prophet who gave it to us:

> Blessed be he that shall bring this thing to light;
> for it shall be brought out of darkness unto light,
>> according to the word of God;
> yea, it shall be brought out of the earth,
> and it shall shine forth out of darkness,
>> and come unto the knowledge of the people
> and it shall be done by the power of God.
> (Mormon 8:16).

3. Captivity and Deliverance

Joseph who saved his family in Egypt foretold that the Messiah would bring latter-day Lamanites "out of darkness unto light—yea, out of hidden darkness and out of captivity unto freedom" (2 Nephi 3:5). Here we see the contrast between darkness and light linked with captivity and deliverance. Both sets of images communicate to us a process, a movement, a rebirth through which humans become whole by coming either to a physical or to a spiritual promised land or condition.

Again and again, individuals or people in the Book of Mormon were delivered from being captives. Sometimes they were politically and physically in slavery; other times the captivity was of the mind and spirit, and the two may be connected. In the wilderness Nephi broke the cords his brothers used to tied him up. Later, on board the ship, he was freed by a miracle from the ropes binding him. The first case of physical deliverance was followed by Lehi's vision of the tree of life, which promises spiritual deliverance; after the ship incident, the group was physically delivered and arrived at the land of promise.

Other individuals put into bondage, especially through being cast into prison, are Abinadi, Alma and Amulek, Ammon and his brethren, Nephi and Lehi, and the Three Nephites. What happened to them parallels the freeing of Moses and the Israelites by God's intervention, just as God took direct action to save Lehi and his family (often linked together, as in 1 Nephi 4:2 and Alma 36:28–29), Limhi and his people, and Alma and his followers. In each case, bondage was associated with the powers of Satan and his prisons of death and hell, while deliverance came through the power of God.

Bondage is often considered in the Book of Mormon to be a necessary condition as preparation for conversion or salvation. After Aaron was freed (Alma 21:14–15), he and his brothers were tremendously successful—as though they somehow needed to go through the experience of physical captivity as a price to be paid in order to deliver others from spiritual bondage. Further, the bondage suffered by peoples such as Alma's group was beyond what humans could do to solve it, requiring the power of God to be shown directly: "They were in bondage, and none could deliver them except it were the Lord their God" (Mosiah 24:21). Similarly, the most oppressive spiritual bondage has to be overcome miraculously by the power of God himself. This is the core of the testimony of Alma the Younger, and it is also the experience of the Lamanites whom Ammon and his brethren taught. Through their teaching, they were moved out of the imprisoning power of Satan and into the refuge of God's love (see Alma 26:15).

4. Wilderness or Wandering

When God frees people from bondage, leading them out into and then through the wilderness often seems to be the way he does it. The pattern of escape into a wilderness is found in the Book of Mormon in the stories of Moses, Lehi, Nephi, Mulek, Mosiah, Limhi, Alma, the Anti-Nephi-Lehies, Jared, and King Omer.

Responses to the wilderness were dramatically different. It seemed to be a spiritual as much as a physical testing ground. For righteous Nephi, the wilderness was a place for receiving revelation, but Laman and Lemuel feared perishing in it. Nephi's experience taught him faith, the rewards of obedience, and gratitude to God: "He hath led me through mine afflictions in the wilderness" (2 Nephi 4:20). For Laman and Lemuel and their posterity, on the contrary, it was where they became a "wild, and ferocious, and a blood-thirsty people, . . . dwelling in tents, and wandering about in the wilderness with a short skin girdle about their loins and their heads shaven" (Enos 1:20).

The essential difference is that the Lord intended his people to go through the wilderness (the command to Lehi) or else to civilize it (as in the case of Alma in the land of Helam), not simply to remain in it, as the priests of Noah did. Living in a tent is necessary for a time, but building a temple is preferred, for it symbolizes permanence. Even the most righteous saints may wander through the land for a while (see Jacob 7:26 and Alma 26:36), but a different sort of wandering ("losing one's way" is the root meaning of the word) is even more dangerous. This is having lost one's spiritual way. Many descendants of Laman and Lemuel (see Mormon 5:18) were lost in this sense. The way out is to have the word of Christ as guide, like a Liahona, to point "a straight course to eternal bliss" and to show that man's final destination is no spot in any earthly wilderness but the heavenly promised land (see Alma 37:44–45).

5. Water or Fruitfulness

In accordance with the Book of Mormon's system of op-positions, it is appropriate that in his dream Lehi had to go through "a dark and dreary wilderness" to reach the tree of life "whose fruit was desirable to make one happy" (1 Nephi 8:4, 10). This tree is a rich, complex symbol. In different parts of the Book of Mormon, it is linked with water, vineyards, and olive trees. The people who listened to Alma at Zarahemla were invited to come to the tree of life and also to drink freely of "the waters of life." Approaching the tree is a holy matter, like taking the sacrament: "Come unto me," Alma quoted the Lord, "and ye shall partake of the fruit of the tree of life; yea, ye shall eat and drink of the bread and the waters of life freely; yea, come unto me and bring forth works of righteousness." On the other hand, those who refuse will be like dead trees that are "hewn down and cast into the fire" (Alma 5:34–35).

The fertility of land and water can have their negative aspects, too. The fountain of living waters in Lehi's dream is opposed by the river of filthy waters. Being whole and safe from storm is communicated by Ammon's image of the converted Lamanites being a ripe field from which a harvest of sheaves has been safely gathered in. They would not be beaten down by the storm at the last day, but "they are in the hands of the Lord of the harvest" (Alma 26:5–7). On the other hand, the wicked, like that leader in wickedness King Noah, are like the dry stubble of the field after the harvest is done, which is run over by beasts and crushed under their feet (see Mosiah 12:11–12). Another opposite of the tree of life is the tree on which the rebel Zemnarihah was hanged (see 3 Nephi 4:28–29).

The key forces of water, fire, and earth are involved in the destruction of the Nephite and Lamanite cities recorded in 3

138

Nephi 8 and 9: cities were sunk beneath the sea, Zarahemla was burned, and Moronihah was covered with earth. Yet in 3 Nephi 11, uplift and even salvation are said to come through those same three elements: being baptized in water, being visited by fire and the Holy Ghost, and being built upon Christ's rock.

6. Dust

The extreme opposite of water and fruitfulness is dust. This image is associated in the Book of Mormon with mortality, humiliation, captivity, obscurity, destruction, and death. The wicked, Nephi prophesied, would be "brought low in the dust," and the Jaredites, unless they repented, would be destroyed and their bones should become "as heaps of earth upon the face of the land" (1 Nephi 22:23; Ether 11:6).

Yet out of the dust come life and blessings. The Book of Mormon itself was prophesied to come "out of the dust." Echoing Isaiah, Moroni cried: "Arise from the dust, O Jerusalem; yea, and put on thy beautiful garments" (Moroni 10:27, 31). Laman and Lemuel were exhorted to "arise from the dust," that is to "awake from a deep sleep, yea, even from the sleep of hell" (2 Nephi 1:14, 13).

After the Nephites have been brought "down low in the dust, . . . yet the words of the righteous shall be written," and the Lord God shall speak concerning them "even as it were out of the ground; and their speech shall whisper out of the dust" (2 Nephi 26:15–16). In other words, the latter-day Lamanites shall be awakened to repentance by a voice considered dead. Life shall come out of death, words of eternal life from the voice out of the dust.

Finally, at the very core, the book's six major kinds of images appeal to our senses so that we more intensely *feel* the atoning power of Christ, which our minds cannot rationally grasp. The Lord acts as "a refiner's *fire*," "the *light* of Israel," guide and deliverer of his children who wander in the *wilderness*, "the fountain of living *waters*," and creator of humans from the *dust* of the earth, and the one who will retrieve us from dust again at the last day.

139

Chapter 13

THE IMAGE OF THE HAND OF GOD IN THE BOOK OF MORMON AND THE OLD TESTAMENT

David Rolph Seely

The image of the hand of God in both the Old Testament and the Book of Mormon stands for the Lord's power to intervene in the affairs of men and the events of history. Comparison between the ways this image is used in the two scriptures supports what the Book of Mormon claims about its own origin.

The hand of God is referred to frequently in both the Old Testament and the Book of Mormon. In fact, it is used with the same frequency in both volumes. Reference to the hand of God, or to the arm or finger of God, occurs 345 times in the 1184 pages of the 1979 Latter-day Saint edition of the Old Testament in English, an average of once every 3.4 pages. Those same images occur 153 times in the 531 pages of the 1981 LDS edition of the Book of Mormon in English (printed in the same format as the Old Testament), again an average of once every 3.4 pages.

The image of the hand of God is connected with important themes in both scriptures. For example, it is prominent in reference to the Creation: "We are the clay, and thou our potter; and we all are the work of thy hand" (Isaiah 64:8), and "By his hand were they all created from the beginning" (Alma 18:32). In the Old Testament, the image of the hand of God is used often in connection with the movements of God's people. The Lord "by the strength of his hand" brought Israel out of Egypt

140

in order to bring them into the promised land (see, for example, Exodus 13:3, 9, 14, 16). In the Book of Mormon, the groups who come to the promised land in the New World are "brought by the hand of the Lord" (2 Nephi 1:5–6; Omni 1:16).

The hand of God is also cited often as the agent of judgment as well as the means of deliverance. The Lord will punish his covenant people with his "outstretched hand" (Isaiah 5:25 = 2 Nephi 15:25). Restoration and gathering will begin when "the Lord shall set his hand again the second time to recover his people" (Isaiah 11:11 = 2 Nephi 21:11; 25:17). In the Book of Mormon, the phrase "his arm of mercy is extended" also signals the Lord's power on behalf of the penitent and the believer (Jacob 6:5; Mosiah 29:20; Alma 19:36).

The hand of God was what afflicted Job (see Job 19:21) and at the same time had the power to heal him (see Job 5:18). The hand of the Lord was what once made the Jaredites prosperous (see Ether 10:28) but later destroyed them (see Ether 1:1). Moroni, quoting words of the patriarch Jacob that are lost from our present-day Old Testament, prophesied the preservation of the seed of Joseph "by the hand of God" (Alma 46:24; see also 1 Nephi 5:14). Throughout the Book of Mormon, prophets were assured that the records would be "preserved by the hand of the Lord" (Alma 37:4; see also Mosiah 1:5), and so would the interpreters necessary to translate them (see Mosiah 28:15).

Often the hand imagery should be understood symbolically. Still, the Book of Mormon reminds us that the Lord really does have a hand, providing a material basis so that our minds can grasp and interpret these metaphors. God has the ability and intention to intervene actively and concretely in the affairs of mortal men if he so chooses, even to the point of taking literal action with his hand. (Recall that the Brother of Jared saw the actual finger of the Lord touching the stones that were to give light to the Jaredites in their barges—see Ether 3:6. Alma 10:2 also reports that certain words seen on the wall of a Nephite temple had been "written by the finger of God.")

Categories of Images in the Two Scriptures

Imagery of the hand of God in the Book of Mormon can be divided into three groups according to how that record uses it in comparison to Bible usage: (1) the Nephite record uses the same images as the Bible; (2) sometimes the uses are similar, although they show certain differences; and (3) certain ways in which the hand of God is spoken of are unique in the Book of Mormon.

Since the Book of Mormon claims to come directly from the Israelite tradition of record-keeping, these three categories are what we would expect: (1) The basic idea and some particular ways of speaking about the hand of God at work among men would have continued. Lehi and his family were familiar with the biblical tradition when they left Jerusalem, bolstered by the scriptures on the plates of brass that they carried with them to America. (2) We could expect them through their history in the New World to develop variations on the biblical ways of speaking of God. (3) Having their own literary tradition in the American promised land, they would have created expressions not known to us from the Bible. They may have either originated these themselves or known and used ancient Near Eastern images not in the Old Testament as we now have it. By reviewing examples of hand-of-God imagery from each of these three categories, we will be able to appreciate that the Book of Mormon both connects with its ancient Israelite heritage and shows us independent Nephite development.

The Same Imagery

Here both the form of the language and the use to which the images are put are similar in both volumes of scripture.

Direct quotations from Isaiah. The largest set of references to the hand of God consists of thirty-six passages in the Book of Mormon quoted from Isaiah. For example, Isaiah 52:10 says, "The Lord hath made bare his holy arm in the eyes of all the nations; and all the ends of the earth shall see the salvation of our God." This is found quoted in four places in the Book of Mormon: Mosiah 12:24 and 15:31, and 3 Nephi 16:20 and 20:35.

Similar images in passages not quoted from the Old Testament.
There are also examples of hand-of-God images in the Book of
Mormon that are not quotes from the Bible yet are so similar as
to suggest a direct relationship. Sometimes these statements
occur in passages that seem to refer to or partially quote from
Bible passages. As an example, note Nephi's comment on the
passage in Isaiah 52:10 where the Lord is said to have "made
bare his holy arm." Nephi uses this same figure twice in 1 Nephi
22:10–11, referring to the latter-day restoration and missionary
work: "All the kindreds of the earth cannot be blessed unless
he shall make bare his arm in the eyes of the nations. Wherefore,
the Lord God will proceed to make bare his arm in the eyes of
all the nations, in bringing about his covenants and his gospel
unto those who are of the house of Israel."

The phrase "holy arm" also occurs in Enos 1:13, which talks
about the coming forth of the Book of Mormon: "Even if it so
be by the power of his holy arm, that it might be brought forth
at some future day unto the Lamanites, that, perhaps, they might
be brought unto salvation." Note that in Isaiah 52:10 this expression also occurs in the context of the prophet writing about the
future restoration, and the phrase is accompanied by the word
salvation.

In another place, Lehi speaks of writing done by the finger
of God when he tells of the vision the Lord had given to Joseph
of Egypt: "I will write unto him my law, by the finger of mine
own hand," no doubt referring to Moses (2 Nephi 3:17). This
same image is of course found in Exodus 31:18 and Deuteronomy
9:10, which refer to "tables of stone written with the finger of
God."

It is true that prominent kinds of hand-of-God imagery in
the Old Testament do not appear in the Book of Mormon (just
as some images in the Book of Mormon do not occur in the Old
Testament). For example, consider the well-known expression
that celebrates the Lord's saving of the children of Israel from
Egypt through defeating Pharaoh's army. The statement is that
he led them out of Egypt with a "mighty hand and outstretched

143

arm." This occurs ten times in the Bible but never occurs in the Book of Mormon. If we had the full Book of Mormon record (Joseph Smith was allowed to translate only a portion of the plates), these missing instances might well show up.

Images Similar but Modified

Many Book of Mormon expressions involving the hand of God differ from those in the Bible but are similar enough to have apparently developed from Bible phrasing.

The image of the lengthened arm. One of these speaks of God's arm being "lengthened." A Hebrew phrase meaning lack of strength or power is "short of hand." This occurs three times in the Old Testament. In each of these cases, the Lord poses a rhetorical question whether mortals think that his hand is shortened; that is, whether men consider that God is powerless to save his people. Obviously, the question is a roundabout way of stating that the Lord does have power to save. For example, in Isaiah 50:2 (= 2 Nephi 7:2), the Lord asks, "Is my hand shortened at all, that it cannot redeem? or have I no power to deliver?" In the Book of Mormon, reference to the shortened hand is made only in this quotation from Isaiah.

Later however, Nephi uses a phrase that may be a reverse of the hand that is shortened. At 2 Nephi 28:32 we find, "Wo be unto the Gentiles, saith the Lord God of Hosts! For notwithstanding I shall lengthen out mine arm unto them from day to day, they will deny me; nevertheless, I will be merciful unto them, saith the Lord God, if they will repent and come unto me; for mine arm is lengthened out all the day long." The picture of the Lord's hand being "outstretched" is common in the Old Testament and the Book of Mormon, and the Book of Mormon frequently uses the image "the arm of mercy extended." Yet the specific word *lengthen* (with *arm* instead of *hand*) occurs only in verse thirty-two. In English, *lengthen* is the precise opposite of *shorten*, suggesting that Nephi intended this image to be the reverse of the shortened hand. Just as in the Bible passages, the Book of Mormon uses this expression in the context of God's power to save.

Interestingly, the statement about the hand of God being lengthened as a symbol of his power is known elsewhere in the ancient Near East, despite being absent from the Bible. In the Ugaritic language we read: "El's hand is lengthened like the Sea's." So perhaps Nephi was using a phrase that already existed in related Semitic cultures but happened not to make it into the Old Testament.

The image of an instrument in the hand of the Lord. This phrase occurs twelve times in the Book of Mormon but not at all in the Old Testament. It refers to servants of the Lord who help bring souls to Christ, often through missionary work. Among these are Nephi, who brought his people across the sea to the promised land (see 2 Nephi 1:24), Joseph Smith in the last days (see 2 Nephi 3:24), and Alma the elder and his converts (see Mosiah 23:10). The phrase appears several times for the younger Alma and the sons of Mosiah (see Mosiah 27:36; Alma 2:30; 17:9, 11; 26:3, 15; 29:9; 35:14). The sense of this expression is perfectly logical in relation to other biblical hand-of-God expressions.

Only a few Old Testament references to the hand of God suggest a person being "in" the hand of God. One of the most prominent is in Isaiah referring to the Suffering Servant (whom Latter-day Saints usually interpret as Christ, or perhaps any prophetic messenger). This is quoted by Nephi: "He hath made my mouth like a sharp sword; in the shadow of his hand hath he hid me, and made me a polished shaft; in his quiver hath he hid me" (Isaiah 49:2 = 1 Nephi 21:2). The most likely Hebrew equivalent to the English term "instrument" would be *kly,* which can refer to either a weapon or a tool. Explicit military words used in this verse ("sharp sword," "polished shaft," and "quiver") certainly seem to make the Servant in this passage an instrument or weapon in the hand of the Lord. Thus the Book of Mormon expression "an instrument in the hand of God" is a possible development from the picture of the Servant as potential conqueror.

The image of trusting in the arm of the Lord, not in the arm of flesh. In the Bible the idea of trusting in the arm of the Lord occurs only in Isaiah 51:5, quoted by Nephi in 2 Nephi 8:5. But phrased a little differently—the divine arm as superior to the mortal arm—a similar idea is used in other places in the Old Testament. Exodus 15, the poem celebrating the Lord's victory at the Red Sea, pictures the climax of the great contest between the hand of God and the might of Pharaoh in terms of hand imagery. The poet praised the Lord in this way: "Thy right hand, O Lord, is become glorious in power: thy right hand, O Lord, hath dashed in pieces the enemy" (v. 6). This is paralleled by the boast of Pharaoh, "I will draw my sword, my hand shall destroy them" (v. 9). The poem concludes with a final image of the Lord's might: "Thou stretchedst out thy right hand, the earth swallowed them" (v. 12). Thus the result of relying on the arm of flesh, in this case the might of Pharaoh and his army, is destruction.

Psalm 44:3 applies the same kind of image to the conquest of the promised land: "For they got not the land in possession by their own sword, neither did their own arm save them: but thy right hand, and thine arm, and the light of thy countenance." In 2 Chronicles 32:8, King Hezekiah says of the approaching Assyrians led by Sennacherib, "With him is an arm of flesh; but with us is the Lord our God to help us, and to fight our battles." In Jeremiah 17:5 we read, "Thus saith the Lord; Cursed be the man that trusteth in man, and maketh flesh his arm, and whose heart departeth from the Lord." This passage may have been among the prophecies of Jeremiah preserved on the plates of brass; thus its language would have been known to Nephi and his descendants.

The idea of trusting in the arm of flesh occurs in two statements by Nephi that could be developments from Jeremiah 17:5. The first says, "O Lord, I have trusted in thee, and I will trust in thee forever. I will not put my trust in the arm of flesh; for I know that cursed is he that putteth his trust in the arm of flesh. Yea, cursed is he that putteth his trust in man or maketh flesh his arm" (2 Nephi 4:34). The other is "Cursed is he that putteth his trust in man, or maketh flesh his arm, or shall hearken unto the precepts of men, save their precepts shall be given by the power of the Holy Ghost" (2 Nephi 28:31).

This concept of the Lord's strength as a source for humans is important throughout the Book of Mormon and is not limited to "the hand." For example, those who have forgotten God "boast in their own strength" (see Mosiah 11:19; Mormon 3:9; 4:8), and this inevitably leads to their destruction. All these examples combined show us that the picture of trusting in "the arm of God" was common in the Old Testament, so we are not surprised to find it also in the Book of Mormon.

An interesting play on this image is found in the story of Ammon. In defense of king Lamoni's flocks, he contended against the Lamanite rustlers, cut off their arms, and "caused them to flee by the strength of his arm" (Alma 17:37). King Lamoni then wanted to know about a man that had "such great power" that he could kill and smite off the arms of bandits. In response, Ammon explained that his arm was not the arm of God—the Great Spirit—but rather that "a portion of that Spirit dwelleth in me, which giveth me knowledge, and also power according to my faith and desires which are in God" (18:35).

Images Unique to the Book of Mormon

I will discuss just two unique images, which are part of a larger set, that explain and illustrate the Atonement.

The arm of mercy. The first is the image of the arm of mercy extended. The phrase "arm of mercy" is not in the Old Testament. The closest phrase that suggests such an image is in Psalm 94:18: "When I said, My foot slippeth; thy mercy, O Lord, held me up." Mercy can also be extended (see, for example, Psalm 109:12), but it seems to be used in the same sense as *show mercy.*

The phrase occurs eight times in the Book of Mormon. It appears first when Jacob explains Zenos' allegory of the olive tree: "While his arm of mercy is extended towards you in the light of the day, harden not your hearts" (Jacob 6:5). If read in context, this phrase is a continuation of the hand imagery that Jacob had introduced three verses earlier: "The day that he shall set his hand again the second time to recover his people, is the day, yea, even the last time, that the servants of the Lord shall go forth in his power, to nourish and prune his vineyard" (6:2).

The image of the arm of mercy also occurs in Mosiah 16:12; Alma 5:33; 19:36; 29:10; and 3 Nephi 9:14. Each time, the Lord is offering "to all people who will repent and believe on his name" (Alma 19:36) the chance to take full advantage of the Atonement. For example, "Behold, he sendeth an invitation unto all men, for the arms of mercy are extended towards them, and he saith: Repent, and I will receive you" (Alma 5:33).

The embrace of Christ. Many of the images of God touching man with his hand in the Old Testament denote sickness, plague, judgment, destruction, and so forth. Yet his hand is also shown to reach out to man in a positive way. Often the hand of the Lord is "upon" or "with" his prophets, showing inspiration and protection (see, for example, 1 Kings 18:46; 2 Kings 3:15; Ezekiel 1:3). Also the hand of God touched Jeremiah's mouth so that he could speak for God (see Jeremiah 1:9). It also "lifted" Ezekiel by his hair to take him to Jerusalem in a vision (Ezekiel 8:3). Elsewhere we read that the hand of the Lord "leads" and the right hand "holds" David (Psalm 139:10; see 63:8; 73:23–24); these images suggest either a handclasp or taking the person by the hand to lead him along.

The Book of Mormon has a significantly different set of imagery regarding God's positive contacts with man. This set is consistent and well developed throughout the book. Central to it is the image of an embrace, of being circled about by the arms of Christ. The Book of Mormon invites all to "come unto Christ" (1 Nephi 6:4; Moroni 10:32). A profound picture of what this means is frequently given of Christ waiting to embrace—to encircle with his arms—his children who come to him.

Nephi expressed it this way: "The Lord hath redeemed my soul from hell; I have beheld his glory, and I am encircled about eternally in the arms of his love" (2 Nephi 1:15). Alma emphasizes the safety of the embrace: "Thus mercy can satisfy the demands of justice, and encircles them in the arms of safety, while he that exercises no faith unto repentance is exposed to the whole law of the demands of justice" (Alma 34:16). And Mormon, at the end of his ministry, is saddened by the final destruction of his people because "this people had not repented that they might have been clasped in the arms of Jesus" (Mormon 5:11). "O ye fair ones," he exclaimed, "how could ye have rejected that Jesus, who stood with open arms to receive you!" (Mormon 6:17).

Hugh Nibley has traced the origins of this atonement imagery to a Semitic word that in the Bible is usually translated "atonement." Nibley finds one of the primary meanings of this term to be *encircling* or *surrounding*. This means that the embrace imagery in the Book of Mormon is a continuation or variant of a Near Eastern way of speaking.

However, the Book of Mormon also uses the figure of being encircled to show the consequences of following Satan—a reverse play on the embrace by the Savior. Instead of an embrace of love, Satan waits to "encircle you about with his chains, that he might chain you down to everlasting destruction" (Alma 12:6; see also Alma 5:7, 9). In 2 Nephi 1, language about the "awful chains [of hell] by which ye are bound" (1:13) is contrasted with the faithful's being "encircled about eternally in the arms of his love" (1:15).

Alma and the sons of Mosiah, at first, are set forth as examples of those "encircled about by the bands of death, and the chains of hell" (Alma 5:7). But they were set free through the Atonement. Through their missionary labors, others who "were encircled about with everlasting darkness and destruction" (Alma 26:15) accepted the invitation of Christ's extended arms of mercy: "He has brought them into his everlasting light, yea, into everlasting salvation; and they are encircled about with the matchless bounty of his love" (Alma 26:15).

The representation of the hand of God in the Book of Mormon has a consistent purpose. It helps us understand the Lord's power and willingness to touch us and save us. That purpose is the same in the Old Testament. Overall, the connections between the way the image of God's hand is used in the Book of Mormon and in the Old Testament support the Book of Mormon's own claim that it is an ancient record in the tradition of the Israelites.

IDEAS AND THEMES

Chapter 14

"MEANS UNTO REPENTANCE": UNIQUE BOOK OF MORMON INSIGHTS INTO CHRIST'S AT-ONE-MENT

Eugene England

The most terrible human reality is that we sin, and the most crucial human problem is what to do about it. The most important claim of Christianity is that it offers a unique solution to that problem through the atonement of Christ. That claim has not, of course, been accepted by non-Christians; it remains, in the Apostle Paul's words, "unto the Jews a stumblingblock, and unto the Greeks foolishness" (1 Corinthians 1:23). And Christians themselves differ greatly in their understanding of *how* Christ's life, death, and resurrection can free them from sin.

The main reason for traditional Christian uncertainty is that, as one theologian has written, "There is not a single New Testament Doctrine of the Atonement. There is simply a collection of images and metaphors . . . from which subsequent tradition built its systematic doctrines and theories."[1] Those metaphors range from a captain gaining military victory over sin and death, to a judge and prisoners in a law court, to payment of ransom. From these metaphors have come quite different, even contradictory, doctrines among Christian believers.

But theories do not matter as much as the individual's experience of escaping from sin through faith in Christ. What actually takes place in that process is much richer than any theory in words about it. Despite having very different theories about the Atonement, many people have experienced it. But theories do matter to some extent—some can interfere with experiencing it, while more correct understandings can aid the experience. In this regard, the Book of Mormon, Another Testament of Jesus Christ, while it provides no single doctrine or metaphor of the Atonement, can give us the basis for a uniquely logical and persuasive explanation. I know from experience that this explanation of the Atonement is particularly helpful to people in our time.

One of the more popular Christian theories of the Atonement is the "satisfaction" theory: sin offends God's honor and justice; God cannot forgive sin without undermining his authority and the force of justice, so Christ's sacrifice paid or satisfied the debt to God's justice and honor. But this theory seems to make God less able to forgive than we are. We are able to forgive each other without conditions or satisfaction. Surely our omnipotent God can do the same.

Another popular theory gets around this problem but has problems of its own. The "moral-influence" theory denies the legalistic framework of having to satisfy the demands of God's justice; instead, it teaches that Christ's sacrifice exerts a moral influence on us by making us aware of our guilt and moving us to change our lives—we respond to the love he has shown for us by loving him and changing our lives to follow him. But this theory apparently removes the necessity of the Atonement. It makes Christ's influence "only" moral and not necessary for salvation, and the scriptures insist that it is necessary.

Many Christians and their churches have seen the fall of Adam as a great mistake that ruined God's plan and offended him. They have assumed that God was unhappy with humanity for what Adam did in Eden. This led to the idea that we must win back his love and favor. If we could not do that by our own actions, then it had to be by Christ's suffering, as a kind of gift that would please God. But the scriptures are clear that God did not reject us; rather, mankind rejected him. We do not need to win back God's love; he is always ready. Instead, we need to be reconciled to God (see 2 Corinthians 5:18–19).

English Christians back in the days when the Bible was first being translated into English seem to have understood this clearly. The word they used for reconciliation was *at-one-ment*, that is, to get back into a condition of oneness. In the sixteenth century, for example, the noted Bible translator William Tyndale even called Christ the "at-one-maker." Only later, in response to changing theology, did a new verb, *atone*, develop, with a different pronunciation, and the meaning that *at-onement* once had gradually changed. The changed meaning and pronunciation continued to express the growing emphasis of theologians on Christ's payment of a debt.

But there has been continuing uneasiness with this change. Modern translations of the New Testament do not use the word *atonement*. The word that was so translated in the King James version is regularly written *reconciliation*. One reason is because of what the modern meaning of *atonement* implies about the nature of God as one who demands payment. Another reason is that *atone* seems to remove Christ's at-onement from our personal experience into a matter that only theologians claim fully to understand. Somehow it came to involve Adam and God (and perhaps the Devil), but not particularly you and me and our need for forgiveness and personal response to Christ.

The Book of Mormon, along with modern revelations, lays the groundwork for clearly understanding this matter. Its unique insights into the At-onement emphasize two concepts: (1) that the fall was not a mistake, and (2) that people were able to experience the At-onement *before* Christ died, in fact, that Adam and Eve became Christians.

According to Latter-day Saint readings of the scriptures, Adam's and Eve's actions in no way spoiled God's plan but were, in fact, part of the plan. Their fall may even be thought of as part of the process of the At-onement. According to the book of Moses in the Pearl of Great Price, after Eve and Adam

155

have left the Garden and been taught by an angel about Christ, Eve exclaims, "Were it not for our transgression we never should have had seed, and never should have known good and evil, and the joy of our redemption, and the eternal life which God giveth unto all the obedient" (Moses 5:11). The two sinners repent and are baptized and recognize that they have been fully forgiven (see Moses 6:51–68). In this they become the model for all their descendants.

A Book of Mormon prophet explains the point in these words: "Adam fell that men might be; and men are, that they might have joy. And the Messiah cometh in the fulness of time, that he may redeem the children of men from the fall. And because that they are redeemed from the fall they have become free forever, knowing good from evil; to act for themselves and not to be acted upon" (2 Nephi 2:25–26).

These verses tell us that the process by which humans became separated from God and then can be brought back into his presence through the At-onement is not an accident. What Adam and Eve did was not against God's plan but the very key to it. We learn that, by our nature as mortals, we had to leave the easy life in the Garden so that we could grow. Only by the hard experiences of life could we do that—reach the depths but also the heights of our soul's capacity.

But why must we go through such a painful fall and rise, and how does it happen, even to those who lived before Christ's mortal ministry? The Book of Mormon provides insights that answer those questions. But the answers are unlike the answers claimed by Christian thinkers in Joseph Smith's day and since.

About six hundred years before Christ was born, Nephi was given a remarkable vision:

> I looked and beheld the great city of Jerusalem, and also other cities. And I beheld the city of Nazareth; and in the city of Nazareth I beheld a virgin. . . . I saw the heavens open; and an angel came down and stood before me; and he said unto me: Nephi, what beholdest thou? And I said unto him: a virgin most beautiful and fair

156

above all other virgins. And he said unto me: Knowest
thou the condescension of God? And I said unto him: I
know that he loveth his children; nevertheless, I do not
know the meaning of all things. And he said unto me:
Behold, the virgin whom thou seest is the mother of the
Son of God, after the manner of the flesh. . . . And I
looked and beheld the virgin again, bearing a child in
her arms. And the angel said unto me: Behold the Lamb
of God, yea, even the Son of the Eternal Father! (1 Nephi
11:13–21).

After the angel explained further, Nephi continued, "The angel
said unto me again: Look and behold the condescension of God!
And I looked and beheld the Redeemer of the world, of whom
my father had spoken" (1 Nephi 11:26–27).

This vision of Jesus Christ's mortal birth provides an important insight into the At-onement. One word given by Joseph
Smith in his translation of Nephi's account is crucial: *condescension,* which means, literally, "descending with." Christ, we are
told here, is God "descending with" us into all that we experience
in mortality. This includes our separation from the Father and
our suffering because of sin. It seems also to say that Christ's
coming down to be like and among us is because of his love for
us. This love is the heart of the power of his at-onement.

Many years afterward, one of Nephi's descendants, the
prophet-king Benjamin, gathered his people together as he approached his death. His aim was to teach them a great revelation
of understanding that had come to him. He reminded them
vividly that they, and he, shared the human tendency to commit
sin, "which doth cause him [the sinner] to shrink from the presence of the Lord, and doth fill his breast with guilt, and pain,
and anguish, which is like an unquenchable fire, whose flame
ascendeth up forever and ever" (Mosiah 2:38). But Benjamin also
gives them the solution by describing his vision of Christ's birth,
then 125 years in the future:

The time cometh, and is not far distant, that with
power, the Lord Omnipotent who reigneth, who was,

and is from all eternity to all eternity, shall come down from heaven among the children of men, and shall dwell in a tabernacle of clay. . . . Lo, he shall suffer temptations, and pain of body, hunger, thirst, and fatigue, even more than man can suffer, except it be unto death; for behold, blood cometh from every pore, so great shall be his anguish for the wickedness and the abominations of his people. And he shall be called Jesus Christ, the Son of God, the Father of heaven and earth, the Creator of all things from the beginning; and his mother shall be called Mary. And lo, he cometh unto his own, that salvation might come unto the children of men even through faith on his name (Mosiah 3:5, 7–9).

In all the scriptures known to us, this is the earliest point in time that we have a clear reference to that part of the Atonement directly connected to our individual sins: "Blood cometh from every pore, so great shall be his anguish for the wickedness and the abominations of his people." This is not a description of what occurred on the cross but of what went on in the garden of Gethsemane the night before his crucifixion. That was the time when Christ suffered fully the fearful loneliness that comes to those who are separated from God. Through capabilities that only he had as the Son of God, Christ "descended" to the ultimate depth of human suffering for sin.

We begin to get clearer insight into what occurred in Gethsemane through a revelation given to Joseph Smith in 1830. It provides the most remarkable and moving description that we have of Christ's experience of at-onement, because it is spoken, in first-person directness, by the Lord himself. We can feel, in some measure, his pain through these words:

I command you to repent—repent, lest . . . your sufferings be sore—how sore you know not, how exquisite you know not, yea, how hard to bear you know not. For behold, I, God, have suffered these things for all, that they might not suffer if they would repent; but if they would not repent they must suffer even as I; which suffering caused myself, even God, the greatest of all, to tremble because of pain, and to bleed at every pore, and to suffer both body and spirit—and would that I might not drink the bitter cup, and shrink— (Doctrine and Covenants 19:15–18).

My reading of these words indicates to me that the Lord broke off his sentence without completing it, shrinking even from the memory of the awful moment, as if remembering and reliving the pain were too great to bear even in A.D. 1830. That is, for me, the precise point where the central act of the Atonement occurs, where I am moved most fully to experience atonement with Christ and rejoice with him as he then goes on to say, "Nevertheless, glory be to the Father, and I partook and *finished my preparations* unto the children of men" (Doctrine and Covenants 19:19; italics added).

Of course we cannot understand all that happened in Gethsemane, especially *how* it happened. Yet we can feel the impact in our hearts of the love Jesus and his Father both expressed there—for each other and for us. Jesus Christ has created the greatest possibility we can imagine: that our common feelings of meaninglessness and separation from God can be removed, that we need not suffer if we would repent. The Father who planned our earth experience, who sent us here into risk and suffering only so we could further grow toward his likeness, has sent his Son to share the experience with us. He came down not only to guide and teach us through his revelations and his example, but also to experience willingly the full range of man's living and dying, his joy and anguish. These were the "preparations" he had to finish to become completely and successfully our Savior.

This in itself is not a new idea. The New Testament hints at it. Paul taught, "For our sake he [the Father] made him [the Son] to be [that is, to see at first hand] sin who knew no sin, so that in him we might become the righteousness of God" (2 Corinthians 5:21; Revised Standard Version).

In his Epistle to the Hebrews, Paul explained the idea more fully. Keep in mind that, in the following verses, "high priest" refers to a person ordained to intercede for us and to act on our behalf: "In all things it behoved him [Christ] to be made like unto his brethren, that he might be a merciful and faithful high priest in things pertaining to God, to make reconciliation for the sins of the people. For in that he himself hath suffered being tempted, he is able to succour them that are tempted" (2:17–18). In other words, "we have not an high priest which cannot be touched with the feeling of our infirmities" (4:15). Paul explained the reason Christ had to descend below all things: "Though he were a Son [of God], yet learned he obedience by the things which he suffered; and being made perfect, he became the author of eternal salvation unto all them that obey him" (5:8–9).

But the Book of Mormon is plainer, especially in a vision of the future Christ that the prophet Alma received about 83 B.C.: "He shall go forth, suffering pains and afflictions and temptations of every kind; . . . he will take upon him the pains and the sicknesses of his people. . . . He will take upon him their infirmities, that his bowels may be filled with mercy, according to the flesh, that he may know according to the flesh how to succor his people according to their infirmities" (Alma 7:11–12).

The Book of Mormon here provides the clearest insight into how only Christ could perform the At-onement: though he is divine, he does not offer us a solution to the problems of separation from our God without knowing the pain himself. This unconditional love is given to us by the same person who gave us the law and who will eventually judge us. Therefore, it has the unique power—available from no other source—to release us from the barrier of our own guilt and give us the strength to repent.

This insight is repeated and developed further throughout the Book of Mormon. We see it in the account of what happened among King Benjamin's people as soon as they grasped the meaning of what he had taught them about sin and at-onement.

> They all cried with one voice, saying: Yea, we believe
> all the words which thou hast spoken unto us; and also,
> we know of their surety and truth, because of the Spirit

of the Lord Omnipotent, which has wrought a mighty change in us, or in our hearts, that we have no more disposition to do evil, but to do good continually. And we, ourselves, also, through the infinite goodness of God, and the manifestations of his Spirit, have great views of that which is to come. . . . And it is the faith which we have had on the things which our king has spoken unto us that has brought us to this great knowledge, whereby we do rejoice with such exceedingly great joy. And we are willing to enter into a covenant with our God to do his will, and to be obedient to his commandments in all things that he shall command us, all the remainder of our days (Mosiah 5:2–5).

King Benjamin responds:

Ye have spoken the words that I desired . . . and now, because of the covenant which ye have made ye shall be called the children of Christ, his sons, and his daughters; for behold, this day he hath spiritually begotten you; for ye say that your hearts are changed through faith on his name. . . . Under this head ye are made free, and there is no other head whereby ye can be made free. There is no other name given whereby salvation cometh; therefore, I would that ye should take upon you the name of Christ, all you that have entered into the covenant with God that ye should be obedient unto the end of your lives (vv. 6–8).

A great and revealing thing occurred here—a truly Christian community was being formed 125 *years before Christ actually lived.* Struck to the heart by the power of God's love, these Nephites experienced a mighty change in their hearts that led them to covenant that they would be obedient to God.

Fifty years later, another prophet among these people, clearly influenced by the prophecies and experiences that had been part of his people's history, again talked about Christ's sacrifice and made clearer what had happened among Benjamin's group:

It is expedient that there should be a great and last

> sacrifice, and then shall there be . . . a stop to the shed-
> ding of blood; then shall the law of Moses be ful-
> filled. . . . This is the whole meaning of the law, every
> whit pointing to that great and last sacrifice; and that
> great and last sacrifice will be the Son of God, yea, infinite
> and eternal. And thus he shall bring salvation to all those
> who shall believe on his name; this being the intent of
> this last sacrifice, to bring about the bowels of mercy,
> which overpowereth justice, and bringeth about means
> unto men that they may have faith unto repen-
> tance. . . . Only unto him that has faith unto repentance
> is brought about the great and eternal plan of redemption
> (Alma 34:13–16).

This prophet, Amulek, said that it is *knowledge* of Christ's sacrifice that alone can penetrate the barrier in our natures keeping us from being at-one with God. This barrier seems to consist of our insisting on judgment and punishment, for ourselves as well as others. This is the force that has prevented us from overcoming our separation from God.

Here we must remind ourselves of an amazing contradiction in ourselves. When our sense of justice is stirred, it makes us aware of sin and of the fact that we must begin to repent, yet it also interferes with our attempts to repent. We feel that every action must suffer its consequences and that we must justify our actions to ourselves. Since there is often a contradiction between our beliefs and our actions, we feel guilt and an unbearable division within ourselves.

The Book of Mormon alone gives us the insight that this division was created *by God himself*. It is part of his plan, for it requires that we consider good and evil and choose between them. Our growth comes by making the right choices. The Book of Mormon prophet Alma taught this clearly to his sinful son Corianton:

> Repentance could not come unto men except there
> were a punishment, which also was eternal as the life of
> the soul should be, affixed opposite to the plan of hap-

piness, which was as eternal also as the life of the soul. Now, how could a man repent except he should sin? How could he sin if there was no law? How could there be a law save there was a punishment? Now, there was a punishment affixed, and a just law given, which brought remorse of conscience unto man (Alma 42:16–18).

This moral nature makes us want to improve our lives. But it also makes us insist that we pay the full penalty for our sin. But of course there is no way that we can fully do this.

However, Alma also taught his son Corianton another essential role God plays in the At-onement, besides giving us law and conscience. Alma taught that justice requires repentance, "for except it were for these conditions, mercy could not take effect except it should destroy the work of justice" (Alma 42:13). He described how this works:

Thus we see that all mankind were fallen, and they were in the grasp of justice; yea, the justice of God, which consigned them forever to be cut off from his presence. And now, the plan of mercy could not be brought about except an atonement should be made; therefore God himself atoneth for the sins of the world, to bring about the plan of mercy, to appease the demands of justice, that God might be a perfect, just God, and a merciful God also (42:14–15).

So God does two things that at first glance look contradictory. He creates "remorse of conscience" by giving the law and judging us and by stirring us to judge ourselves, but he also brings about "the plan of mercy, to appease the demands of justice." The contradiction is escaped because God also provides the solution. He "himself atoneth for the sins of the world." This refers, of course, to Jesus Christ, the Son, who willingly came to earth to provide a way for us to escape justice if we would have faith in him and repent. If we respond to Christ's at-onement, it becomes possible for us to personally experience both separation and reconciliation. This opens to us the full meaning of both evil and good. It bring us to a condition of meekness and lowliness of heart whereby we can freely accept from God the power to be a god.

This love from the Father and the Son is unconditional. As Paul expressed it, "While we were yet sinners, Christ died for us" (Romans 5:8). Christ's love was not conditional upon our actions or our qualities. He expressed this love to us while we were yet in our sins. He did not complete the process of forgiveness, which depends upon our response; he *initiated* it in a free act of mercy. This love is quite independent from the notion of justice. It is entirely unmerited, unearned, unrelated to the worthiness of the object (except in that each person has intrinsic worth through our eternal existence and God-like potential).

The Book of Mormon helps us understand why this unique love that God extends to us can save us. God takes a risk on the possibility that his love will stir in each of us the necessary response, repentance. His love, expressed in the At-onement, gets directly at that barrier in us, the God-given sense of justice Alma taught his son about. That barrier makes us unable to forgive ourselves. Because of that, we are unable to unconditionally love ourselves, unable to respond positively to our own potential, unable to be at peace with ourselves. But he breaks down that barrier in suffering for our sins because of his love for us.

The demands of justice that Alma and Amulek are talking about, which must be overpowered, are at least in part from our own sense of eternal justice, especially our own demands on ourselves. These demands cause us to feel guilt and division within ourselves. They begin the process of repentance, but they cannot complete it. So the At-onement gives us an escape from the burden of sin that we are utterly incapable of escaping by any other means.

Thus the "moral influence" of Christ's at-onement, understood properly, *is necessary* for salvation. Nothing else can fully motivate us to repent and nothing else can break down the barriers that prevent us from forgiving ourselves. There is no condition in which we can imagine God being unable to forgive. But what effect will the forgiveness have? Although the At-onement is necessary, it is not enough. Forgiveness is meaningless unless it leads to repentance. Forgiveness must be accepted by free agents to be effective. We must respond to the At-onement and complete the process.

The Book of Mormon teaches that the At-onement is reconciliation as much as payment or satisfaction of justice. We may try to repent so that God will forgive us and atone for our sins; yet the power to repent comes ultimately from recognizing that God freely atones for our sins and begins the process of forgiveness by extending unconditional love to t ɔ. He does this in order that we might repent and thus bring to conclusion the process of forgiveness. God's forgiveness is at least as much a freely given power to help us repent as it is a subsequent reward for repenting.

The center of our experience of the At-onement is Christ's love breaking through the barrier of justice within us. That experience comes to us only through our knowledge of his love and suffering and through the gospel ordinances that remind us of that At-onement and recommit us to respond with repentance and obedience. The process is a complex one. Particular events may trigger it, and it may have climaxes, but essentially it is a lifelong process.

When I began serving as a missionary, I had not yet experienced the At-onement in a decisive personal way. While I was serving in Hawaii, I faced the most difficult spiritual challenge of my life to that point. A man we were teaching had come to believe the gospel was true, but he couldn't find the strength to repent. He would make promises to change his habits, behavior, and feelings that were very harmful to himself and his family, but he would break his promises and then suffer terribly from guilt. He felt ashamed, not good enough for Christ, and too weak to become good.

We tried all kinds of ways to help him be strong. We told him about the hell he was making for himself and about the heaven with his family he was destroying. We made hourly calls to check up on him. We went over and over the logical "steps" of repentance. Nothing worked. His family members, who had already joined the Church, and we missionaries were all near despair.

Then I remembered Joseph Smith's statement that the Book of Mormon was "the most correct book" in the world and that its principles provided the best way to get near to God.[2] I studied it looking for ways to help our friend. As I did, I went back over my notes from religion classes, which I remembered had stressed the new vision of salvation through the *means unto repentance* provided by Christ's at-onement as explained in the Book of Mormon.

Slowly I found again the key I had been taught earlier, but which had not meant enough until now when it was needed so badly. We read the main passages about Christ from the Book of Mormon with our friend, and he came to feel the spirit of complete love his Savior had for him. I remember when we came to the sermon of Amulek, in Alma 34, where he taught that the suffering of Christ brings about the bowels of mercy, enough to break through the bands of justice and give us the means to have enough faith to repent.

This was exactly what our friend needed — to see clearly that there was a source for the power he needed. As he read the Book of Mormon passages, he finally understood and *felt* that power and thus was able to accept Christ's love and repent. Those around him helped the process, but the turning point was when he felt love from Christ, conveyed by the promises and spirit of the Book of Mormon. He said, "If Christ can have this kind of love for me, who am I to refuse to accept it — and to accept myself." With this new strength, he became a new person, almost overnight.

My own life didn't change as much right then, but I saw clearly that the Book of Mormon had, for me and for my friend, the best answer to the chief human question, "What can we do about our sins?" I became convinced that it also contained the best direct help to actually bring people to repent. My experience since then has increasingly vindicated those convictions about the unique insights of the Book of Mormon into the process and power of the At-onement.

Notes

1. William J. Wolf, "The Atonement," in *Encyclopedia of Religion*, 16 vols, ed. Mircea Eliade (New York: Macmillan, 1986), I.496.

2. *Teachings of the Prophet Joseph Smith*, comp. Joseph Fielding Smith (Salt Lake City: Deseret Book Company, 1976), 194.

Chapter 15

THE WAYS OF
REMEMBRANCE

Louis Midgley

Careful attention to one particular word used in the Book of Mormon yields some surprising dividends. For example, Lehi pled with his sons to remember his words: "My sons, I would that ye would *remember;* yea, I would that ye would hearken unto my words" (2 Nephi 1:12; italics added here and in subsequent scriptures). Such language may go unnoticed, or it may seem to be merely a request to recall some teachings. The word *remember* seems rather plain and straightforward. But when looked at more closely, the language about remembrance in the Book of Mormon turns out to be rich and complex, conveying important, hidden meaning.

The Book of Mormon uses terms related to *remembering* and *forgetting* well over two hundred times. The ideas intended with these words must be significant. By looking carefully at what the Book of Mormon says about "the ways of remembrance" (1 Nephi 2:24), we can better understand the book's overall message.

The Lord told Nephi, "They [the Lamanites] shall be a scourge unto thy seed, to stir them up in *remembrance* of me; and inasmuch as they will not *remember* me, and hearken unto my words, they shall scourge them even unto destruction" (2 Nephi 5:25). Since the Book of Mormon ends with the destruction of the Nephites, remembrance seems to have been vitally important, and even decisive, for Lehi's descendants.

Later, King Benjamin "appointed priests to teach the people, that thereby they might hear and know the commandments of

God, and to stir them up in *remembrance* of the oath they had made" (Mosiah 6:3). This was after he had indicated that the original members of the Lehi colony had failed to prosper precisely because part of them had "incurred the displeasure of God upon them; and therefore they were smitten with famine and sore afflictions, to stir them up in *remembrance* of their duty" (Mosiah 1:17).

The first thing to note is that "ways of remembrance" does not mean simply inner reflections, or merely awareness of or curiosity about the past, or even detailed information to be recalled. True, in a number of places the idea of remembrance in the Book of Mormon seems to carry the meaning of recalling information about the past (see, for example, Ether 4:16; Alma 33:3). More commonly, however, remembrance refers to action. This action springs from realizing the meaning of past events. Thus, in the Book of Mormon, remembrance results in action.

The call to remember is often a passionate plea to see God's hand in delivering his people from bondage and captivity. Alma clearly explained this connection:

> When I see many of my brethren truly penitent, and coming to the Lord their God, then is my soul filled with joy; then do I *remember* what the Lord has done for me, yea, even that he hath heard my prayer; yea, then do I *remember* his merciful arm which he extended towards me [at the time I repented]. Yea, and I also *remember* the captivity of my fathers; for I surely do know that the Lord did deliver them out of bondage. . . . Yea, I have always *remembered* the captivity of my fathers; and that same God who delivered them out of the hands of the Egyptians did deliver them out of bondage (Alma 29:10–12).

Later Alma said, "I would that ye should do as I have done, in *remembering* the captivity of our fathers; for they were in bondage, and none could deliver them except it was the God of Abraham" (Alma 36:2; compare v. 29).

Because these Nephites of Alma's time were distant from

169

God's acts of deliverance in the past and from the redemption promised in the future to their descendants, they had to rely on the words of prophets, the visions of seers, and what was recorded in the sacred texts. So formal remembrance took on crucial significance for them. Acts of remembering could let them feel as if they were participating in the past events that saved their forefathers. Meanwhile, remembering the prophecies could help them look forward to events that had not yet taken place. Through remembering the bondage and captivity and then the deliverance of their fathers—from Egypt and from Jerusalem as well as from the desert wilderness and ocean—the Nephites would have their minds turned ahead to the atoning sacrifice of Jesus Christ—the central event in the overall plan of redeeming men from bondage to sin and death.

From the perspective of the Nephites, remembrance included active participation in some form. For them, it meant recalling not simply with the mind but also with the heart. To remember was to place the event upon the heart, or to turn the heart toward God—to repent or return to him and his ways as righteous forefathers had done. As in the Hebrew Bible, remembering often carries the meaning of acting in obedience to God's commands. Remembering God and thereby prospering so as to be lifted up at the last day (as in 3 Nephi 15:1 and Alma 38:5) are contrasted with forgetting and then perishing, or being cut off from God's presence (as at Alma 37:13 and 42:11). These opposites remind us of the grand law of opposition Lehi described in 2 Nephi 2.

Since remembering involved action, what specific actions were the Nephites told to take? The Book of Mormon tells us they were to awaken, soften the heart, see, hear, believe, or trust, as the examples below demonstrate. Overall these actions involved turning to God. People showed this by keeping his commandments: "They did remember his words; and *therefore* they went forth, keeping the commandments of God" (Helaman 5:14).

On the other hand, when people forget, they "do harden

their hearts, . . . and do trample under their feet the Holy One" (Helaman 12:2). Forgetfulness is also pictured as a dreadful sleep from which one needs to awake (see 2 Nephi 1:12–13). The person who does not remember suffers from blindness and disbelief (see 3 Nephi 2:1–2). To forget is also to fasten one's heart upon or worship riches (see Helaman 13:22). It means to engage in wickedness and to become involved deeply in iniquity (see Helaman 11:36). Being "cut off and destroyed forever" (2 Nephi 1:17) is the ultimate and dreadful fruit of forgetfulness.

The Book of Mormon links remembrance with covenants. Remembering is to keep the terms of the covenant between God and his people. The visible way to do that is simply to keep the commandments. At the same time, keeping the commandments strictly leads to remembering. Thus rebellious Israel, the prophet Abinadi tells us, had always been "quick to do iniquity, and slow to remember the Lord their God; therefore there was a law given them [by covenant at Mount Sinai], yea, a law of performances and of ordinances, a law which they were to observe strictly from day to day, to keep them in remembrance of God and their duty towards him" (Mosiah 13:29–30).

Like the Hebrew Bible, the Book of Mormon uses the expressions *keep* and *remember* interchangeably. For example, in Deuteronomy 5:12 the command is given to "keep the sabbath," while in Exodus 20:8 Israel is required to "remember the sabbath day, to keep it holy." The same connection is found in Jarom 1:5 and Mosiah 18:23, where the expression is "to keep," and Mosiah 13:16–19, where it is "to remember." Occasionally "remember to keep" joins both expressions. Thus Nephi pleads with his brothers to "give heed to the word of God and remember to keep his commandments always in all things" (1 Nephi 15:25). The point is that one remembers by actually doing something, not by merely recalling the past out of curiosity or for any other reason than to serve God.

For this reason the Israelite festivals and "performances" were observed, in order to remember and so "keep the commandments." (This expression occurs eighty-five times in the

Book of Mormon, often in connection with remembrance, as in Alma 36:1 and 30.) From the perspective of the Book of Mormon, one does not act only in order to remember. The two ideas are connected in both directions: a person remembers in the deepest sense only by acting in conformity with the will of God, and the action then stirs remembrance, as Abinadi indicated.

Genuine memory or remembrance occurs in the faithful response to the claims of the covenant God has made with Israel to make Israel his people. Much like the teaching found in Deuteronomy 8:18–19, remembering God, keeping his commandments, and prospering are linked, and then they are contrasted with forgetting him and perishing (see 2 Nephi 9:39; 10:22–23). Memory and covenants are thus constantly linked in the Book of Mormon. "Rememberest thou the covenants of the Father unto the house of Israel?" (1 Nephi 14:8; compare, for example, 17:40; 19:15; 2 Nephi 3:5, 21; 29:1–2, 5, 14).

So it is not surprising to find in certain instances the word *remembrance* as part of the covenant blessing and cursing formula (see Alma 37:13; compare 36:1, 29–30; Mosiah 1:5–7; and 2:40–41). The Book of Mormon is not a secular but a covenant history, that is, one written from the perspective of the promised blessings for keeping the commandments, and also the cursings that follow from their neglect.

God's demands upon Israel cannot be understood apart from the ways of remembrance. The mighty acts of God on their behalf, including delivering Israel from bondage in Egypt and, finally, atoning for their sins, are crucial. Without his dramatic acts on their behalf, they would be nothing but another little Near Eastern tribe. The commandments he gave them recall and are based in his actions. Therefore the commandments are not just an expression of vague heavenly laws, but are grounded in the key events in their history.

God is carrying out a plan (see 2 Nephi 9:6, 13; Jacob 6:8) that includes the testing of his people Israel—they are on probation (see 1 Nephi 10:21; Mormon 9:28). Part of the plan is to provide a way for their redemption from sin and darkness. But they must trust God, repent, and keep the commandments, or the plan fails. The importance of memory, in the Book of Mormon sense, is to bring about their obedience and so allow them to claim the promised blessings and avoid the cursings.

As in the Hebrew Bible, the language of remembrance includes warnings, promises, threats, pleas, complaints, and so forth. Furthermore, as in the Hebrew Bible, remembering the covenant sometimes is equivalent to possessing a land promised to the descendants of the one who first made the covenant with God, or to those who might be "grafted in" among the literal descendants (see Jacob 5; Alma 16:17). In that regard, Lehi's dealings with God are shown to us on the model provided by Abraham, and much attention is given in the Book of Mormon to the promise connected to the land.

To this point we have noted little about God remembering. In the Book of Mormon, for God to remember always implies action. God is pictured as remembering, or forgetting, because of a covenant he once made with his people. By forgetting the sins of men, God grants a blessing or gives a gift in accordance with the covenant, which includes mercy or forgiveness (see Mosiah 26:22, 29–30). When God remembers, he does something, just as he expects his people to act when they remember him. He may punish, deliver, preserve, heal, sustain, warn, forgive, or otherwise intervene in human affairs as a result of his remembering or forgetting. For God to remember always implies his working through real events, molding situations and circumstances to further his "eternal plan of deliverance" (2 Nephi 11:5), or "plan of redemption" (Jacob 6:8; Alma 34:9, 16, 31). God's remembering is more than God merely recalling in his thought—it is rather to act, finally by giving life or death.

The close links between thought and action can also be seen in the way in which remembering in the Book of Mormon is tied to the heart of man (see, for example, Alma 1:24; 10:30). It is also demonstrated in the giving of names. To remember someone is to know or believe on his name. "I would that ye should remember also, that this is the name that I said I should give

173

unto you that never should be blotted out, except it be through transgression; therefore, take heed that ye do not transgress, that the name be not blotted out of your hearts. I say unto you, I would that ye should remember to retain the name written always in your hearts" (Mosiah 5:11–12). For man, remembering is to awake, to hearken, to heed, to pray, and to obey by keeping the commandments and by knowing, pondering, and being willing to take a name upon them.

The Book of Mormon emphasizes the need to have records (such as the plates of brass) and to preserve them. It also stresses continuing to keep sacred records. In this we may see the kind of connection found in the Hebrew (and Arabic) language between the verb meaning "to remember" and the noun form of that verb which means "record." There is a "book of remembrance" mentioned in the Book of Mormon (see 3 Nephi 24:16), as well as a "book of life" that records the names of the righteous (see Alma 5:58; 3 Nephi 27:26). To record is to make a memorial of deeds or sayings, that is, to inscribe in a book (Exodus 17:14).

In the Book of Mormon remembering is clearly dependent upon the possession of records (see especially Mosiah 1:3–4). This connection is part of the reason for the obsession with records that the Nephite prophets had. Throughout the Book of Mormon, the fate of the people of God depends on their memory of their past. Without careful attention to the message of historical records, they would fail to fulfill their role in the plan of salvation.

King Benjamin taught his sons

> concerning the records which were engraven on the plates of brass, saying: My sons, I would that ye should remember that were it not for these plates, which contain these records and these commandments, we must have suffered in ignorance, even at this present time, not knowing the mysteries of God. For it were not possible that our father, Lehi, could have remembered all these things, to have taught them to his children, except it were for the help of these plates. . . . Were it not for

these [records], which have been kept and preserved by
the hand of God, that we might read and understand of
his mysteries, and have his commandments always before our eyes, that even our fathers would have dwindled
in unbelief, and we should have been like unto . . . the
Lamanites (Mosiah 1:5).

King Benjamin, using a common expression for instructing
sons in the Book of Mormon, teaches his sons:

I would that ye should remember that these sayings
are true, and also that these records are true. And behold,
also the plates of Nephi, which contain the records and
the sayings of our fathers from the time they left Jerusalem until now, and they are true. . . . Now, my sons,
I would that ye should remember to search them diligently, that ye may profit thereby; and I would that ye
should keep the commandments of God, that ye may
prosper in the land according to the promises which the
Lord made unto our fathers (Mosiah 1:6–7).

Clearly the memory that is expected of the people of God in both
the Bible and Book of Mormon is not mere curiosity; neither is
it a matter of being able simply to recall. Rather, the key is
righteous deeds.

The covenant that God made with Lehi was renewed from
time to time through rituals involving the entire community.
Those rituals taught and in fact constituted "ways of remembrance," as they did with ancient Israel. Remembering the terms
of the covenant made with God included the constant stressing
of the blessings and cursings that flow from keeping or not
keeping the commandments, from the broken hearted and contrite offering of sacrifices as memorials (or fruits) of repentance.

The history found in the Book of Mormon of God's contin-
uously saving or delivering the people is given to enlarge the
memory (see Alma 37:8) of the covenant people. It shows a
passion for preserving the crucial story of the divine dealings
with humans and our halting responses. The heart of that story
is the conflict between obedience and rebellion, liberty and bon-

dage, prosperity and suffering. Remembrance thus teaches and warns Israel, although it does not inflate reputations or pride. The people of God need to know how they came to be that; they also need to know how they have strayed, both as a people and as individuals, from the correct path, and how they might once again regain favor in God's eyes by turning away from sin and showing repentance.

We are to remember, as the Nephites of old remembered. We are to remember the curses brought upon the Nephites, which they inflicted upon themselves by forgetting the terms of the covenant. We must understand that to the extent that we fail to remember and keep our covenants we are or will be cut off from God's presence. At that point we are carnal, sensual, and devilish, chained in bondage and captivity.

The sacred records translated as the Book of Mormon provide us with direction from prophets who warn us to preserve and enlarge our own memory of God's mighty deeds and with the terms of the covenant that make us the people of God. These records teach us that we must neither forget what God has done nor what we have covenanted to do. The result of forgetting is to begin following some unholy tradition into darkness and sin. Instead, we must "always remember him, and keep his commandments" (Moroni 4:3) and be willing to take upon us the name of Jesus Christ, for to forget the sacrifice offered by our Lord for our sins by not keeping the commandments is to offend God.

Chapter 16

JESUS' COVENANT
TEACHINGS IN THIRD NEPHI

Victor L. Ludlow

The title page of the Book of Mormon states that the first purpose of the book is "to show unto the remnant of the House of Israel what great things the Lord hath done for their fathers; and that they may know the covenants of the Lord, that they are not cast off forever." This means that the Book of Mormon is intended, in part, to teach Lehi's descendants about the covenants that the Lord has made with them. The key covenant they will learn about is that they would be a blessing for all nations — a consecrated people of God. Beyond teaching about the covenants, the Book of Mormon also prophesies key signs and events that will demonstrate when the promised covenant is being fulfilled in the latter days.

To fulfill this purpose, the Book of Mormon contains many important teachings about the Lord's covenants with his people. There are at least 113 references in the Book of Mormon to the Lord's covenants with Israel. Some references can be found in nearly every part of the book, but they are concentrated most heavily at the beginning, in 1 Nephi and 2 Nephi, and at the end, in 3 Nephi and Mormon. Seventy percent of the references to covenants come from just three people. Nephi at the beginning of Book of Mormon history and Mormon at the end refer to covenants twenty-one times each. But by far the greatest emphasis is in the words of the Lord himself, especially in 3 Nephi, as he specifically mentioned covenants thirty-seven times.

Jesus gave three major sermons or discourses recorded in 3 Nephi. The first is the American version of the Sermon on the

Mount (see chapters 12–14), which is basically the same talk recorded in the New Testament book of Matthew, with a number of important changes. The 3 Nephi version of the Sermon on the Mount clarifies one important puzzle that has bothered some people as they have read in Matthew. Was he speaking to all humans or to only a special group? The Nephite account makes plain that the Savior was directing his sermon to those who had already been baptized. That is, they had already covenanted with the Lord to keep his commandments (see 3 Nephi 11:21–28; 12:1–2). It is safe to conclude that when Jesus gave the Sermon on the Mount that Matthew has passed on to us, the Lord was there speaking to a similar set of believers, not just to everyone who happened to be listening.

The second of Jesus' sermons to the Nephites teaches the people of Israel about the law and the covenant that Jehovah established long ago with the early fathers of the house of Israel (see 3 Nephi 15–16). It includes material also found in the Old and New Testaments, but with greater detail.

The last and most crucial of the three sermons is what I think of as his "Covenant People Discourse," which runs from 3 Nephi 20:10 to 23:5. This discourse is particularly valuable because it contains teachings unique to the Book of Mormon. Jesus may have taught them elsewhere, but they have not been recorded and passed down to us anywhere else.

Jesus Teaches about the Law and the Covenant

In the second discourse, starting in 3 Nephi 15, Jesus clarified some misunderstandings the Nephites had about the law of Moses. Earlier, when signs were given to the Nephites confirming that Jesus had been born, some of them thought that they no longer needed to keep the requirements of the law of Moses, since the Son of God was now on the earth and a new religious era had begun. However, their prophets told them that they needed to live the law until instructed otherwise. About thirty years later, Christ appeared at the city Bountiful and told them that the law had been fulfilled now that he had been slain and

178

resurrected: "Behold, I say unto you that the law is fulfilled that was given unto Moses" (3 Nephi 15:4). How could they be sure of that? He continues:

> I am he that gave the law, and I am he who covenanted with my people Israel; therefore, the law in me is fulfilled, for I have come to fulfil the law; therefore it hath an end. Behold, I do not destroy the prophets [and their prophecies], for as many as have not been fulfilled in me, verily I say unto you, shall all be fulfilled. And because I said unto you that old things have passed away, I do not destroy that which hath been spoken concerning things which are to come. For behold, the *covenant* which I have made with my people *is not all fulfilled;* but the *law* which was given unto Moses *hath an end in me* (3 Nephi 15:5–8; italics added).

He told them that the law Moses gave them was fulfilled, but that the covenant was not, so the two are not the same thing. The original covenant with Abraham was established over five hundred years earlier than the law through Moses was received among Abraham's descendants, the twelve tribes.

The Abrahamic covenant was established about 1900 B.C. At that time God made special promises to Abraham, then later renewed those to Abraham's son Isaac and grandson Jacob. Parts of the promises were fulfilled in earlier times, while other parts were not fulfilled until after Joseph Smith had begun this gospel dispensation. But some of the covenant promises have yet to be fulfilled. Indeed, the last of them will not be completed until Christ begins to rule the earth at the Millennium.

The law of Moses, that is, the statutes and regulations covering hundreds of situations of everyday life (Torah), was given to Israel about 1300 B.C. All those ceremonial details were intended to lead the Israelites to think of Jesus Christ and look forward to his great sacrifice. That law was fulfilled in Christ's actions at Gethsemane and Golgotha.

Jesus continued his teaching to the Nephites by discussing some of the covenant promises that remained to be fulfilled and what needed to be done to fulfill them. He discussed for example the unification of all Israel under the Messiah's leadership in their lands of inheritance. Starting in 3 Nephi 16:17, the Lord told us: "Then the words of the prophet Isaiah shall be fulfilled." He then quoted the last three verses from chapter fifty-two of Isaiah, which foretell that the watchmen (leaders) of Zion will sing joyfully and the inhabitants will rejoice because Zion, the Lord's city, has been established.

This short but profound discourse as recorded by Mormon and translated by Joseph Smith is consistent with the historical context and with passages of the Bible. It serves as a bridge between the simple, broad expectations of the Sermon on the Mount and the profound, specific requirements of what I call the "Covenant People Discourse."

Jesus' "Covenant People Discourse"

The rest of 3 Nephi 17, all of 18 and 19, and the first part of 20 all record what Christ did before leaving that day and what he did upon returning the following day. In chapter twenty we pick up where he started teaching the people on the next day. Here he began his unique "Covenant People Discourse":

> When they had all given glory unto Jesus, he said unto them: Behold now I finish the commandment which the Father hath commanded me concerning this people, who are the remnant of the house of Israel. Ye remember that I spake unto you [yesterday], and said that when the words of Isaiah should be fulfilled—behold they are written, ye have them before you, therefore search them—and verily, verily, I say unto you, that when they [the words of Isaiah] shall be fulfilled then is the fulfilling of the covenant which the Father hath made unto his people, O house of Israel (vv. 10–12).

The prophecies of Isaiah referred to include events concerning the second coming of the Lord and the start of the Millennium. At that time the covenant is to be finally and completely fulfilled. Jesus did not, of course, tell us the specific time when

180

this would take place, but he did point us to a kind of checklist of prophecies in Isaiah that would mark the fulfillment of the covenant.

Before getting to Isaiah directly, Jesus renewed the promises that the remnants of Israel would be gathered to their promised lands and given power over the unrepentant Gentiles (see 3 Nephi 20:13–20). He also reviewed prophecies given to Moses that tell of the coming of the Messiah and the covenant promises made to Abraham (see vv. 21–31). But Isaiah is the one who receives Jesus' emphasis. At verse thirty-two, without announcing it, Jesus starts quoting from Isaiah 52. Toward the end of his discourse, he also quotes all of chapter 54 of Isaiah (see 3 Nephi 22).

I have found it challenging to try to grasp why the Lord emphasized Isaiah so much at this point. Years ago, I studied these pages segment by segment, analyzing and reviewing this part over and over. I knew there was something unusually valuable in his teachings that I was not comprehending. For a long time I felt frustrated with these three chapters (20–22). I reviewed dictionaries and commentaries and studied the Hebrew roots of Isaiah's words. I cut and pasted the verses into clusters. I studied the passages in different translations. After all this work, I had to confess that I still did not see how the teachings all fit together.

A Key: The Fulfillment of the Abrahamic Covenant

Finally, while I was reading in chapter twenty-one, the whole structure of the discourse came into focus. The insight started with verse seven. Here the Lord says: "When these things come to pass that thy seed shall begin to know these things—it shall be a sign unto them." The word *sign* rang a bell in my mind. He continued: "That they may know that the work of the Father hath already commenced unto the fulfilling of the covenant." Here was another key word, *covenant*, and a sign was to be given that its fulfillment had commenced.

I backtracked to verse one, "I give unto you a sign [there was that key word again], that ye may know the time when these things shall be about to take place" (3 Nephi 21:1). When what things would take place? That Christ would gather Israel in from their long dispersion and fulfill his promises to them (see 20:46).

Reading verses seven and one a little more closely reveals one important distinction. In verse one a sign was to be given "when these things shall be *about to take place.*" These last four words tell us that something is almost ready to start—but not quite yet. In verse seven a sign was to be given "that they may know that the work of the Father *hath already commenced.*" The final three words describe something that has already started. Somewhere between verse one and verse seven the verb tense had shifted from future to past.

I looked more closely to see how the first and the seventh verses connect to each other. The first sentence of the chapter starts in verse one and does not conclude until the end of verse seven. The promised sign is actually within one long, very complex sentence. The longer I studied this complicated sentence, the clearer its subtle and profound messages became, and I realized that this was not a haphazard, convoluted sentence thrown together by Joseph Smith, but an eloquent declaration of the Lord. First, the Lord promised a sign so we would know when the promised covenant was about to be fulfilled, then he revealed the sign, and finally he testified that, after the sign was given, we would know that the Father's covenant promises were nearing fulfillment.

To clarify this complicated statement, I have pulled out the central core of the sentence (without noting the lengthy omissions, for the sake of clarity):

> I give unto you a sign: when these things [the Book of Mormon] shall be made known unto the Gentiles and shall come forth from them unto a remnant of your seed [the Lamanites], [so] that the covenant of the Father may be fulfilled which he hath covenanted with his people, O house of Israel; therefore, when these works [the Book of Mormon] shall come forth from the Gentiles, unto

your seed [so] that your seed shall begin to know these
things, [then] it [the Book of Mormon record] shall be a
sign unto them, that they may know that the work of
the Father hath already commenced unto the fulfilling
of the covenant which he hath made unto the people
who are of the house of Israel.

The core of this sentence comes through very clearly when
all the secondary concepts and explanatory notes, which make
up the bulk of the sentence, are dropped out. Note that the key
sign that will mark the beginning of the fulfillment of the Lord's
promises to Israel is that the Book of Mormon will go from the
Gentiles to the Lamanites, so that the Lamanites will begin to
know its teachings.

After saying what the sign is to be, Jesus continued his
"Covenant People Discourse" by promising marvelous blessings
not only to the native Israelites, but also to the Gentiles who
would join them by accepting the gospel in the period when the
sign was becoming visible. In chapter 20, verses 10–46, the Lord
summarized the great work to be done among the Gentiles as
well as among his covenant people (see 3 Nephi 21:8–11). In
21:26–29 he summarized the Father's work in gathering the dis-
persed of Israel. He prophesied the blessings to be enjoyed by
Zion (the Church) and her stakes in the last days by quoting all
of Isaiah 54 (in 3 Nephi 22).

The covenant with Israel would finally be fulfilled by Christ's
kingdom being established over the whole earth, as stakes are
organized and Israel – both the original Israelites by descent and
also the additional converted Gentiles – settle down in peace.
Jesus concluded his discourse in 3 Nephi 23 by telling us to
search the words of Isaiah, since they contain the key promises
given to Israel (see 3 Nephi 23:1–5)

Has the Key Sign Been Fulfilled Yet?

The fulfillment of this prophesied sign becomes a barometer
by which Latter-day Saints can measure how much of the Father's work with his children on earth has been completed in

preparation for the Second Coming. Was this sign—the Lamanites knowing the Book of Mormon message—fulfilled early in this dispensation? Granted, Joseph Smith sent missionaries with the Book of Mormon to a few Lamanite groups, but very little success resulted. The early converts to the Church instead came from scattered Israel among the Gentile nations—the United States and Canada, the British Isles, Scandinavia, and Germany. At least through the Church's first century, little progress had been made among the Lamanites, the native Americans.

When I went on my first mission in 1962, I was sent to West Germany, where there were six missions. We had over eleven percent of the Church's missionary force there. At that same time, the Church had only six missions in all of South America and three in Mexico. Thus even in the early 1960s, the Lamanites were apparently not receiving and accepting the Book of Mormon message in sufficient numbers so that we could say that the promised sign had been fulfilled.

When I served as a mission president in Germany a generation later, there were only three missions in Germany. But by then the Church in Central and South America had vaulted ahead. As of 1990, there were seventeen missions in Mexico, and any one of them baptized more than all the missions in Germany, Austria, Switzerland, Finland, Norway, Sweden, Denmark, Holland, Belgium, and Iceland combined. There were, in 1990, seventy missions in Central and South America compared to ten in the same area when I went on my first mission in 1962.

The Fulfillment of the Covenant Promise

The covenant with Israel is beginning to be fulfilled. The descendants of Abraham are to be a blessing to the nations of the earth—by leading out in carrying the gospel to all peoples. This promised sign of success was to start among the remnants of the Lamanite part of Israel. The Savior's words in 3 Nephi 22 are being brought to pass dramatically in our day.

It seems that 1975 may have been the pivotal year, after

which nobody should fail to see that the prophesied sign—the marvelous missionary work among the House of Israel in the Americas—has unmistakably appeared. At that time President Spencer W. Kimball stated three times that "Now is the time of the Jew" or Israelite in the unfolding of God's work among his children. Since then, success among the Lamanites and peoples of Central and South America has truly blossomed.

The key sign promised in 3 Nephi indicates the beginning of the end for the final prophetic period immediately prior to the Millennium. It appears that this sign has now been given. God's work is rolling forth to bring about the promises given to the patriarchs regarding their descendants.

The teachings about the covenant laid out in Christ's words in 3 Nephi are complex and subtle. They include and integrate prophecies given over thousands of years. At the same time they clarify how all those prophecies connect to the restoration of the Book of Mormon and the Lord's kingdom in modern times. For us individually, they help us catch the vision and recognize the signs that were recorded so long ago.

This is a marvelous time to be on the earth, a period the ancient prophets foresaw and yearned for. As they prophesied about our age, they told of servants in the vineyards and workers in the fields of God's final harvest scenes. Rather than ignoring or resisting God's expanding kingdom, we share the possibility of actually bringing to reality the things that the prophets promised so long ago. The acts of Christ at the time of his life and death on the earth fulfilled the old law and ushered in a new religious age. In a similar way, he now invites our action in fulfilling his covenant promises so we can help usher in his millennial reign.

Chapter 17

THE GATHERING OF ISRAEL IN THE BOOK OF MORMON: A CONSISTENT PATTERN

Robert L. Millet

The Book of Mormon is holy scripture. It is a key witness of the divine Sonship of Jesus Christ and a convincing testimony that salvation is to be found only through him. The Book of Mormon's primary message, that Jesus Christ came to earth to redeem mankind, is closely tied to the history of the house of Israel. One of the primary purposes of the Nephite record, according to its title page, is "to show unto the remnant of the House of Israel what great things the Lord hath done for their fathers; and that they may know the covenants of the Lord, that they are not cast off forever."

The ancient American scripture contains repeated promises about the gathering of Israel that together yield a complex picture of the role the twelve tribes are to play in the latter days. The picture of gathering that the record presents is entirely consistent within the book and between it and the Bible. This picture assures readers that God has a plan for his chosen people and that they have a crucial mission to perform. Moreover, the Nephite record tells us how Israel will be identified and unified.

What the Book of Mormon teaches about Israel includes such diverse topics as the physical and spiritual aspects of scattering and gathering, the relation of the natural or genetic Israelites and those who are adopted, the timetable and geography of the gathering, and the special situations of three groups—the Jews, the descendants of Lehi, and the lost ten tribes. Here I focus only on one topic, the relation between the physical and spiritual aspects of scattering and gathering.

Background: Jew and Gentile

The Book of Mormon assumes that its readers know about the origins of Israel; God's covenant with Abraham, Isaac, and Jacob; and the promises of priesthood power and eternal life for the chosen seed. At no place in the Book of Mormon does a writer specifically define "the house of Israel," although everything said is consistent with their being the descendants of the patriarch Jacob. What we have, rather, are insightful comments and explanations about the scattering and gathering of Israel.

Book of Mormon writers often speak in a generalizing, black-and-white, clearly defined fashion. Thus there are said to be only two churches on earth—the church of the Lamb and the church of the devil (see 1 Nephi 14:10). The same generalizing viewpoint can be seen when we read in Alma 34:33–35 that individuals either receive and live up to gospel laws here or else they face at death a time of "darkness" when no action is possible. Latter-day revelation makes clear that, while this is broadly true, a number of important qualifications apply to that picture. We also are told that partial judgment at death divides all mortals into just two camps, called paradise and outer darkness (see Alma 40:12–14). Again, the details revealed in our day expand on that loose characterization of the afterlife.

This same uncomplicated manner of labeling is also used in referring to major classes of people in the prophetic view of history presented in the Book of Mormon. In particular, two major historical groups are of concern to Nephi—Jews and Gentiles. To him, Jews are those descended from the inhabitants of the kingdom of Judah at the time Lehi left Jerusalem, regardless of whether individuals might have had ancestors not of the tribe of Judah (see 2 Nephi 33:8). In terms of this very generalized definition, even one who happened to be descended from one of the ten tribes but who lived around Jerusalem in 600 B.C. would be called a Jew (see 2 Nephi 25:6, 14–15 and 33:8). So in this framework, the Lehite colony—whether Nephite or "Mulekite"—is a subcategory of the Jews.

In these terms, it is perfectly appropriate for Nephi to speak of the reception of the Book of Mormon by the latter-day descendants of Lehi as follows: "Then shall the remnant of our seed know concerning us, how that we came out from Jerusalem, and that *they are descendants of the Jews*" (2 Nephi 30:4; italics added). Later Nephi explained: "I have charity for the Jew—*I say Jew, because I mean them from whence I came*" (2 Nephi 33:8; italics added; compare D&C 19:27).

Further, the Book of Mormon prophets spoke often of the latter-day restoration of the gospel among "the Gentiles" in the New World promised land and of the gospel message those Gentiles would take to the house of Israel in the latter days (see 1 Nephi 15:17; 22:7–8). In this sense, people may be Israelite by descent but Gentile by culture. Joseph Smith thus prayed as a part of the dedicatory services in the Kirtland Temple: "Now these words, O Lord, we have spoken before thee, concerning the revelations and commandments which thou hast given unto us, who are identified with the Gentiles" (D&C 109:60).

The Scattering of Israel

The Old Testament makes clear the causes for the scattering of Israel. Speaking on behalf of Jehovah, Moses warned ancient Israel that, if they rejected God, they would be scattered among the nations: "If thou wilt not hearken unto the voice of the Lord thy God, to observe to do all his commandments and his statutes which I command thee this day; . . . thou shalt . . . be removed into all the kingdoms of the earth" (Deuteronomy 28:15, 25). "The Lord shall scatter thee among all people, from the one end of the earth even unto the other; and there thou shalt serve other gods, which neither thou nor thy fathers have known" (v. 64).

The Lord spoke similar words through Jeremiah more than half a millennium later: "Because your fathers have forsaken me, saith the Lord, and have walked after other gods, and have served them, and have worshipped them, and have forsaken me, and have not kept my law; and ye have done worse than your fathers; . . . therefore will I cast you out of this land into a land that ye know not, . . . where I will not shew you favor" (Jeremiah 16:11–13). The cause of Israel's scattering is plain: she had forsaken the God of Abraham, Isaac, and Jacob and no longer deserved his blessings.

The Book of Mormon presents the same message. In writing of the Jews, who here symbolize all the house of Israel (see 1 Nephi 15:17, 20; Mormon 5:14), Jacob taught that "after [the Lord] should manifest himself they should scourge him and crucify him. . . . And after they have hardened their hearts and stiffened their necks against the Holy One of Israel, behold, the judgments of the Holy One of Israel shall come upon them," such that "they [will be] driven to and fro." In short, they "shall be scattered, and smitten, and hated" (2 Nephi 6:9–11). Jacob later explained that, "because of priestcrafts and iniquities," the Jews "will stiffen their necks against him [Christ], that he be crucified. . . . And they who shall not be destroyed shall be scattered among all nations" (2 Nephi 10:5–6). Of course the same result was prophesied for the Nephites. Nephi the son of Helaman predicted that, unless the Nephites repented of their wickedness, the God of Israel would, instead of gathering his people, scatter them (see Helaman 7:19).

The Gathering of Israel

The gathering of Israel is to result from the scattered remnants of Israel repenting and returning to the worship of the Lord Jehovah. Old Testament references to the gathering of Israel are numerous. They underline the essential fact that a chosen people are a people who make appropriate choices. They must choose the God of their fathers and strictly obey his counsels and teachings if they are to be gathered and blessed (see, for example, Isaiah 43:1–7; Jeremiah 3:12–23; 16:11–21).

The Book of Mormon is even more specific in clarifying this principle of gathering: the people of Israel will be gathered again to the degree that they return to Christ and become formally associated with the Saints of God. That is, people are gathered first spiritually and second temporally, first to the Lord and his church and then to the lands of their inheritance or to the congregations of the Saints. Nephi wrote that "after the house of Israel should be scattered they should be gathered together again; or, in fine, after the Gentiles had received the fulness of the Gospel [i.e., after the restoration through Joseph Smith had taken place], the natural branches of the olive-tree, or the remnants of the house of Israel, should be grafted in, or come to the knowledge of the true Messiah" (1 Nephi 10:14). Nephi later explained to his rebellious brothers some of the words of their father concerning Israel's destiny:

> Now, the thing which our father meaneth concerning the grafting in of the natural branches through the fulness of the Gentiles, is, that in the latter days, when our seed shall have dwindled in unbelief, yea, for the space of many years, and many generations after the Messiah shall be manifested in body unto the children of men, then shall the fulness of the gospel of the Messiah come unto the Gentiles, and from the Gentiles unto the remnant of our seed—and at that day shall the remnant of our seed know that they are of the house of Israel, and that they are the covenant people of the Lord; and then shall they know and come to the knowledge of their forefathers, and also to the knowledge of the gospel of their Redeemer, which was ministered unto their fathers by him; wherefore, they shall come to the knowledge of their Redeemer and the very points of his doctrine, that they may know how to come unto him and be saved (1 Nephi 15:13–14; compare 2 Nephi 30:5; Mormon 7:1–10).

Jacob reminded his people that the Lord God "has spoken unto the Jews, by the mouth of his holy prophets, even from the beginning down, from generation to generation, until the time comes that they [the Jews, or the house of Israel] shall be *restored to the true church and fold of God;* when they shall be gathered home to the lands of their inheritance, and shall be established in all their lands of promise" (2 Nephi 9:2; italics added).

The sequence of gathering—first to Christ and his Church and then to specific locations—is clear in Jacob's words. Having taught that the people of Jerusalem who reject the Savior will be "scattered among all nations," he added: "Thus saith the Lord God: When the day cometh that they shall believe in me, that I am Christ, then have I covenanted with their fathers that they shall be restored in the flesh, upon the earth, unto the lands of their inheritance" (2 Nephi 10:6–7). Among his American Israelites, the resurrected Lord spoke of the day when the gospel of Jesus Christ would be had among his people:

> I will remember the covenant which I have made with my people; and I have covenanted with them that I would gather them together in mine own due time, that I would give unto them again the land of their fathers for their inheritance, which is the land of Jerusalem, which is the promised land unto them forever, saith the Father. And it shall come to pass that the time cometh, when the fulness of my gospel shall be preached unto them and they shall believe in me, that I am Jesus Christ, the Son of God, and shall pray unto the Father in my name. Then shall their watchmen lift up their voice, and with the voice together shall they sing; for they shall see eye to eye. Then will the Father gather them together again, and give unto them Jerusalem for the land of their inheritance (3 Nephi 20:29–33).

In short, the restoration of Israel is primarily their restoration to the knowledge of Christ (see Mormon 9:36). "It is not the *place* of gathering that will save the scattered remnants," Elder Bruce R. McConkie has written, "but the *message* of salvation that comes to them in their Redeemer's name. . . . Salvation is not in a *place* but in a *person*. It is in Christ."[1]

President Spencer W. Kimball likewise summarized this principle as follows: "Now, the gathering of Israel consists of joining the true church and their coming to a knowledge of the true God. . . . Any person, therefore, who has accepted the restored gospel, and who now seeks to worship the Lord in his own tongue and with the Saints in the nations where he lives, has complied with the law of the gathering of Israel and is heir to all of the blessings promised the saints in these last days."[2]

Joseph Smith, the Book of Mormon, and the Gathering

The Book of Mormon and Joseph Smith play key roles in the gathering of Israel in the final dispensation. Not only does the Book of Mormon describe with exactness the process by which Israel was to be scattered then gathered, it also spells out the *means* by which that gathering is to take place. People are to become converted to the restored gospel and be gathered into the true church of God particularly through the Book of Mormon.

Some six hundred years before Christ, Nephi saw that in the future a powerful church would take many plain and precious truths from the Bible writings as Jewish writers originally recorded them. He also saw the work that Joseph Smith would set in motion and gloried in the fact that through the Book of Mormon, as well as "other books" of scripture, plain and precious truths and "many covenants" of the Lord would be restored (1 Nephi 13:20–40).

His father Lehi, drawing on the writings of Joseph of old as contained on the brass plates, prophesied about the coming of Joseph Smith, a "choice seer" who would do much to bring the scattered Israelites to a knowledge of the promises made to their ancestors. "Thus prophesied Joseph [in Egypt], saying: Behold, that seer will the Lord bless; and they that seek to destroy him shall be confounded; . . . and his name shall be called after me; and it shall be after the name of his father. And he shall be like unto me; for the thing, which the Lord shall bring forth by his hand [the Book of Mormon and the Restoration], by the power of the Lord shall bring my people unto salvation" (2 Nephi 3:7, 14–15).

In addition, while he was among the Nephites, the risen Lord spoke of the latter-day work of gathering and of the vital role of this leader, Joseph Smith.

> For in that day, for my sake shall the Father work a
> work, which shall be a great and a marvelous work
> among them; and there shall be among them those who
> will not believe it, although a man shall declare it unto
> them. But behold, the life of my servant shall be in my
> hand; therefore they shall not hurt him, although he shall
> be marred because of them. Yet I will heal him, for I will
> show unto them that my wisdom is greater than the
> cunning of the devil. Therefore it shall come to pass that
> whosoever will not believe in my words, who am Jesus
> Christ, which the Father shall cause him [Joseph Smith]
> to bring forth unto the Gentiles, and shall give unto him
> power that he shall bring them forth unto the Gentiles,
> (it shall be done even as Moses said) they shall be cut
> off from among my people who are of the covenant (3
> Nephi 21:9–11).

President Ezra Taft Benson has emphasized the obligations
resting upon those who have been given the Nephite scripture:
"The Book of Mormon is the instrument that God has designed
to 'sweep the earth as with a flood, to gather out His elect unto
the New Jerusalem.' (Moses 7:62.)"[3] In fact, because of its central
role in the work of gathering in the last days, the Nephite prophets spoke of the Book of Mormon as one of the signs of the times
showing that gathering is underway.

Following his abridgment of the Savior's teachings in America, Mormon advised his readers "that when the Lord shall see
fit, in his wisdom, that these sayings [in the Book of Mormon]
shall come unto the Gentiles according to his word, then ye may
know that the covenant which the Father hath made with the
children of Israel, concerning their restoration to the lands of
their inheritance, is already beginning to be fulfilled" (3 Nephi
29:1; compare 21:1–7). His son Moroni added, after discussing
the great vision of the Brother of Jared: "When ye shall receive
this record ye may know that the work of the Father has commenced upon all the face of the land" (Ether 4:17).

Elder McConkie stated that "the process of gathering is one
in which the scattered remnants of Jacob—those of all tribes—

believe the Book of Mormon, accept the restored gospel, and come to the latter-day Zion. . . . This gathering will be one person here, and two there, and a few somewhere else—all by the power of a book, the stick of Joseph joined with the stick of Judah."[4] Almost four hundred years after Christ's birth, the prophet-editor Mormon, knowing that his compilation would one day reach all peoples, spoke with fervor:

> Therefore I write unto you, Gentiles, and also unto you, house of Israel, when the work shall commence, that ye shall be about to prepare to return to the land of your inheritance; yea, behold, I write unto all the ends of the earth; yea, unto you, twelve tribes of Israel. . . . These things doth the Spirit manifest unto me; therefore I write unto you all. And for this cause I write unto you, that . . . ye may believe the gospel of Jesus Christ, which ye shall have among you; and also that the Jews, the covenant people of the Lord, shall have other witness besides him whom they saw and heard, that Jesus, whom they slew, was the very Christ and the very God (Mormon 3:17–21).

The Millennium: The Final Work of Gathering

The Book of Mormon provides a consistent message regarding the final "work of the Father." It tells us that part of the gathering of Israel will not take place until after the return of Christ and the beginning of the millennial era. Nephi, apparently quoting the prophet Zenos, told of the destruction of the wicked at the time of the Second Coming: "For behold, saith the prophet, the time cometh speedily that Satan shall have no more power over the hearts of the children of men; for the day soon cometh that all the proud and they who do wickedly shall be as stubble; and the day cometh that they must be burned" (1 Nephi 22:15). The righteous would be delivered through the destruction of the wicked by fire. Those who fought against Zion and the Saints would be destroyed, and Moses' prophecy would be fulfilled that those who reject the Lord and his servants would be cut off from among the people of the covenant (see vv. 16–20).

Using language borrowed from Zenos, Nephi then described the millennial day and one phase of gathering: "The time cometh speedily that the righteous must be led up as calves of the stall, and the Holy One of Israel must reign in dominion, and might, and power, and great glory. And he gathereth his children from the four quarters of the earth; and he numbereth his sheep, and they know him; and there shall be one fold and one shepherd; and he shall feed his sheep, and in him they shall find pasture" (vv. 24–25).

Jesus himself explained about this phase of gathering:

> Then shall they [the "Gentiles" of the Latter-day Church] assist my people [natural Israel] that they may be gathered in, who are scattered upon all the face of the land. . . . Then shall the power of heaven come down among them; and I also will be in the midst. And *then shall the work of the Father commence at that day,* even when this gospel shall be preached among the remnant of this people. Verily I say unto you, at that day shall the work of the Father commence among all the dispersed of my people, yea, even the tribes which have been lost, which the Father hath led away out of Jerusalem (3 Nephi 21:24–26; italics added).

Further, the Savior said: "Then shall the work commence, with the Father among all nations in preparing the way whereby his people may be gathered home to the land of their inheritance. And they shall go out from all nations" (3 Nephi 21:28–29).

Conclusion

How the scattered people of Israel will return to the God of their fathers and then return to their lands of inheritance is consistently presented within the pages of the Book of Mormon. The process of gathering is also consistent with what the Old and New Testaments and the Doctrine and Covenants say about it. The Book of Mormon could not have contained such a sweeping and orderly picture of Israel—its scattering, gathering, and

195

destiny—without divine inspiration to the prophets who gave it to us. No New York farmer on his own could have woven these threads together throughout such a large and complex book. The Book of Mormon bears the marks of antiquity; it evidences the yearnings of a people of long ago whose hopes and dreams were for a united Kingdom of Israel under the gentle command of the Holy One of Israel.

Surely, as Moroni affirmed on the title page of the Book of Mormon, God has done great things for Israel; he has not forgotten her. In fact, one of the overarching messages of the allegory of Zenos about Israel's history (see Jacob 5) is that God has no intention of letting Israel go. After centuries of long-suffering and endurance with an often stubborn, hardhearted people, the Lord's merciful hand is stretched out still—he will not let Israel go! Jacob said that the Lord "remembereth the house of Israel, both roots and branches; and he stretches forth his hands unto them all the day long" (Jacob 6:4–5). The Book of Mormon provides an invaluable doctrinal interpretation of Israel's past, as well as a sacred lens through which to scan Israel's possibilities.

Notes

1. *The Millennial Messiah* (Salt Lake City: Deseret Book, 1982), 200; italics added.

2. *The Teachings of Spencer W. Kimball,* ed. Edward L. Kimball (Salt Lake City: Bookcraft, 1982), 439.

3. *A Witness and a Warning: A Modern-day Prophet Testifies of the Book of Mormon* (Salt Lake City: Deseret Book, 1988), vii.

4. *A New Witness for the Articles of Faith* (Salt Lake City: Deseret Book, 1985), 457.

Chapter 18

ISAIAH – KEY TO THE BOOK OF MORMON

Avraham Gileadi

The book of Isaiah and the Book of Mormon teach us much about each other. The better we understand the one, the better we will understand the other. And the more we learn about what both have to say, the more we will learn about the time in which we live.

The Book of Mormon offers four keys essential for understanding Isaiah: (1) the spirit of prophecy or the Holy Ghost; (2) the letter of prophecy or the manner of the Jews; (3) diligent searching of Isaiah's words; and (4) types, or the idea that events in Israel's past foreshadow events in the latter days. When we apply these four keys to Isaiah's writings, a message unfolds there that is immediately applicable and recognizable to Latter-day Saints. The developing spiritual and political shape of the world in which we live parallels precisely the prophetic scenario Isaiah drew up millennia ago.

Knowing these four Book of Mormon keys, we understand Isaiah in a new light. Isaiah speaks to us – to our generation – like a voice from the dust. Isaiah shows us where we as Latter-day Saints fit into the Lord's plan of salvation. He tells us the role we must play in redeeming Israel's ancient covenant people, or else be swept away by the Lord's judgments. The last days portend both good and evil: Isaiah describes a glorious salvation on the earth for the Lord's long-suffering people; but he also portrays a world ripening in iniquity that the Lord will destroy in a fiery holocaust, a war to end all wars. Isaiah identifies the chief actors in this modern drama by means of ancient names and key words. Matching these with their latter-day counterparts resembles putting together a jigsaw puzzle — every piece fits and adds to the picture.

Isaiah's thought also permeates the Book of Mormon. At many key points we find references to Isaiah or sections from his prophecies. Book of Mormon prophet-writers quote from Isaiah in numerous instances. They express their own thoughts in Isaiah's words, often without mentioning him as their source. They use Isaiah's systematic way of employing terms and expressions. They reproduce whole chapters of Isaiah in strategic parts of their narratives, their doctrinal explanations, or their prophesyings. The words of Isaiah, far beyond those of any other Old Testament writer, are significant for them.

The Book of Mormon's emphasis on Isaiah leads us to believe that his words furnish a key to understanding the Nephite record. As we appreciate Isaiah's influence on Book of Mormon prophet-writers, we understand the Book of Mormon better. We realize that the Book of Mormon is not simply the story of what happened to Lehi's family and others who journeyed to the Western hemisphere. The book does tell that story, but it tells it in a way intended to teach us things about our time also. One of the ways it does that is by recording especially those events that parallel and reinforce Isaiah's teachings about the last days. These events are included in the Book of Mormon, chosen out of the many that could have been included, to help the Lord's people in our time understand events that are to come — events that will fulfill Isaiah's prophecies about our modern day.

An example of how the Book of Mormon gives us a key for understanding Isaiah can also show how understanding Isaiah aids our understanding of the Book of Mormon. As we study the Book of Mormon more closely, we find that it paints a living portrait of the *types* of things Isaiah prophesied for the last day. Let us look at the exodus theme, which appears prominently in the book of Isaiah.

Isaiah prophesied a literal new exodus for some of the Lord's people in the last days that resembles the ancient exodus out of

Egypt. He predicted that the Lord's people will exit "Babylon" on the eve of a cataclysmic destruction, a destruction like that which struck Sodom and Gomorrah. To Isaiah, however, "Babylon" in the latter days consists of a world ripening in iniquity and the wicked who make up its citizenry. Both the exodus out of Egypt, therefore, and also the name Babylon serve as types. First, the Lord will miraculously intervene to save his people from bondage and destruction as he did in Egypt. Second, the ancient Babylonian world, which was known for its idolatry and oppression, here becomes a symbol of latter-day wickedness. Third, there will occur a Sodom-and-Gomorrah type of destruction (by fire rained down from the sky) in the last days.

Isaiah used this method of prophesying throughout his writings. He prophesied new things based on the old. Events that have set important precedents qualify as types and shadows for the last days. In addition to a new exodus, Isaiah predicted a new passover, a new descent of God on the mount (not Mount Sinai this time but Mount Zion), a new wandering in the wilderness, and a new conquest of the promised land—all new versions of things similar to what happened in Moses' day.

These ancient types are keys to understanding the book of Isaiah. My reading tells me that more than thirty major events that are reported in the Old Testament serve as types for the future, that is, for our day. So, when Book of Mormon writers quote so much from Isaiah, we expect that they will share Isaiah's use of types. We find, in fact, that Book of Mormon writers build on this aspect of Isaiah's thought more than any other.

Many Book of Mormon stories are inspired by types. Why did Book of Mormon writers choose to tell about certain events in their history and not others? For the same reason that Isaiah described certain events of his day and not others. The reason is that those events had special meaning as lessons through which those who would live many generations later could learn what they must watch for and do.

What standard did Book of Mormon writers use to decide what was appropriate to include and what was not? Often it was

Isaiah's standard: types. Whatever in their history best served as a type and shadow for the latter days, they included in their narratives. What would not serve effectively as a type, they left out, just as Isaiah did. Their aim was not to give an exhaustive history but rather to teach certain lessons to us and to their descendants.

The Book of Mormon commences with an exodus: the people in Jerusalem were ripening in wickedness; the Lord sent Lehi and others to prophesy a coming destruction and captivity. When the people sought Lehi's life, the Lord commanded him to take his family and flee into the wilderness. Soon Ishmael's family joined them, and they traveled together in the wilderness, then crossed the sea to a promised land. Nephi drew numerous parallels between the families' exodus out of the land of Jerusalem and the Israelites' exodus out of Egypt. Nephi in many instances functioned as a new Moses, preserving his people and leading them to the promised land.

Not long after they arrived in the promised land, Nephi led another exodus. When their father died, Laman and Lemuel sought to kill Nephi. The Lord warned Nephi to flee into the wilderness with all who would join him. They journeyed for days, then reestablished themselves as a righteous people (see 2 Nephi 5:1–11). As the Lamanites increased in numbers and warred incessantly against the Nephites, Mosiah led yet another exodus. His remnant of the Nephites traveled through the wilderness until they discovered the people of Zarahemla and united with them (see Omni 1:12–19). The people of Zarahemla themselves had participated in an exodus from Jerusalem at the time King Zedekiah of Judah was taken captive into Babylon. They had journeyed in the wilderness and crossed the sea to the promised land much like Lehi's group (see Omni 1:15–16).

Alma led an exodus of believers to escape wicked King Noah's wrath. The Lord warned Alma, their high priest, to flee into the wilderness. They discovered the land of Helam and settled there (see Mosiah 23:1–5). After Amulon persecuted Alma and his people, putting them into hard bondage, the Lord again commanded Alma to depart into the wilderness. Many days later his people reached safety in the land of Zarahemla (see Mosiah 24:8–25). King Limhi's people, in bondage to the Lamanites, similarly escaped by an exodus. With Ammon leading the way, they traveled from the land of Nephi through the wilderness and arrived in the land of Zarahemla (see Mosiah 22:11–13). Later, the Lamanites whom the sons of Mosiah converted (the Anti-Nephi-Lehies) also had to flee. When the unconverted Lamanites killed many of them, Ammon led them in yet another exodus through the wilderness to Zarahemla (see Alma 27:2–26).

A classic exodus in the Book of Mormon involves Jared and his brother and their friends. They departed from the "great tower" in Mesopotamia when the Lord confounded the people's language. The brother of Jared obtained the Lord's promise of a new land of inheritance. They wandered through the wilderness and crossed seas, eventually arriving in the promised land (see Ether 1:40–42; 2:5–7; 6:4–12). There are six features common to this exodus and others in the Book of Mormon: First, the Lord is personally involved in the exodus. Second, a prophet-leader communicates with the Lord on behalf of his people. Third, the Lord guides his people as to when they should leave and which direction they should take. Fourth, they gather up and bring with them seeds and livestock of all kinds. Fifth, they dwell in tents during a prolonged journey through the wilderness. Sixth, they arrive safely and prosper in the land of promise. All of this reminds us of Moses and the Israelites leaving Egypt and journeying to the promised land.

To make sure the reader recognizes the exodus theme in the Book of Mormon, its writers quote many of Isaiah's prophecies of the latter-day exodus out of Babylon (see 1 Nephi 20:20; 2 Nephi 8:10–11; 21:15; 3 Nephi 20:41–42). The Book of Mormon illustrates by a series of types what the exodus predicted by Isaiah will be like. What the Nephite prophet-writers have chosen to mention about each exodus, particularly the commonly shared elements, teaches us about the nature of exoduses. Yet an exodus is not an abstract idea, a figure of speech, or merely a point of historical interest. Instead, it is a literal and dramatic event, one that changes people's lives forever. It involves the Lord's intervention in behalf of his righteous people when only his help can deliver them from calamity.

An exodus means irrevocable separation from those, perhaps loved ones, who do not merit the Lord's deliverance. It signals a fresh beginning, the replanting of a community, the restoring of a righteous civilization. The Book of Mormon leaves no doubt about the kind of candidates who qualify for the Lord's deliverance. Nor does it leave us in the dark about who the oppressors are. As the latter-day exodus draws near that Isaiah prophesied, the Book of Mormon is there to teach us about conditions preceding it. Knowing with what faithfulness the Lord acts in times of great judgment will inspire us to act in faith toward him, to endure with long-suffering the oppressions that must come. Having received from the past "a pattern in all things" (D&C 52:14), and having received latter-day prophecies of an exodus by the Saints (D&C 103:15–20), we will not easily be deceived.

We thus see that what Isaiah prophesied directly about the last days by drawing on ancient types, the Book of Mormon prophesied indirectly by highlighting certain aspects of its history that reinforce or echo the types used by Isaiah. One further example will help to make this point. The Lord's judgments in the last days possess a twofold dimension: at his coming, the Lord will both deliver (by an exodus) the righteous and destroy the wicked. The righteous will inherit the land vacated by the wicked who perish. This reversal will take place in two stages: first, when his people ripen in wickedness, the Lord will raise up enemies to invade their land and destroy many of them; and second, when the Lord's purpose of punishing the wicked has been served, he will empower a righteous remnant of his people to overthrow the invaders. Those who remain to inherit the land will be the Lord's righteous, proven people.

Isaiah projected this as the pattern of deliverance and destruction for the last days. Using ancient Assyria as the type of an oppressive latter-day superpower, Isaiah predicted that the Lord will raise up a new "Assyria" as his instrument for destroying and taking captive his people. This "Assyria," after invading and ravaging the promised land, will prevail until it fully accomplishes the Lord's purpose of cleansing the wicked from the land. But "Assyria's" own wickedness will prove its downfall also. Its armies will perish when the Lord smites them at the hands of a righteous Ephraimite army whom he will lend his own power.

Like the exodus theme, the Book of Mormon emphasizes this pattern of invasion and reconquest. Why do Book of Mormon writers take up so much space on precious gold plates with stories of warfare? They tell us that not a hundredth part of their history is recorded in the Book of Mormon, so this pattern of invasion and reconquest must have been important for them to emphasize so much. Why do Book of Mormon writers play up certain episodes of their military history, such as the wars Moroni waged, and yet deliberately downplay others, such as King Benjamin's great victory over the Lamanites (see Words of Mormon 1:13)? Is it because in King Benjamin's case no actual conquest by the Lamanites had occurred? Is it because at that time few dissenting Nephites were destroyed in the war? The typical military stories of the Book of Mormon feature both wickedness by the Lord's people and conquest of their land by enemies.

The Lord permits enemies to destroy and take away the promised lands when his people do not keep his commandments. This is a key lesson that they must learn. The Nephites' wickedness constitutes *the* reason for the wars that are emphasized. That much the Lord had shown Nephi before they reached the promised land (see 1 Nephi 2:24). The Lord raised up the Lamanites as "a scourge" against the Nephites when the Nephites ripened in iniquity (see 2 Nephi 5:25). By means of wars, the Lord often destroyed the more wicked part of the Nephites but spared the righteous (see Omni 1:5–7; Alma 50:22).

Alma the Younger's battle against the Amlicites and Lamanites is a good example of this pattern of wars. Those Nephites who sought to change the constitution of their government allied themselves with the Nephites' arch-enemies, the Lamanites. The combined forces of these two groups caused much destruction. After many perished, the Lord strengthened the Nephites, and they overthrew their enemies and ousted them from the land (see Alma 2:1–3:3). Another war occurred after Alma and Amulek preached to the people of Ammonihah. The inhabitants of that city burned to death all who believed in the words of the prophets. Very soon a Lamanite army succeeded in utterly destroying the city, killing every inhabitant, before the Nephites rallied an army sufficient to overpower them. With the Lord's intervention, however, the Nephites defeated their enemies and delivered their captives (see Alma 16:1–10).

Classic military encounters in the Book of Mormon occurred in the days of Moroni, the Nephite chief captain. Zoramite dissenters joined forces with the Lamanites and invaded the land of the Nephites. Moroni inspired his forces to fight for their freedom, and they called on the Lord to aid them. Moroni's superior technology and strategies allowed the Nephites to rout a much larger force than theirs. The Lamanites made a covenant of peace with Moroni never to come against the Nephites again (see Alma 43:3–44:20).

A further effort to destroy the Nephites' freedom by changing the government led to war. Amalickiah, attempting to become king, caused internal dissension among the Nephites, even in the church. Moroni raised the title of liberty and put down the dissenters. Amalickiah, however, fled with a small band and succeeded in becoming king of the Lamanites. He send an innumerable army to attack the Nephites in their cities. But Moroni's methods again took them by surprise, and the Lamanites went home in defeat (see Alma 46:1–49:30).

Amalickiah returned at the head of another Lamanite army, just as Moroni was putting down the king-men who had attempted to alter the government. Amalickiah's armies captured many Nephite cities, and a long war ensued. The Nephite armies under Moroni, Lehi, Teancum, Helaman, and others fought under difficult conditions. Further dissensions by king-men weak-ened Nephite efforts. Peace was restored only after much suf-fering and loss of life (see Alma 51:1–62:52).

Other battles receive much less attention in the Book of Mormon. The great victory King Benjamin achieved over the Lamanites, discussed earlier, is reported in only two verses (see Words of Mormon 1:13–14). Later, a tremendous battle between the Nephites and Lamanites took place when many Lamanites converted to the Lord. The loss of life in these battles exceeded any up to that time (see Alma 28:1–3). But both episodes receive little prominence in the Book of Mormon, possibly because they do not follow the pattern of wickedness leading to destruction, followed by victory by the righteous.

All the Nephite-Lamanite wars that follow the pattern I men-tion occur from 87–51 B.C., a thirty-six year period. When we look at these wars as a series of types, we should not necessarily assume that as many wars will repeat themselves in our time. Just as several exoduses in the Book of Mormon may prefigure a single latter-day exodus—the exodus of which Isaiah proph-esied—so several Nephite-Lamanite wars may prefigure a single war between the Lord's people and an alien power. Remember that Isaiah's code name for this latter-day power is Assyria.

Elements the Book of Mormon battles have in common teach us about this great last war of which Isaiah prophesied: First, internal dissensions and secret combinations will weaken and divide the Lord's people. Second, an alien power will invade the land, conquering and destroying, and seeking to impose its oppressive rule over the Lord's people. Third, a righteous prophet-commander will lead an army of the Lord's people against their enemies. Fourth, their cause will be to defend their freedom, their religion, and their families. Fifth, they will call on the Lord to assist them. Sixth, the hand of the Lord will be with them so that they will succeed in defeating their enemies and restoring peace.

Each set of parallels in the Book of Mormon (of the exodus and war stories) foreshadows the events Isaiah prophesied. I expect that many of these parallels particularly concern the Lord's people on the American continent. That makes the Book of Mormon an informative guide to the future. It helps us to see a deeper meaning behind Nephi's statements that his people may "liken" Isaiah's words to themselves (see 1 Nephi 19:23–24; 2 Nephi 11:2, 8). Since Nephi saw the last days in vision, he established a pattern for recording history that would best serve the Lamanites in that latter day. I believe the source of Nephi's prophetic pattern is Isaiah. The chronicling of those things that will most typify and benefit a future generation of the Lord's people constitutes the difference between sacred and secular history. The Book of Mormon's wide use of such types helps to establish its authenticity as an ancient, sacred record written by prophets for the instruction of the Lord's people in the last days.

SOCIETY, POLITICS, AND WAR

Chapter 19

KING, CORONATION, AND COVENANT IN MOSIAH 1–6

Stephen D. Ricks

The first six chapters of Mosiah are remarkable in several ways. They contain King Benjamin's farewell address, one of the most memorable sermons we have on record. They also give us a picture of how Mosiah succeeded his father, Benjamin, to the Nephite throne. Many features of the ceremony that was involved reflect the traditions of ancient Israelite culture. First is the significance of the office of king. Second is the coronation ceremony for the new king. The details of this ceremony have parallels in Israel and other ancient Near Eastern societies and even in other parts of the world. Finally, the order of events reported in these chapters reflects the "treaty-covenant" pattern well known in ancient Israel and the ancient Near East. My discussion of these three sets of features will show how faithfully the Book of Mormon reflects these Old World practices and beliefs.

Kingship

The Meaning of Kingship. Nearly every ancient and medieval civilization had a king, who it was believed had been appointed by heaven. Kingship is a political institution whose origins are lost to history. The Egyptians believed that kingship had existed as long as the world itself; to the Sumerians, this form of rule was a gift of the gods. In Israel, kingship came to be a vital element of the society's organization through the four hundred years leading up to Lehi's departure. In the American promised land, among the Nephites, Lamanites, and people of Zarahemla, kings were again an essential part of political life for centuries. Mosiah 1–6 gives us some of the clearest information on the ideals of royal government in the Book of Mormon.

Choosing the King. The Book of Mormon presents a pattern for choosing kings that matches customs in ancient Israel. It was considered necessary that God choose the man to be king. Thus, Solomon, not his older brother Adonijah, succeeded his father David as king, since, as Adonijah himself said, "it [the kingship] was [Solomon's] from the Lord" (1 Kings 2:15). The Nephite King Benjamin believed that God had called Mosiah, his son: "On the morrow I shall proclaim . . . that thou art a king and a ruler over this people, whom the Lord our God hath given us" (Mosiah 1:10).

In Israel, the eldest son of the king usually became the next ruler, although the king was not obligated to choose him if he believed God desired otherwise. Jehoshaphat gave the kingdom to Jehoram "because he was the firstborn" (2 Chronicles 21:3). However, as noted above, Solomon succeeded David even though Solomon was not the eldest son. The Book of Mormon does not say whether Mosiah was Benjamin's firstborn son, although this probably was the case since his name is given first in the list of names of Benjamin's sons (see Mosiah 1:2).

In Israel, both Solomon and Jotham became king while their fathers were still alive because their fathers were old or ill (see 1 Kings 1:32–40; 2:1–10; 2 Kings 15:5). This is also why Benjamin installed Mosiah when he did: "[Benjamin] waxed old, and he saw that he must very soon go the way of all the earth; therefore, he thought it expedient that he should confer the kingdom upon one of his sons" (Mosiah 1:9). Then, after he "had consecrated his son Mosiah to be a ruler and a king over his people, . . . king Benjamin lived three years and he died" (Mosiah 6:3, 5).

Conflicting Views of Kingship. In Mesopotamia and Egypt, kingship was the only form of government, as far as we know. The king there was viewed as descended from a god, or at least he had been adopted as an offspring of deity. To the writers of history in those lands, no other type of rule was conceivable.

On the other hand, in Israel, while the king was ruler "by the grace of God," an alternative view recognized the dangers of kingship. When the Israelites demanded of the prophet Samuel, "Make us a king to judge us like all the nations," Samuel painted a grim picture of what would happen under a king:

> He will take your sons, and appoint them for himself, for his chariots, and to be his horsemen; and some shall run before his chariots. And he will appoint him captains over thousands, and captains over fifties; and will set them to ear [plant] his ground, and to reap his harvest, and to make his instruments of war, and instruments of his chariots. And he will take your daughters to be confectionaries, and to be cooks, and to be bakers. And he will take your fields, and your vineyards, and your oliveyards, even the best of them, and give them to his servants. And he will take the tenth of your seed, and of your vineyards, and give to his officers, and to his servants. And he will take your menservants, and your maidservants, and your goodliest young men, and your asses, and put them to his work. He will take the tenth of your sheep: and ye shall be his servants. And ye shall cry out in that day because of your king which ye shall have chosen you; and the Lord will not hear you in that day (1 Samuel 8:11–18).

The Nephites were torn between the same conflicting views of kings. Benjamin's description of how he ruled could hardly contrast more with Samuel's description:

> [I] have not sought gold nor silver nor any manner of riches of you; neither have I suffered that ye should be confined in dungeons, nor that ye should make slaves one of another. . . . And even I, myself, have labored with mine own hands that I might serve you, and that ye should not be laden with taxes, and that there should nothing come upon you which was grievous to be borne (Mosiah 2:12–14).

Mosiah followed his father Benjamin in farming "the earth, that thereby he might not become burdensome to his people" (Mo-

211

siah 6:7). He took great pains to avoid abusing the royal power. Yet, near the end of his reign, Mosiah gives the most damning criticism to be found anywhere in scripture on the perils of kingship: "Because all men are not just it is not expedient that ye should have a king or kings to rule over you. For behold, how much iniquity doth one wicked king cause to be committed, yea, and what great destruction!" (Mosiah 29:16–17; see all of 29:5–36).

The King as Guardian of the Covenant of the Lord. The king in the Near East was obliged to maintain justice generally and to protect the rights of the weakest members of society. Benjamin does not discuss this responsibility directly, but several points in his sermon imply that he understood and abided by the principle of protecting the rights of the weak (for example, see Mosiah 2:17–18; 4:13–16, 24).

The king in Israel had an added responsibility of acting as guardian of the covenant between the Lord and his people—a concept that seems to have no parallel among neighboring peoples. He was expected to be an obedient follower of God and to lead his people to obey the covenant.

Kingship and covenant are also closely connected in Mosiah 1–6. Benjamin's command to his son to prepare for this grand occasion had two parts to it, to proclaim the son the new king, and to "give this people a name" (Mosiah 1:10–11). The name was "the name of Christ." This was to be accepted by all "that have entered into the covenant with God that [they] should be obedient unto the end of [their] lives" (Mosiah 5:8).

The association of the two concepts in the agenda indicates that they were linked in Nephite thinking. Kingship and the covenant of the people with God are again combined in Mosiah 6:3. After Mosiah had been consecrated king, he appointed priests "to teach the people, that thereby they might hear and know the commandments of God, and to stir them up in remembrance of the oath [or covenant] which they had made." The record notes that following Benjamin's death, Mosiah very strictly observed the covenant and the commandments that his father had passed on to him (see Mosiah 6:6).

Coronation

The coronation of the king is the most important ritual act associated with kingship in the ancient Near East. A comparison of Mosiah 1–6 with coronation ceremonies recorded in the Old Testament and with such rites among other ancient Near Eastern peoples reveals striking parallels.

The Sanctuary as the Site of the Coronation. A society's most sacred spot is the location where the holy act of royal coronation takes place. For Israel, the temple was that site. So we read that, during his coronation, Joash stood "by a pillar [of the temple], as the manner was" (2 Kings 11:14). However, the temple had not been built when Solomon became king, so he was crowned at Gihon (see 1 Kings 1:45). Gihon was made sacred by the presence of the Ark of the Covenant (which contained the sacred objects from Moses' day) within the special tabernacle that David had made to shelter it. The priest Zadok took "out of the tabernacle" the horn containing oil, from which he anointed Solomon (1 Kings 1:39). In the Nephite case, the temple at Zarahemla was the site chosen for Benjamin's address to the people and for the consecration of his son Mosiah as king (see Mosiah 1:18).

Installing in Office with Insignia. At the coronation of Joash, Jehoiada the priest conferred upon him two objects, called the *nezer* and the *'edut.* The meaning of the first term is certain; it means *crown* (2 Kings 11:12). What *'edut* means is far less certain. It may have been a piece of writing that affirmed the king's adoption by God and promised the new king victory over his enemies, as Psalm 2:7–9 suggests, or it may have been a document that the ruler was to wear containing the basic terms of Yahweh's covenant with the house of David (the line of the kings).

The transfer of power to Mosiah involved something similar. Benjamin gave him certain objects. He passed on the official records of the people (the plates of brass and the plates of Nephi), the sword of Laban, and the miraculous ball, called also the director or Liahona (see Mosiah 1:15–16). Of course, the royal documents were the most important records in the kingdoms of the ancient world, and a sword was a frequent sign of kingship in Europe and Asia. In addition, an orb or ball was commonly held in the hand of Old World rulers, from early modern times at least back to the Roman Empire. Although the Bible does not mention such an object, it still might have been part of the Israelite set of artifacts copied from their neighbors.

Anointing. To anoint the king with oil was a significant part of the coronation ceremonies in ancient Israel and in the ancient Near East generally. The Bible records the anointing of six of the kings: Saul, David, Solomon, Jehu, Joash, and Jehoahaz. Indeed, the name *Messiah,* which was used to refer to several of the kings of Israel, means *anointed,* no doubt referring to the rite of anointing the king during his installation.

The Hittites, a northern neighbor of the Israelites, also had a ceremony that included anointing the king with oil. Although there is no clear evidence that the Egyptian king was anointed when he became king, he apparently was anointed every morning before entering the temple to perform daily chants.

Following Benjamin's address and the people's renewal of the covenant, Benjamin "consecrated his son Mosiah to be a ruler and a king over his people" (Mosiah 6:3). The context does not indicate whether this "consecration" included anointing. However, some ritual act was evidently involved, and back almost at the beginning of Nephite history, Jacob indicates that the coronation included anointing. He reported that his brother Nephi, the first king, "began to be old, and he saw that he must soon die; wherefore, he anointed a man to be a king and a ruler over his people now, according to the reigns of the kings" (Jacob 1:9). "According to the reigns of the kings" clearly refers to the pattern of kingship in Judah, with which Nephi was personally familiar.

Receiving a Throne Name. In many societies, a king received a new name or throne name when he was crowned king. Several Israelite kings had two names, a "birth name" and a throne name. It may be that all the kings of Judah received a new name when they came to the throne. During the Middle Kingdom period, each king of Egypt had no less than five names and received a throne name at the time he became king. Kings in Mesopotamia also received a new name. Each Parthian king (in ancient Iran) assumed the same throne-name, "Arsak," at his crowning, a fact that has made it hard for historians to identify one ruler from another.

Use of the same royal title marks the early Nephite kings. Jacob wrote that, "The people having loved Nephi exceedingly . . . wherefore, the people were desirous to retain in remembrance his name. And whoso should reign in his stead were called by the people, second Nephi, third Nephi, and so forth, according to the reigns of the kings; and thus they were called by the people, let them be of whatever [original] name they would" (Jacob 1:10–11). While we do not know that this new name was given to the rulers over the Nephites as part of the coronation rite, there is every reason to expect that it was.

The Assembly of Mosiah 1–6 as a Covenant Renewal

Mosiah 1–6 mentions several interesting features of this assembly: the pilgrimage of whole families to the temple site, the sacrifice of animals, and the people's dwelling in tents. These elements are so typical of the Israelite Feast of Tabernacles that they strongly suggest to me that the events recorded in these chapters took place during a Nephite observance of that festival. From the Old Testament, it seems most likely that the Feast of the Tabernacles was when the Israelites renewed their covenant with God, and that appears to be what the Nephites were doing in the assembly reported in Mosiah 1–6.

Six elements of covenant renewal can be found in Exodus, Deuteronomy, and Joshua: (1) the king/prophet gives a preamble that introduces God as the one making the covenant or that introduces his prophet as spokesman for God; (2) the king/

215

prophet gives a brief review of God's relations with Israel in the past; (3) the king/prophet notes the terms of the covenant, listing specific commandments and obligations that God expected Israel to keep; (4) the people bear witness in formal statements that they accept the covenant; (5) the king/prophet lists the blessings and curses for obedience or disobedience to the covenant; and (6) the king/prophet makes provisions for depositing a written copy of the covenant in a safe and sacred place and for reading its contents to the people in the future.

In addition, the ideal was that the new king take office before the death of the old one, and this transfer of power was connected with the ceremony where the people make or renew their covenant with God. Interestingly, each of these features is found in Mosiah 1–6 (see Table 1).

1. Preamble. The passages in the Bible dealing with the renewal of the covenant sometimes introduce God as the maker of the covenant: "God spake all these words saying . . . " (Exodus 20:1). At other times, a prophet is introduced to act for God: "Joshua said unto all the people, Thus saith the Lord God of Israel . . . " (Joshua 24:2). Similarly, Benjamin's covenent assembly in the book of Mosiah begins: "These are the words which [Benjamin] spake and caused to be written, saying . . . " (Mosiah 2:9). Although Benjamin is speaking, he is clearly acting as the mouthpiece of God. In fact, a sizable part of his address consists of words that had been made known to him "by an angel from God" (Mosiah 3:2).

2. Review of God's Relations with Israel. At this point in the covenant renewal, according to the Bible, the people hear of God's mighty acts on behalf of his people Israel. For example, Jehovah says through Moses, "Ye have seen what I did unto the Egyptians, and how I bare you on eagles' wings, and brought you unto myself" (Exodus 19:4; cf. Exodus 20:2; Joshua 24:11–23). The Mosiah passage includes a long account of the past relations between King Benjamin and his people (Mosiah 2:9–19).

3. Terms of the Covenant. Each of the biblical covenant passages states the commandments that God expects his people Israel to keep. A prime example is in Exodus 20–23 where God first briefly lists the Ten Commandments (Exodus 20:3–17) and then spells out in greater detail what the people are to obey (Exodus 21:1– 23:19). Benjamin's address also contains numerous commandments; for example, "Believe in God. . . . Believe that ye must repent of your sins and forsake them, and humble yourselves before God; and ask in sincerity of heart that he would forgive you" (Mosiah 4:9–10).

4. *Formal Witness.* One time in the Old Testament, an object, a particular stone, was made witness to the covenant, "for it hath heard all the words of the Lord which he spake unto us: it shall be therefore a witness unto you, lest ye deny your God" (Joshua 24:27). In general, though, the people themselves were the witnesses. For instance, they say "All that the Lord hath spoken we will do" (Exodus 19:8). Following King Benjamin's address, the people express their desire "to enter into a covenant with [their] God to do his will, and to be obedient to his commandments" (Mosiah 5:5). They further witness their willingness to obey by allowing their names to be listed among those who have "entered into a covenant with God to keep his commandments" (Mosiah 6:1).

5. *Blessings and Cursings.* The end of biblical covenants often contains a list of curses and blessings for those who enter into the covenant: "Cursed be the man that maketh any graven or molten image. . . . And all the people shall answer and say, Amen. Cursed be he that setteth light by his father or his mother. And all the people shall say, Amen" (Deuteronomy 27:15–17). "Blessed shalt thou be in the city, and blessed shalt thou be in the field. Blessed shall be the fruit of thy body, and the fruit of thy ground, and the fruit of thy cattle" (Deuteronomy 28:3–4).

More often the Old Testament just implies the curses and blessings: "Joshua said unto the people, . . . If ye forsake the Lord, and serve strange gods, then he will turn and do you hurt, and consume you, after that he hath done you good" (Joshua 24:19–20). The curses and blessings in Benjamin's speech are also implied rather than stated outright: "Whosoever doeth this shall be found at the right hand of God. . . . Whosoever shall not take upon him the name of Christ must be called by some other name; therefore, he findeth himself on the left hand of God" (Mosiah 5:9–10).

6. *Reciting and Depositing the Covenant.* The Bible frequently mentions that the covenant was read aloud: "He [Moses] took the book of the covenant, and read in the audience of the people" (Exodus 24:7). Other passages mention that the covenant was written and put in a safe and sacred place: "Joshua wrote these words in the book of the law of God, and took a great stone, and set it up there under an oak, that was by the sanctuary of the Lord" (Joshua 24:26). The words of King Benjamin were written and sent out among the people, not only so they could study and understand what had gone on, but also as a permanent record of the assembly (see Mosiah 2:8–9). At the end of Benjamin's address, when all of the people expressed a willingness to take upon themselves Christ's name, their names were recorded (Mosiah 6:1).

Hugh Nibley has noted that one of the best means of establishing a text's authenticity is to examine the degree to which it accurately reflects in its details the culture from which it claims to derive. The Book of Mormon claims to derive from ancient Israel. Mosiah 1–6 reflects in considerable detail the Israelite customs and beliefs that we know are part of the process of choosing and placing a new king on the throne.

Table 1

Treaty/Covenant Pattern in the Old Testament and in Mosiah

Elements	Ex. 19: 3b–8	Ex. 20–24	Deut.	Josh. 24	Mosiah 1–6
Preamble	Ex. 19:3b	Ex. 20:1	Deut. 1:5 (Deut. 1:1–5)	Josh. 24:2a (Josh. 24:1–2a)	Mosiah 2:9a (Mosiah 1:1–2:9a)
Review of God's Relations with Israel	Ex. 19:4	Ex. 20:2	Deut. 1:6–3:29	Josh. 24:2b–13, 16b, 17–18a	Mosiah 2:9b–21, 23–24a, 25–30
Terms of the Covenant	Ex. 19:5–6	Ex. 20:3–23:19	Deut. 4–26	Josh. 24:14, 18b, 23	Mosiah 2:22, 24b, 31–41; 4:6–30
Formal Witness	Ex. 19:8	Ex. 24:3		Josh. 24:16a, 19a, 21–23	Mosiah 5:2–8
Blessings and Curses		Ex. 23:20–33	Deut. 27:9–28:68	Josh. 24:19b–20	Mosiah 5:9–15 (3:24–27)
Reciting and Depositing of the Covenant	Ex. 19:7	Ex. 24:4–8	Deut. 27:1–8; 31:9, 24–26	Josh. 24:25–27	(Mosiah 2:8, 9a) Mosiah 6:1–3, 6

Chapter 20

NEPHI'S POLITICAL TESTAMENT

Noel B. Reynolds

The writers of the Book of Mormon talked a lot about their government and political beliefs. Most of us look only at the Nephite system of judges and the Gadianton robbers, however. Few of us have looked closely at Nephi's political testament and the traditions among the Nephites and the Lamanites about ruling.

The great political question among Book of Mormon peoples was "Who has the right to rule?" Did Nephi's descendants and those who followed them have a legitimate right to rule? Or should the right have belonged to Lehi's oldest son Laman and his descendants? This quarrel is the cause of centuries of political and military struggle. But this was not the only problem. Even within Nephite society, an endless number of dissenters challenged the government. They often split away to join the Lamanites when they could not win control inside the Nephite system. These dissenters typically argued for the Lamanite view, in part because they thought they could line their own nests that way.

By paying close attention to how this struggle was waged, we can see one of the reasons the Book of Mormon was written. Of course it is a witness for Christ and his teachings. But in addition, it provides reasons why we should believe that the tradition of the Nephites was just and correct. The two messages of the book are tied together in such a way that whoever accepts the teachings of Christ accepts that Nephi was a legitimate ruler, and vice versa.

Every group of people wants to be assured that its government is lawful and was founded properly. This is, in part, why stories of national origins and city foundings have been so important to human societies. The stories explain the origins of their laws and their rulers. Such traditions often deal with conflicting versions of the founding, explaining away all but one "authorized" account.

Nephi undertook late in his life to write an account of his people on the small plates. Though we don't know what the large plates — the political history — contained, we can guess from his version of how his people originated that a major issue was who had the right to govern. His small plates defend the Nephite tradition and refute the account advanced by the Lamanites and dissenters. Nephi carefully constructed what he wrote to convince his own and later generations that the Lord had selected him over his older brothers to be Lehi's successor. Thus, one interesting way to read the account is as a political tract produced to show that his rule was authoritative.

We would not expect to find this kind of political argument in Nephi's writings if they were only a journal of what happened to Nephi and his family. Nephi's entries on the small plates were not written as the events happened. Instead, he wrote years after the events, drawing on the journal or notes that he had kept plus "the record of [his] father" (1 Nephi 1:17). Furthermore, all of it was seen through his memory and mature reflections. What we tend to read as a story of flight from Jerusalem is really a carefully designed account explaining to his successors why their religious faith in Christ and their political tradition — the kingship of Nephi — were both true and legitimate.

Several times in the text, Nephi mentioned the competing tradition of Nephite dissenters and Lamanite spokesmen. Essentially, the Lamanites taught their people the following about their ancestors and the "right way" of government:

1. "They were driven out of the land of Jerusalem because of the iniquities of their fathers" [Lehi and Ishmael].

2. "They were wronged in the wilderness by their brethren" when Nephi "took the lead of their journey in the wilderness."

3. "They were also wronged [by Nephi?] while crossing the sea."

4. "They were wronged while in the land of their first inheritance" when Nephi led part of the people away, taking "the ruling of the people out of their hands."

5. "They said that he robbed them" when Nephi "took the records which were engraven on the plates of brass" (Mosiah 10:12–17).

Five hundred years after Nephi wrote his record, a Zoramite dissenter, Ammoron, stated the Lamanite charge simply, "Your fathers [Nephi and ruling descendants] did wrong their brethren, insomuch that they did rob them of their right to the government when it rightly belonged unto them [the Lamanites]" (Alma 54:17).

Zeniff was one of the first to defend the tradition of Nephi's rule. He explained that the younger brother took the lead because he was righteous and was called of God: For "the Lord heard [Nephi's] prayers and answered them, and he took the lead of their journey in the wilderness." Zeniff further claimed that Laman and Lemuel had hardened their hearts while on the sea, and that Nephi "departed into the wilderness as the Lord had commanded him, and took the . . . plates of brass" (Mosiah 10:13–16). This version of the Nephite political tradition seems to have been standardized early in their history.

The tradition was an officially accepted one because it was repeated on ceremonial occasions. For example, when the Nephites met under King Benjamin's direction to offer sacrifices and give thanks to the Lord their God, Mormon listed in the prayers of thanksgiving the key features of the Nephite tradition:

1. The Lord had brought them out of Jerusalem.

2. The Lord had delivered them from their enemies.

3. The Lord had appointed just men to be their teachers.

4. The Lord had given them a just man to be their king, who

had established peace in Zarahemla and had taught them to keep the commandments of God (Mosiah 2:4).

The Book of Mormon describes the Lamanites as constantly seeking to dominate the Nephites. From the first, Nephi claimed, they tried to kill him (1 Nephi 7:16). Hundreds of years later, Zeniff reported that the Lamanites were still teaching their children to hate Nephi's offspring, to murder and rob them, and even to "have an eternal hatred" toward them. From what he had learned growing up in the Nephite kingdom, Zeniff (a descendant of Mulek) said that all this hatred was because Laman and Lemuel "understood not the dealings of the Lord" and had "hardened their hearts against the Lord" (Mosiah 10:14–17). No doubt the older brothers had ground into their families these anti-Nephi teachings. By the second generation, the teachings had resulted in the Lamanites' deadly intention to destroy not only the Nephites, but also their records and traditions (Enos 1:14).

Now, we might think that destroying the Nephites would have been enough. Why would they be concerned about destroying the Nephite records too? Perhaps it was because the Lamanites remembered Nephi's and Lehi's prophecies that those records would be a powerful tool in converting Lamanites to the Nephite beliefs. If so, they would want to eliminate even that possibility by wiping out the books. Samuel the Lamanite knew already before the time of Christ the power in the Nephite records: "As many of them [the Lamanites] as are brought to the knowledge of the truth, and to know of the wicked and abominable traditions of their fathers, and are led to believe the holy scriptures, yea, the prophecies of the holy prophets, which are written . . . are firm and steadfast in the faith" (Helaman 15:7–8). We also have several missionary stories that describe the liberation that took place when the Lamanites allowed themselves to learn of the "incorrectness of the traditions of their fathers" (Alma 9:17; 17:9; 24:7).

Statements of Nephite apostates emphasize how politically powerful the correct records were. For example, while living

223

among the Lamanites, Mosiah's missionary sons encountered the Amalekites, who had apostatized from the Nephite beliefs. One Amalekite spokesman rejected the Nephite teaching that a Redeemer would come, at the same time belittling all other Nephite traditions: "We do not believe that thou knowest any such thing. We do not believe in these foolish traditions. We do not believe that thou knowest of things to come, neither do we believe that thy fathers and also that our fathers did know concerning the things which they spake, of that which is to come" (Alma 21:8). The famous apostate Korihor displayed this same skepticism (see Alma 30:16).

So did the Zoramite leaders who were angry with Alma for challenging their schemes. The Zoramites even went to the extreme of inserting their denial of the Nephite tradition, "which was handed down to them by the childishness of their fathers," into their one ritual prayer. Instead, they thanked God that they had not been "led away after the foolish traditions" of the Nephites, which "bind them down to a belief of Christ" (Alma 31:16–17). Furthermore, their religious rebellion was soon reflected in a political revolt against Nephite rule, whereby they "became Lamanites" (Alma 43:4).

The Nephites were clear about the link between their religious and political traditions. Mormon wanted us to notice how the Zoramites changed their worship and their political loyalties at the same time because he pointed out the connection of political structure and religion among the Nephites. Five verses later he informed us that the Nephites' only intent was to "preserve their rights and their privileges, yea, and also their liberty, that they might worship God according to their desires. For they knew that if they should fall into the hands of the Lamanites, that whosoever should worship . . . the true and the living God, the Lamanites would destroy" (Alma 43:9–10).

The aims of the religious apostates are clearest in the revolt of Amalickiah and his followers. Amalickiah's intention was to convert the Nephites' free government into a monarchy, with himself as king. The writer indicated that this was first phrased as a religious argument and that by his flatteries Amalickiah won dissenters from the church (see Alma 46:5–7). Amalickiah's intent was "to destroy the church of God, and to destroy the foundation of liberty" (Alma 46:10). Captain Moroni responded by rallying the Christians to support both their religion and their political system. On his banner, he wrote a "title of liberty," calling upon the people to battle for "our God, our religion, and freedom, and our peace" (Alma 46:12).

In spite of Moroni's quick victory and Amalickiah's flight to the land of Nephi, the struggle continued. After Amalickiah was slain, the Nephites had to face newly recruited Lamanite armies under the leadership of Amalickiah's brother and heir, Ammoron. In answer to Moroni's letter calling on him to repent and give up fighting the Nephites, Ammoron challenged both Nephite authority and religious teachings, saying: "As concerning that God whom ye say we have rejected, behold, we know not such a being; neither do ye; but if it so be that there is such a being, we know not but that he hath made us as well as you. . . . But behold these things matter not" (Alma 54:21–22).

Like Amalickiah and his followers, many of "these dissenters" had "the same instruction and the same information" as the Nephites, even "having been instructed in the same knowledge of the Lord." Yet after dissenting, they adopted "the traditions of the Lamanites; giving way to indolence, and all manner of lasciviousness; yea, entirely forgetting the Lord their God" (Alma 47:36). Like Ammoron and Amalickiah, many of them waged war against the Nephites "to avenge their wrongs, and to maintain and to obtain their rights to the government" (Alma 54:24). In fact, Nephite apostates "became more hardened and impenitent . . . than the Lamanites" (Alma 47:36). Thus, a main factor that determined the group a person felt he belonged to was whether he accepted or rejected the traditions of the Nephite fathers, particularly Lehi's and Nephi's prophecies about the coming of Christ.

The Nephite tradition centered on the message about Christ. As Nephi often stated, his purpose was to persuade his children to believe in Christ, that they might be saved (see 1 Nephi 6:4; 19:18; 2 Nephi 25:23). Mosiah also recorded that those who grew up after the time of Benjamin's national meeting "did not believe the tradition of their fathers" about either the "resurrection of the dead" or the future "coming of Christ" (Mosiah 26:1–2). From statements like these, we can see that the Nephites built their political position and their religion on the same basis — that the Christ who would come among them had designated Nephi to be their leader.

When a person accepted the religious teachings, he or she also acknowledged Nephi as the Lord's spokesman and designated leader over Lehi's people. Thus, when Nephi determined on his small plates to persuade his descendants and all later readers to believe in Christ, he felt he also had to include proof that he was rightful heir to the office of prophet and that his father had passed on the right to govern. This amounted to proving that the Nephite traditions were correct and that the Lamanite traditions were mistaken. This proof rested upon the central plank of the Nephite tradition, the belief that the Son of God would come down to earth and atone for the sins of all men.

This is at the core because it justifies all other beliefs. Nephi intertwined the argument for Christ with evidence that his own authority as ruler was divinely given. They stand or fall together. Nephi, like Lehi, saw and heard Christ, and he testified that the Savior would come among Lehi's progeny. Furthermore, Christ had spoken to Nephi, appointing him "a ruler and teacher" over his brothers while delivering him from their treachery. Without Christ, the argument for Nephi's authority had no basis; and without Nephi's authority, the Nephite political claims would have collapsed in the face of Laman's seniority in the family.

There are six major stories in 1 Nephi that Nephi seems to have selected to explain and justify his position as leader. Each story has these features:

1. God gave commands to Lehi or Nephi as leader of the party.

226

2. Laman and Lemuel murmured and rebelled because they lacked the faith to follow the commands and resented what they had lost by leaving Jerusalem.

3. Their disobedience brought a group crisis.

4. The crisis was resolved through God's unmistakable help to Nephi.

5. All repented and were reconciled, having recognized God's hand over them.

On the small plates, Nephi reported how Laman was given chance after chance to obey the Lord and so assume his rightful role as head of the family after Lehi's death. Had he followed Christ, he could properly have led the party. But his (with Lemuel's and the sons of Ishmael's) rebellion, stiff-neckedness, and murmuring caused the Lord to reject them and to choose Nephi in their place. By these accounts, Nephi showed us he was chosen by the Lord, by Lehi, and even by his grumbling brothers, who then followed him—and once even bowed in subjection to him—of their own choice.

Mormon, the editor of much of the Book of Mormon as we now possess it, used material from Nephi's small plates as a key for understanding Nephite politics many centuries later. The difference in time did not mean that Nephi's points had lost meaning, for being a Nephite always depended on accepting the Nephite traditions and records: "Whosoever would not believe in the tradition of the Lamanites, but believed those records which were brought out of the land of Jerusalem, and also in the tradition of their fathers, which were correct, who believed in the commandments of God and kept them, were called the Nephites, or the people of Nephi" (Alma 3:11).

Nephi also supported his claim to authority by indirectly comparing his situation to those of Old Testament leaders. The story of Joseph the son of Jacob and Nephi are similar, for example. Like Joseph, Nephi was resented by his older brothers, for he too was his father's favorite. As Joseph learned by revelation that he would rule over his brothers, so God let Nephi know that he would teach and rule over his brothers. Nephi's brothers felt the same murderous rage toward Nephi that caused Joseph's brothers to throw Joseph into a pit in the wilderness to die. Like Joseph, Nephi credited his escape to God's power.

In case we might fail to make the Nephi-Joseph connection on our own, Nephi mentioned in three places that Joseph was their ancestor. One place he even reviewed the story for our benefit: "That Joseph who was the son of Jacob, who was sold into Egypt, and who was preserved by the hand of the Lord, that he might preserve his father, Jacob, and all his household from perishing with famine" (1 Nephi 5:14; see 1 Nephi 6:2; 2 Nephi 3:4). Nephi stressed their lineage even though he wrote that he did not want to use precious space on the plates with genealogy. Remember that Nephi told how, by means of his bow, he provided food and saved his father's family from starvation (1 Nephi 16:23). (Note that the bow was anciently a symbol connected with Joseph—see Genesis 49:23-24.)

Nephi also accused his brothers of doing what Joseph's brothers had done—bringing "down [their father's] gray hairs with sorrow to the grave" (1 Nephi 18:18; compare Genesis 42:38). Lehi, like Jacob, gathered his people together to receive his final blessings. Both of these patriarchs rebuked their older sons for faithlessness and promised the birthright to the younger sons, who had already become the families' actual leaders. These subtle comparisons between Nephi and Joseph are scattered throughout the text and can easily be missed. Together they reveal a subtle but unmistakable pattern.

Nephi also compared himself more openly to Moses, leader of the Exodus from Egypt and the founder of the Israelite nation. The overall pattern is the same as the Exodus: Lehi's family escaped from a wicked land and trekked through wilderness to their promised land. The similarities are numerous: Moses struck down an Egyptian overseer smiting an Israelite slave; Nephi began his career as a leader by killing wicked Laban. Following this, he fled into the wilderness, as Moses had done. Nephi described Laban's death after telling how he had exhorted his brothers to follow him without fearing Laban or his soldiers.

Nephi said that the Lord would protect them as he protected Moses and the Israelites against the Egyptians (see 1 Nephi 4:3).

Also like Moses, Nephi had to deal with murmuring and faithlessness among his people. Again, both leaders went up into a mountain to receive the word of God (1 Nephi 17:7–10). Still later, Nephi compared himself to Moses when his brothers refused to help him build the ship. On that occasion he listed details of the experience of Moses and the Israelites similar to their own history. While he did not explicitly draw a comparison between himself and Moses, the parallels are evident (see 1 Nephi 17:23–47). Thus, like Moses and Joseph, Nephi bolstered his position as the legitimate leader because the Lord chose and supported him.

I have reported elements of the Book of Mormon in which the Nephites' argument for Christ's divinity and for the origin of their own government are tied together. These arguments helped later generations of Nephites to be determined to defend their freedoms and traditions against the Lamanites and Nephite dissenters. Although the arguments that Nephi presented are subtle, they are clear and persuasive, according to the Hebrew style of writing. He recorded numerous incidents proving that God chose him and elevated him above his brothers because of their disobedience. Nephi also referred repeatedly to Israelite heroes who set patterns that parallel his case and thereby justify his cause. Nephi is shown to be like a new Moses and a new Joseph, saving a portion of Israel from captivity and darkness by prophetic teaching and divinely appointed government.

Chapter 21

THE COVENANT TRADITION IN THE BOOK OF MORMON

Blake T. Ostler

All societies have festivals, rituals, and traditions that reoccur on specific days of the calendar. In the United States, for example, we celebrate Christmas, Easter, Memorial Day, and Halloween. There are certain things that we always do on these days in the same way. Ancient societies were no different from our own in this respect. One common festival, for example, that the Egyptians, Babylonians, Hittites, Greeks, and Phoenicians all observed was the New Year's festival, which followed standard patterns of ceremony and language.

The Israelites also observed certain festivals (Shavuot, Passach, and Sukkot) that they kept as a matter of covenant with Yahweh (Jehovah); that is, by these events they renewed that covenant. The purpose of such festivals in Israel was to aid the people to become a holy community, a nation of priests, God's own people (see Exodus 19:6). The covenant made at such festivals gave Israel a sense of special identity before God: "You should enter into the covenant of Yahweh your God, and into His oath, which Yahweh your God is making with you today; so that He may establish you today for a people to Himself, and He Himself be your God, as He has spoke to you, and He has sworn to your Fathers, to Abraham, Isaac and Jacob" (Deuteronomy 29:12–13, New Jerusalem Bible Translation).

The Book of Mormon displays examples of ceremony or ritual that accurately reflect the ritual tradition followed by the ancient Israelites. Many similarities are found, in addition to some differences. It is highly unlikely that any person could accurately write about Israel's rituals and covenants without having been directly and intimately familiar with them.

From knowledge available in the Bible or in any other source at that time, no nineteenth-century writer, such as Joseph Smith, could have made up the picture of rites and covenants among the Nephites and Lamanites that would so accurately reflect the Israelite tradition. This is strong confirmation that the Book of Mormon is what it claims to be—an ancient record brought to light through Joseph Smith by the gift and power of God.

The ritual tradition reflected in the Book of Mormon is not an exact and unchanging duplication of Israelite ceremonial events found in the Bible. Instead, the record shows that it gradually changed and developed over time. Still, one type of sacred festival found in the Book of Mormon—whereby the people renewed their covenant with God—appears to be based upon Israelite traditions.

Like our own traditions, Book of Mormon traditions followed a definite pattern. For example, nearly everyone in the United States who celebrates Christmas observes a common tradition. We put up and decorate evergreen trees, give and receive gifts, picture a figure called Santa Claus, and visit friends and family members. The Christmas tradition differs somewhat in various nations—Sweden, Italy, Holland, Britain, and so on—and it doesn't occur at all in largely non-Christian societies like China. Further, the Christmas traditions in the United States have changed and developed mostly since 1900. But despite the obvious variations, there is a definite pattern for Christmas celebration that gradually changes over time.

Real traditions and real societies are like that. They follow a pattern that changes and develops over time. Moreover, when a certain tradition is described, we can sometimes pinpoint a particular culture and the general time in which the actions occurred. As we would expect, then, traditional celebrations spoken of in the Book of Mormon followed a pattern that changed and developed over time. As we would also expect, the Nephites were able to maintain certain aspects of their traditions and festivals largely unchanged from the way those features existed among the Israelites they left behind.

The Covenant Renewal Tradition in Israel

Covenant renewal is such a basic Israelite tradition. It is reported in the Bible in Exodus, Deuteronomy, Ezra, and Joshua. The pattern included these eight features:

1. *Gathering of the Nation.* The entire nation was called by proclamation to be present (usually at the temple) for an important event, such as the coronation of a new king or the ordination of a new high priest. Such a proclamation is found in Joshua 24:1: "Joshua gathered all the tribes of Israel to Shechem, and called for the elders of Israel, and for their heads, and for their judges, and for their officers; and they presented themselves before God."

2. *Preamble and Designation of Titles.* The covenant ceremony was preceded by a short introduction of the person who would state the terms and conditions of the covenant, standing as the representative of the people before God. We see this in Joshua 24:2: "Joshua said unto all the people, Thus saith the Lord God of Israel."

3. *Covenant Speech/Mighty Acts of God.* The king or high priest next gave a speech reminding the people of the mighty deeds that God had done for them. The purpose was to demonstrate that they were obligated to enter into a covenant to recognize God as their God and king and to do all things commanded by him. Such a speech is found at Joshua 24:2–13, where Joshua listed the numerous times God had delivered his people from bondage, protected them, made them victorious over their enemies, and given them a promised land by covenant.

4. *The Terms of the Covenant.* After this speech, the leader listed the terms of the covenant, usually specifying obedience. For example, Joshua said to his people: "Therefore fear the Lord, and serve him in sincerity and in truth: and put away the gods which your fathers served on the other side of the flood [Red Sea], and in Egypt; and serve ye the Lord" (Joshua 24:14).

5. *Curses and Blessings.* As in a modern contract, an ancient covenant included both benefits and obligations. Often, the terms were stated in an if-you-do-this, God-will-do-this proposition. Obeying the covenant entitled Israel to promised blessings, just as a person receives specific benefits by keeping a contract made under the rules of our society. However, breaking the covenant would bring curses, just as today one must pay damages for breaching a contract.

The covenant speech in Israel reminded the people of the blessings God had promised them if they obeyed and the cursings he had threatened them with if they failed. See this in Joshua 24:20: "If ye forsake the Lord, and serve strange gods, then he will turn and do you hurt, and consume you" (see also Joshua 8:34). The curses and blessings were sometimes represented by dividing the nation into two camps: those on the left would chant the curses and those on the right would call out the blessings (see Deuteronomy 27:11–13).

6. *Witness Formula.* The people were made witnesses of the covenant and of the events taking place. Witnesses were necessary to make the mutual promises legally binding. A witness formula is found in Joshua 24:22: "Joshua said unto the people, Ye are witnesses against yourselves that ye have chosen you the Lord, to serve him. And they said, We are witnesses."

7. *Covenant Recorded.* The words of the covenant, and sometimes even the names of those entering into the covenant, were written down so that they could be read later as evidence that the covenant had indeed been entered into and was valid (see Deuteronomy 29:20–22). Joshua 24:25–27 states that the covenant was recorded so that the people could remember it: "So Joshua made a covenant with the people that day, and set them a statute and an ordinance in Shechem. And Joshua wrote these words in the book of the law of God, and took a great stone, and set it up there under an oak, that was by the sanctuary of the Lord. And Joshua said unto all the people, Behold, this stone shall be a witness unto us; for it hath heard all the words of the Lord

233

which he spake unto us: it shall be therefore a witness unto you, lest ye deny your God."

8. *Formal Dismissal.* The gathering concluded when the king or high priest dismissed the people to return to their dwellings. A formal dismissal is found in Joshua 24:28: "So Joshua let the people depart, every man unto his inheritance."

Covenant renewal festivals in Israel began at least by the time of Moses and were observed for centuries throughout the period of the kings. By the time of King Josiah (621 B.C.), king of Judah, the custom had almost been lost. But a great renewal did take place at that time, inspired by King Josiah's finding a copy of the almost-forgotten Book of the Covenant inside the neglected temple at Jerusalem. (Most scholars believe that what we know as Deuteronomy comes from the book he found.)

King Josiah and many of the people experienced rekindled interest in the law as a result. This renewed interest came to be observed in a new cycle of covenant-making ceremonies – at least, it was about this time when yearly festivals were begun. The population of the entire nation had to come to the temple to offer sacrifices and gifts to the Lord as part of the renewal of their vows.

The Covenant Renewal Festival in the Book of Mormon

The same pattern and elements of the covenant renewal festivals just outlined appear repeatedly in the Book of Mormon. Although the Nephites' covenant renewal festivals changed over time, the same basic pattern remained, as shown in several places in the Book of Mormon.

The clearest examples of covenant renewal festivals are found at the time King Benjamin gave his speech (see Mosiah 1–6) and at the time of King Limhi's gathering (see Mosiah 7). Both Benjamin's and Limhi's gatherings clearly follow the covenant pattern used among the Israelites from Moses to Josiah. Note that, although King Limhi gathered his people just three years after King Benjamin's speech and assembly, Limhi's people had been separated from the rest of the Nephites and had been in bondage to the Lamanites for perhaps as long as eighty years. Yet the pattern Limhi followed is so similar to the pattern Benjamin used that obviously a strong tradition of ritual existed among the Nephites. It must have been followed long before Limhi's grandfather Zeniff headed to the land of Nephi in the day when Benjamin's father Mosiah was king over the Nephites.

Thus this ritual tradition of renewing the covenant in huge gatherings was quite basic among the Book of Mormon people. For example, the traditional nature of the proclamation by which the king called his people to assemble at the temple is evident from the nearly identical language used in both King Limhi's and King Benjamin's accounts:

King Limhi	*King Benjamin*
Now, it came to pass on the morrow that king Limhi sent a proclamation among all his people that thereby they might gather themselves together to the temple, to hear the words which he should speak unto them (Mosiah 7:17).	[King Benjamin said:] My son, I would that ye should make a proclamation throughout all this land . . . that thereby they may be gathered together; for on the morrow I shall proclaim unto this my people. . . . And [Mosiah] proclaimed unto all the people who were in the land of Zarahemla that thereby they might gather themselves together, to go up to the temple to hear the words which his father should speak unto them (Mosiah 1:10, 18).

The preambles to both Limhi's and Benjamin's speeches are also very similar:

King Limhi	*King Benjamin*
And it came to pass that when they had gathered themselves together that he spake unto them in this wise,	And it came to pass . . . that the people gathered themselves together throughout all the land, that

saying: (Mosiah 7:18)

they might go up to the temple to hear the words which King Benjamin should speak unto them. . . . And these are the words which he spake and caused to be written, saying: (Mosiah 2:1, 9)

The idea underlying covenant renewal in Israel was that God had been merciful to Israel by performing mighty deeds on behalf of his chosen people. He had delivered Israel out of bondage in Egypt and sustained them in their flight from Egypt to Sinai. Thus, the themes of deliverance from bondage and the Exodus were especially prominent when the Israelites renewed their covenant with the Lord (see for example Deuteronomy 4:10–13; 6:20–22). In return for God's grace and the miracles performed on their behalf, the people of Israel were obligated to recognize Yahweh (Jehovah) as their king and their God, and he would in turn recognize Israel as his people and continue his support of them.

Statements of God's acts on behalf of his people were present in both Limhi's and Benjamin's speeches, as we would expect. Benjamin praised God as "him who has created you from the beginning, and is preserving you from day to day, by lending you breath, that ye may live" (Mosiah 2:21). Limhi's speech also reminded his people how much they were in debt to the Lord, reminding them that just as God had delivered the Israelites from bondage in Egypt, so God had also guided Father Lehi to the new world as a type of a second exodus to a promised land.

Moreover, Limhi promised his people that they themselves would soon be delivered miraculously from bondage, just as their Israelite forefathers, if they would obey the covenant that Limhi recited to them:

O ye, my people, lift up your heads and be comforted; for behold, the time is at hand, or is not far distant, when we shall no longer be in subjection to our enemies. . . . Therefore, lift up your heads, and rejoice, and

236

put your trust . . . in the God of Abraham, and Isaac, and Jacob; and also, that God who brought the children of Israel out of the land of Egypt, and caused that they should walk through the Red Sea on dry ground, and fed them with manna that they might not perish in the wilderness . . . That same God has brought our fathers out of the land of Jerusalem, and has kept and preserved his people even until now (Mosiah 7:18–20).

After the leaders had each reminded their people about God's many mighty acts on behalf of his people, both repeated the terms of the covenant that would be binding upon them. Those covenants followed a two-part formula, as all divine covenants do. The first part of this formula tells what the people must do. The second part sets forth what God will do if the people are faithful to their part of the covenant. The two-part format of covenant is clear in both speeches:

King Limhi

If ye will turn to the Lord with full purpose of heart, and put your trust in him, and serve him with all diligence of mind, if ye do this, he will, according to his own will and pleasure, deliver you out of bondage (Mosiah 7:33).

King Benjamin

All that he requires of you is to keep his commandments; and he has promised that if ye would keep his commandments ye should prosper in the land. . . . Secondly, he doth require that ye should do as he hath commanded you; for which if ye do; he doth immediately bless you (Mosiah 2:22–24).

The purpose of the covenant was to establish a permanent, binding relationship between God and his people. Of course, the relationship could not be established if the people violated the terms. So Benjamin warned: "I would that ye should take upon you the name of Christ, all you that have entered into the covenant with God that ye should be obedient unto the end of your lives. Whosoever doeth this shall be found at the right hand of God. . . . Whosoever shall not take upon him the name of

Christ . . . findeth himself on the left hand of God" (Mosiah 5:8–10).

Limhi also recited the cursings and blessings of the covenant to his people. The particular blessing of the covenant that concerned them was deliverance from bondage to the Lamanites. The curse for breach of the covenant was remaining in bondage. Limhi said:

> It is because of our iniquities and abominations that he has brought us into bondage. . . . For behold, the Lord hath said: I will not succor my people in the day of their transgression; but I will hedge up their ways that they prosper not; and their doings shall be as a stumbling block before them. And again, he saith: If my people shall sow filthiness they shall reap the chaff thereof in the whirlwind; and the effect thereof is poison. And again he saith: If my people shall show filthiness they shall reap the east wind, which bringeth immediate destruction. And now, behold, the promise of the Lord is fulfilled, and ye are smitten and afflicted (Mosiah 7:20, 29–32).

After the covenant had been agreed to by the people, Benjamin and Limhi each made their people witnesses to the covenant ceremony. The witness formula emphasized that the people should remember the actions that had taken place because the actions were legally binding. An agreement was not enforceable in ancient Israel unless there were witnesses to it. Both Benjamin's and Limhi's speeches contained a similar witness formula:

King Limhi	King Benjamin
And ye are all witnesses this day, that Zeniff, who was made king over this people . . . (Mosiah 7:21)	And of all these things which I have spoken, ye yourselves are witnesses this day (Mosiah 2:14).

The references to being "witnesses this day" shows that covenants were not taken lightly and that the day they were entered into was a day to be remembered. To help them re-

238

member the covenant, the events of the ceremony were recorded and deposited to be read at later festival occasions when the covenant was to be renewed (see Exodus 19:7; 24:7; Deuteronomy 27:2–4; Joshua 24:26). King Benjamin had the covenant recorded and sealed (Mosiah 6:1). Limhi also renewed the covenant made at Benjamin's coronation ceremony, because he had all of King Benjamin's words read to his people (see Mosiah 8:2–3).

Thus, the Nephites followed the Israelite practice of sealing up the covenant to be read on later occasions. Of course, Limhi's words were recorded and saved, because we have them in the Book of Mormon. The fact that the words of the covenant ceremonies were inscribed on gold plates as a permanent record would have served the same purpose as Joshua's inscribing the terms of Israel's covenant on stone.

King Limhi and King Benjamin dismissed their people to return to their homes in words very similar to those contained in Joshua 24:28. The formal dismissal by the king was necessary because the people had been summoned to the meeting by him. They therefore needed his permission to leave the ceremony.

King Limhi	*King Benjamin*
And it came to pass that after he had done all this, that king Limhi dismissed the multitude, and caused that they should return every one unto his own house (Mosiah 8:4).	It came to pass that when king Benjamin had made an end of all these things . . . he dismissed the multitude, and they returned, every one, according to their families, to their own houses (Mosiah 6:3).

Ancient Background of the Book of Mormon

There are many features of the Book of Mormon that I believe were beyond the capabilities of Joseph Smith — or of any person living in the early nineteenth century — to devise. Some people have suggested that the Book of Mormon is the kind of book someone could and would write if the author lived in a culture saturated by the Bible, as New England was in the early 1800s. If that were true, then why was Joseph Smith the only one to produce such a book? The Book of Mormon is the only writing coming out of the nineteenth century that faithfully reflects the ancient Israelite covenant tradition. None of the books, articles, or sermons written in Joseph Smith's day presents the eight elements of the ritual pattern that I have shown are found in the Book of Mormon. Nor do any of his "everyday" writings contain anything like this pattern.

Further, I think it is clear and convincing from the similarity between King Benjamin's and King Limhi's presentations that the actions were ritual in nature and were repeated on special occasions. The similarity between the Israelite covenant renewal festivals and what we have recorded from among the Nephites in the Book of Mormon is undeniable. Those who are willing to ignore this type of ancient material in the Book of Mormon overlook what I consider to be compelling evidence.

Notwithstanding the fact that the Book of Mormon is available to us only in English and has passed through the hands of Joseph Smith, its ancient background can be detected throughout the book. The evidence that the Book of Mormon shows the Nephites faithfully carrying out the Israelite ritual tradition, even down to fine details, is for me among the most persuasive of all. It isn't possible that Joseph Smith just blindly duplicated the old Israelite covenant tradition through luck because he had read the Old Testament a good deal. Rather, the Book of Mormon repeats the same pattern and features it in almost identical language, over and over again.

Moreover, the evidence demonstrates that those responsible for keeping the Nephite records were conscious of the fact that their actions were part of a ritual tradition. The nature of the actions, the similarity of the language, and the understanding of the ancient Israelite covenant are simply too precise to be accounted for in terms of luck or even as a result of the most profound abilities in comparative literature. It seems to me that this is one aspect of the Book of Mormon that even the most skeptical of critics cannot explain away.

Chapter 22

WARFARE IN THE
BOOK OF MORMON

William J. Hamblin

The wars and battles described in the Book of Mormon include some of the most detailed narratives of the book. Those accounts provide us with an excellent chance to examine how consistent and complex the text is. Joseph Smith lived in an age of warfare with guns, yet the Book of Mormon displays patterns of warfare that made sense only before gunpowder was used. This can be seen in both the general patterns and in the tiny details of the text. Descriptions of weapons and tactics in the Book of Mormon are definitely ancient. Furthermore, the warfare in the Book of Mormon differs from what we read about in the Bible. It differs in the same way that war in ancient Mesoamerica (Mexico and northern Central America) differed from biblical warfare.

Warfare has long played a basic role in history. The threat of war helped to develop central governments and civilization. Conquest often resulted in the movement of culture and religion from one area to another. The spread of the world's great religions, especially Christianity and Islam, was in part based on conquest. Much of the great writing of the past was on military themes. The transport of diseases, plants, and animals to new regions, as well as human migrations, were closely connected with military activity. The expansion and control of trade routes was as much a military as an economic matter.

Thus warfare has always been a major concern of leaders. In ancient times, they considered wars inevitable, so the way they prepared to fight helped determine how their societies were organized. Often, rulers could maintain their power only by using force against their own subjects. Reliance on armies led to huge empires policed mainly through the use of soldiers. Among them were the most famous nations of the past: the Assyrians, Persians, Mauryans of India, Ch'in and Han dynasties of China, the domain of Alexander the Great, and Rome.

Most economic surplus was used by ancient rulers to maintain the military. The values of many ancient peoples glorified military action and heroism, creating a widespread martial mentality. The spoils of war were a major source of prosperity for a victorious state. What we see today as the great cultural achievements of ancient civilizations were, for the most part, built on plunder, blood, and ruins.

The warfare described in the Book of Mormon fits this general pattern. Apart from a remarkable period following Christ's visit to the Nephites, warfare was nearly constant in the records of the Nephites and Jaredites. The writers of the Book of Mormon took war and its results seriously, and finally the Nephite civilization was destroyed by war. Mormon devoted about one-third of his abridgment and all of his own book directly or indirectly to military matters. In its emphasis on warfare, the Book of Mormon accurately reflects the grim reality of early history.

Of course, many features of premodern warfare were still present in Joseph Smith's day. But there were vital differences. A basic change in the nature of war occurred when gunpowder weapons became effective beginning in the fourteenth century. Joseph Smith published the Book of Mormon after the rise of gunpowder weapons and after the war tactics devised by Napoleon. Joseph Smith thus lived in an age when the practice of warfare differed from that in pregunpowder times. If he had written the Book of Mormon himself, what he would have said about battles would be quite different than what was the practice centuries earlier. I will examine six subjects having to do with war where the Book of Mormon reports warfare in ways typical of the ancient Near East and, in many cases, Mesoamerica.

Agriculture and Ecology

Ancient warfare was limited by agriculture. Men were needed to plant and harvest, yet the same men also had to serve as soldiers. So mass armies could be maintained only a few months a year when farming permitted it. Neither were armies equipped to operate in all weather conditions. Only certain months of the year permitted them to move, camp, and fight in the field.

When we come to the time of Napoleon, however, production had improved to the point that warfare was no longer dependent on harvest times. Many men could be used as soldiers, and armies could be maintained through all seasons. John Sorenson has shown that the old-style environmental limits are reflected in the descriptions of warfare in the Book of Mormon, and that they also match the seasonal conditions that existed in Mesoamerica (see, for example, his article in this volume). The Book of Mormon parallels ancient warfare in the areas of ecology and agriculture. It talks of battles limited by farming and harvests and war operations affected by weather.

Weapons and Military Technology

Another important element in premodern warfare was technology. Despite vast differences in detail, all premodern soldiers fought with roughly similar weapons. Face-to-face, personal combat was standard. Hence swords and other hand-held weapons were key, and armor was common. Missiles like arrows, javelins, and spears were all propelled by muscle power in some way. Since improvements in materials for weapons and armor always made a great impact on combat, leaders were constantly searching for new developments. But with the rise of long-range gunpowder weapons, guns replaced swords, spears, and arrows, and armor too was discarded.

The weapons, tactics, and military operations in the Book of Mormon fit this ancient pattern. The Book of Mormon provides a great deal of detail on military technology. As I have explored this area in several articles, I have found weapons and armor in the Book of Mormon to be consistent with patterns in the ancient Near East and Mesoamerica. Nothing in the Nephite record suggests that Joseph Smith could have invented such war stories, based on how fighting was done in his time.

Instead, warfare in the Book of Mormon consistently sounds like that in Mesoamerica before the European conquerors arrived. It differs from the ancient Near East in those features where Mesoamerican warfare differs from the ancient Near East. Coats of mail, helmets, battle chariots, cavalry, and siege engines—elements prominent in Bible lands—are all absent from both the Book of Mormon and Mesoamerica. If Joseph Smith were copying from information in books available to him, like the Bible, Josephus's histories, or books about the Romans, that described ancient wars, he would have included those features. Instead, the Book of Mormon leaves out those features of armament frequently mentioned in biblical and classical sources but absent from ancient Mesoamerica.

Logistics

Warfare, of course, did not involve only combat. In order for armies to compete, ancient societies needed basic resources. They had to obtain food to support the soldiers, cloth and leather for uniforms and armor, stone or metals to make weapons and armor, stone and lumber to build fortifications, and timber and other products to construct ships. They needed gold, silver, and other forms of wealth to purchase these supplies and to ensure officer and troop loyalty. Recruiting, equipping, training, supplying, and moving large groups of soldiers, servants, and animals were major undertakings anciently. As the story of Moroni and Pahoran illustrates, the costs of war put terrible social and economic pressure on Nephite society (see Alma 58–61). Plundering was used to supply many ancient armies, and the Book of Mormon mentions it often.

Warriors were generally organized into kinship or community units. The soldiers served under leaders who fought in battle and whom they knew personally. Units tended to be organized by tens, hundreds, and thousands, a fact reflected throughout the Book of Mormon. Premodern warfare also tended to rely on aristocratic officers. When gunpowder enabled commoners with only limited training to kill the most highly trained aristocrat, leadership shifted from the royalty. On the other hand, governments in Joseph Smith's time (1820s) drafted all men. Soldiers were organized into large administrative units, not just into communal or local formations. Unit size varied greatly and was not based on multiples of a basic number. Noblemen as officers had also become outdated.

The Book of Mormon armies follow the ancient pattern of armies organized along kinship, tribal, and community lines and with its hereditary leadership. The following features in the book also parallel ancient logistics: loyalty based on community, social and economic problems affecting warfare, problems of supply, the importance of plunder, and the lack of use of animals for movement and supply.

Descriptions of Battles

Preparations for battle anciently were complex. Soldiers had to be trained, equipped, and organized into units for marching and fighting. Then they were mobilized at central points to begin operations. Leaders commonly used distinctive banners to summon and identify their troops (like Moroni's title of liberty; see Alma 46:12–22). A wide range of camp followers were usually required to supply the troops with food and equipment. Barracks, arsenals, fortifications, and other base facilities needed to be prepared and maintained. Also, some type of standing army, usually royal guardsmen, was needed in peacetime. When war threatened, getting troops and supplies to key spots could involve extensive marching and maneuvering. Any reader of the Book of Mormon will recall the seemingly endless accounts of marches and countermarches. They may be boring to many, but they reflect the realities of maintaining ancient armies.

Not all conflict involved formal set battles. Much of it was closer to what in modern times we call guerilla war. This style

245

of fighting is clearly described in the Book of Mormon, especially in the account of the Gadianton robbers. Actual battles took only a small part of the time of a campaign, but the battle was of course the most important moment. Battle plans were generally made shortly before meeting the enemy. Frequently a council of officers and veterans would discuss the situation and offer suggestions, which is what Moroni does to prepare for battle (see Alma 52:19). Information from spies was crucial to forming battle plans. Knowledge of the enemy sometimes depended solely upon reports from spies. The Book of Mormon too shows how crucial spying was in its battles.

Battles often began with an exchange of missiles (stones, arrows, spears) to wound and demoralize the enemy. Only when the missiles were spent did the two sides close in for hand-to-hand combat. The battle described in Alma 49 describes such an archery duel preceding a hand-to-hand melee. If panic began to spread in the ranks, a complete and sudden collapse could result. The death of the king or commander could lead to such a collapse, as happened in Alma 49:25. Most casualties occurred during the flight and pursuit, after the main units had broken up. Battles in the Book of Mormon often end with just such rout, flight, and destruction of an army (see Alma 52:28; 62:31).

Laws of War

Laws and customs in ancient societies often controlled international relations and diplomacy. Perhaps the custom that strikes modern readers as strangest is the use of personal oaths. The Book of Mormon's emphasis on oaths of loyalty from troops and oaths of surrender from prisoners shows ancient concepts at work. Once an oath had been made, it had all the power (and more) that a written contract would have among us today. The Book of Mormon also presents a complex pattern of international relations, treaties, and diplomacy consistent with ancient Near Eastern practices.

Most ancient societies also treated robbers as brigands, not thieves. Whereas thieves would be imprisoned or punished short of death, robbers usually were tried as traitors or murderers and executed. So the treatment of robbers in the Book of Mormon reflects ancient law. Another parallel pattern involves prisoners. The taking of prisoners posed problems for ancient armies. Their maintenance depleted the already strained resources needed to support the army. So prisoners were frequently either killed or traded. The Lamanite practice of killing prisoners and the Nephite practice of exchanging them were consistent with the ancient milieu.

The burial of the dead in the Book of Mormon also shows the problems and practices of past societies. One case in particular — the dead from Ammonihah were buried in shallow graves, which caused the area to become desolate — mirrors what happened elsewhere in the past. Another ancient practice mentioned in the Book of Mormon concerns the capture and imprisonment of kings in Jaredite history. The treatment of captive kings is similar to that in Mesoamerican societies as old as the Jaredites.

There is also the parallel of human sacrifice, which nations around Israel and in Mesoamerica practiced. Though strictly forbidden by the Mosaic law, Israelites still fell into that practice several times during their history. The occasions of human sacrifice in the Book of Mormon echo an all too distressing pattern in the Near East and Mesoamerica. In the above-mentioned ways, the Book of Mormon faithfully reflects the ancient laws and customs that dictated what should or should not be done during war.

Religion and Warfare

Nearly all ancient war was connected with religion and was carried out through a complex series of religious ritual, law, and beliefs. Although there were also other motives, premodern warfare was basically a sacred matter. By Joseph Smith's day, war had become mainly secular, arising from political, nationalist, racial, and economic factors. The close connection between religious ideology and warfare is one of the most obvious ancient elements in the Book of Mormon. In numerous details the Book of Mormon unintentionally reveals the close tie between war and religion. Activities such as consulting prophets before battle are mentioned in the Book of Mormon. Likewise, a strict purity code for warriors can be seen in the story of Helaman and the stripling warriors.

Many details of the Mosaic law concerning war are also apparent in the Book of Mormon. For instance, an example of the ritual destruction of apostate cities appears in the Book of Mormon (see Alma 16). The ideology of holy war among the Nephites parallels that of the Israelites. The Nephites also seem to have observed the principles of camp purity and certain ritual behavior before, during, and after battle. For the Nephites and the Lamanites (to a lesser but still crucial extent), warfare was a thoroughly religious matter.

The Book of Mormon manifests clear parallels to ancient patterns of military behavior. I have not mentioned all of them in this review due to space limits. There were also the martial implications of shifting populations, the exhange of written or oral challenges between leaders, and the centrality of war to the elite class of society, to name a few more areas. In so many ways, the Book of Mormon uniquely reflects its dual heritage of the ancient Near East and Mesoamerica.

Chapter 23

SEASONS OF WAR, SEASONS OF PEACE IN THE BOOK OF MORMON

John L. Sorenson

When we look carefully at what the Book of Mormon says about war, we find that the many military activities reported did not take place just anytime during the calendar year. Rather, they occurred according to a definite pattern. Certain months were war months while others were not. The complete consistency of this pattern reminds us of how many details the writers of this scripture kept straight.

Useful information on this matter is found chiefly between Alma 9 and 47. A handful of cases report a specific day and month for a battle. For example, Alma 16:1 says that a Lamanite army attacked around the city of Ammonihah on "the fifth day of the second month in the eleventh year" of the reign of the judges over the Nephites.

Far more frequent is the kind of report given in Alma 44. The account of a huge battle between the Nephites and Lamanites near Manti ends this way: "They did cast their dead into the waters of Sidon, and they have gone forth and are buried in the depths of the sea. And the armies of the Nephites, or of Moroni, returned and came to their houses and their lands. And thus ended the eighteenth year of the reign of the judges" (verses 22–24). These statements indicate to me that this battle took place near the end of the year, probably during the final month. On the basis of statements like this, I count thirty-two cases in which the wording places the action near the end or the beginning of the year.

Finally, in about a dozen other cases, arriving at an approximate date for a military action is possible by noting everything said to have happened during the year, then dividing up the year according to how long each activity might logically have taken. These cases provide us with reasonable month dates, even though they might be off a little.

Unfortunately, all these dates are given only in terms of the Nephite calendar of that time. We would like to know a great deal more about that calendar than the statements about it in the Book of Mormon reveal. But at least we do learn some things and can infer other things. For example, the highest numbered month mentioned is the eleventh (see Alma 49:1). And the highest numbered day mentioned is the twelfth (see Alma 14:23). How many months were there in one year, and how many days did one month contain? If we are to answer those questions and construct a picture of what their calendar was like overall, we must look outside the scripture at the cultural background from which they came. (Keep in mind that the Nephites, and the Lamanites separately, could have made changes in their system over the years. Furthermore, they may have used more than one calendar at a time, as many other ancient peoples did.)

The Near Eastern background of Lehi's people is one place to learn some things about what calendar system they might have carried to America with them. While not as many details on calendars are given in the Bible as we would like, still it appears as if the Jews in Lehi's day used twelve months of thirty days each. (Peoples around the world have thought up and used a surprising variety of other forms of months and years, by the way.) Scholars assume that the Jews probably added five extra ("leap") days at the end of the year (and perhaps another extra one periodically) in order to keep the calendar from getting out of agreement with the sun. (The actual sun year is a little more than 365 and one-quarter days long.) Without discussing here much of the other information on the matter known to scholars, I will assume that the Nephites did observe twelve months to the year, each month thirty days in length.

The forty-five war incidents where a season is indicated are spread through the Nephite year this way:

Number of Military Actions Reported in Each Calendar Month

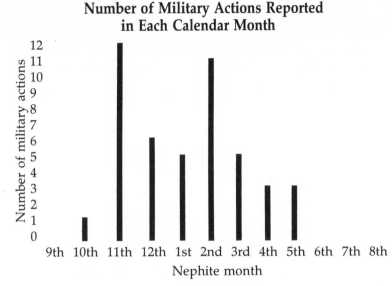

This timing pattern is striking. Clearly, wars went on mainly at the end and beginning of the year, while months six through nine were quiet. Also, what fighting there was in the fourth and fifth months tended to be minor skirmishes, not major wars. What reasons can we find for this pattern?

When we search this same section of Alma for statements about growing or harvesting food and about hunger or the re-supply of armies, a pattern appears that makes sense in relation to the schedule for battles. The fourth through ninth months, when combat was rare or absent, were the months when crop cultivation was reported. Getting food to the armies seems to have been a concern chiefly in the twelfth through second months. So, allowing a couple of months to transport the crop from the fields to where the troops were, it looks as though the harvest was in months ten to twelve. The upshot of this is a picture of the Nephite year arranged something like the following:

Field preparation and cultivation—months 4–9
Main harvest—months 10–12
Time of warfare—chiefly months 11–3

Notice the logic of this calendar. Since the soldiers were also farmers (armies were made up almost totally of the equivalent of today's "reservists"), they were not normally available for war during the season when they had to labor "delivering their women and their children from famine and affliction, and providing food for their armies" (Alma 53:7). Logically, then, war went on after the farm work was done but before the next planting season had begun.

On this basis we can be confident that we know in what months, according to the Nephite calendar, the wars were fought. But we are still left with the question, How do the Nephite months correspond to our months?

The Nephite lands where this fighting went on were most likely in the American tropics. The weather pattern is generally similar anywhere in that warm zone. That region has its main rainy season at the same time as the North American summer. The major reason is that the strong sun heats the land, then the air that is heated at the surface expands and rises. When it goes up, moist air is pulled in off the oceans to replace it, producing rain. This May-through-September period, when there is both heat and moisture, is of course when the chief crops grow. On the contrary, October through April is much drier.

In the civilizations of Mesoamerica (southern Mexico and northern Central America)—the most probable scene for the Nephite society—before the time of Columbus, military campaigns were carried out between late October and about the end of February. The farmers were then mostly free of duties in the fields, and food from the year's crops (harvested from October into December) was at hand either from one's own people or by capturing it from the enemy. At the same time, rivers that had been full from the rain waters and land that was soggy during the wet season had become passable, and living in field camps could then be tolerated.

If we compare the picture of the seasons drawn from the Book of Mormon with what we know about Mesoamerica, the parallels are obvious. The Nephite war season, their tenth or eleventh through second or third months, must coincide with the period for Mesoamerican conflicts, that is, roughly November through February. That means that the Nephite year (at least in the first century B.C. when these wars were recorded) ran from the latter half of December around through December again. A good guess is that their new year would have fallen at the winter solstice, December 21 or 22, when the sun appears to start moving northward again. (Many different ancient peoples followed such a "new year" dating.) Therefore, Nephite month twelve would have ended and month one begun near December 22 — quite close to our own calendar.

The Mesoamerican data and the Book of Mormon account concerning seasons seem to fit so strikingly that it seems to me safe to assume that the matchup is correct. In its light, we can understand how a classic case of war among Book of Mormon peoples fits the facts of calendar and seasons. Alma 51:22–37 reports Amalickiah's sudden attack on the "east borders by the seashore." The Nephite dissenter Amalickiah, who had gained the kingship over the Lamanites by murder, had been getting his troops into position for months. At the same time, Captain Moroni, head of the Nephite armies, was putting down the "king-men" rebellion among his own people (see Alma 51:9–14, 22). The Lamanites struck first at the east (seaward) end of the Nephite defense line, capturing the city of Moroni. Then they headed for the narrow neck of land, staying "down by the seashore . . . driving the Nephites before them and slaying many" (verses 25, 28). Over a few weeks, they captured at least five more cities before the Nephites could stop them.

At that point they were practically at the land and city of Bountiful, the last obstacle before capturing their key objective, "the narrow pass" into the land northward. In this dangerous situation, both armies made camp right next to the beach because they were overpowered by "their much fatigue . . . caused by the labors and heat of the day" (verses 32–33). But Teancum, the leader of the local Nephite army, did not sleep. He sneaked into the enemy camp to Amalickiah's tent, killed him without a sound, and got out without any of the Lamanites knowing about it.

"Thus endeth the twenty and fifth year of the reign of the judges over the people of Nephi; and thus endeth the days of Amalickiah. And now, it came to pass in the twenty and sixth year . . . , when the Lamanites awoke on the first morning of the first month, behold, they found Amalickiah was dead in his tent" (Alma 51:37–52:1).

Our findings about the seasons permit us to pinpoint this operation on our calendar quite closely. The Lamanite forces had had a long haul from their homeland in Nephi to the scene near the city of Moroni where they were to launch their attack. They apparently began moving advance men and supplies well before they attacked, likely by the middle of month nine (the first week in September?). As the rains dried up sufficiently and the most crucial part of the harvest passed, freeing men to be mustered into the army, the main force would have moved from the land of Nephi in the next six weeks. By the beginning of the twelfth month (around November 17?), they would have been in place. (During that time, Moroni had been busy, getting a public vote of approval from key areas around the capital, Zarahemla, to put down the revolt of the king-men, then attacking and defeating those rebels.)

The capture of the city of Moroni and the others that fell would have consumed a few weeks, I suppose, based on the distances separating them. By late November and early December, the rain-swollen rivers would have finally shrunk to a size travelers could manage (the "east borders by the seashore" cannot be anything but a rather wet, low-lying, hot area), and the trails would have become passable. Finally, on the last day of the year (December 21?), they found themselves camped near the shore of the east sea not many miles from their objective, the pass leading north. Even though the hottest weather was several months away, still the bright sun and mugginess had made the soldiers weary, and they slept hard. Then Teancum's daring feat in the middle of the night eliminated the Lamanite leader. The shocking discovery of their dead king on new year's day had a predictable effect on the Lamanites (who seem to have observed the same new year day). They took it as an ill omen for the coming year (but they were already field weary and might have been looking for an excuse to rest), so they hunkered down inside Mulek, the nearest of the cities they had captured.

Perhaps our establishing these dates is not important in understanding this attack or appreciating its results, but the concreteness of the setting, including the date and the weather, makes the entire business more "real" to me, more believable as history.

Over all, we find remarkable consistency in the handling of these highly technical bits of war and calendars. Most of us would not have been alert enough in writing a book about wars to have kept all this straight in our heads. If Joseph Smith had simply made up a "golden Bible" on the basis of his own experience and the locality where he lived, as some critics believe, then the thirty-two battles at the end and start of the year in the Book of Mormon would have fallen in western New York's windy, icy winter, a major error! The "heat" suffered by the Nephite and Lamanite soldiers and Amalickiah's death on new year's eve (Alma 51:33–52:1) would have been a hilarious blunder. Instead, the timing of wars we find in the scripture is part of a consistent pattern. It all agrees with what the Book of Mormon says about itself—that it is a translation from an authentic ancient American record.

LIST OF CONTRIBUTORS

S. Kent Brown, Ph.D., Brown University. Professor of Ancient Scripture, Brigham Young University.

Eugene England, Ph.D., Stanford University. Professor of English, BYU.

Avraham Gileadi, Ph.D., BYU. Writer, Woodland Hills, Utah.

Alan Goff, M.A., BYU. Technical editor, New York.

William J. Hamblin, Ph.D., University of Michigan. Assistant Professor of History, BYU.

Grant R. Hardy, Ph.D., Yale University. Assistant Professor of Asian Studies, Elmira College.

Victor L. Ludlow, Ph.D., Brandeis University. Associate Professor of Ancient Scripture, BYU.

Louis Midgley, Ph.D., Brown University. Professor of Political Science, BYU.

Robert L. Millet, Ph.D., Florida State University. Associate Professor of Ancient Scripture and Dean of Religious Education, BYU.

Blake T. Ostler, J.D., University of Utah. Attorney, Salt Lake City.

Noel B. Reynolds, Ph.D., Harvard University. Professor of Political Science, BYU.

Stephen D. Ricks, Ph.D., University of California, Berkeley. Associate Professor of Asian and Near Eastern Languages, BYU.

Richard Dilworth Rust, Ph.D., University of Wisconsin at Madison. Professor of English, University of North Carolina, Chapel Hill.

David Rolph Seely, Ph.D., University of Michigan. Assistant Professor of Ancient Scripture, BYU.

John L. Sorenson, Ph.D., University of California, Los Angeles. Professor Emeritus of Anthropology, BYU.

Terrence L. Szink, Ph.D. candidate, UCLA.

John S. Tanner, Ph.D., University of California, Berkeley. Professor of English, BYU.

LIST OF CONTRIBUTORS

Melvin J. Thorne, Ph.D., University of Kansas. Executive Editor, Foundation for Ancient Research and Mormon Studies, Provo, Utah.

John A. Tvedtnes, M.A., University of Utah and Hebrew University. Computer specialist and writer, Salt Lake City.

John W. Welch, J.D., Duke University. Professor of Law, BYU.

SCRIPTURE INDEX

259

SUBJECT INDEX

Abinadi, 72, 113

Abinadom, 56

Abrahamic covenant, 179

Adam: Lehi's teachings about, 13–14; fall of, 54–56

Agriculture, effect of, on warfare, 243, 251–52

Allegory of Zenos, 61–62, 147, 196

Alma the elder, 72

Alma the younger, 111–12, 162–63

Alma 36: overall structure, 116–18; the full text, 118–24; relations between paired sections, 124–27; weaving factors, 127–29; degree of chiasticity, 129–30; contrast with same account in Mosiah, 130–31

Alter, Robert, 105

Amaleki, 53, 56

Amalickiah, 224–25

Ammonihah, destruction of, 23–27

Ammoron, 225

Amulon, 71–72

Anointing of kings, 214

Anti-Nephi-Lehies, 26

Apostates, political and religious views of, 224–25

Arm: trusting in, of flesh, 145–47, of mercy, 147–48

Assyria as type for destruction, 203, 205

At-onement of Christ: traditional Christian theories of, 153–55; as means of reconciliation with God, 155, 165; Latter-day Saint understanding of, 155–56; condescension of God in, 157; connection of, to individual sins, 157–59; offers strength for repentance, 160; blessings of, were available before Christ's birth, 160–61; mercy depends on, 163; personal experience with, 165–67

Benjamin, King: teachings of, about Christ, 157–58; people of, experience mighty change, 160–61; holds covenant renewal ceremony, 234–39

Benjaminites, 68–70

Benson, Ezra Taft, 193

Bible: editing in, 16–19; example of chiasmus from, 115–16; truths removed from, 192. See also Old Testament

Bondage, 136–37, 169–70

Book of Mormon: complexity of, 15; studying editing of, 16, 19, 22, 25; colophons in, 32–37; recalling of Exodus in, 49–50; small plates of, 52, 55–56; combination of records in, 53; ancient nature of, demonstrated, 67, 239–40; first edition of, contained more Hebraisms, 78–79; leads investigator to understand Christ,

269

to Christ, 189–92; role of Book of
Mormon and Joseph Smith in,
192–94; to be completed during
Millennium, 194–95
Genealogical records of Jacob's
descendants, 57
Gentiles, Book of Mormon
classification of, 187–88
Gethsemane, Christ's suffering in,
158–59
God: dependence on, 49–50;
reconciliation with, 155, 165;
remembering and forgetting of,
173; Abraham's covenant with,
179; miracles of, cited in covenant
festival, 236–37. *See also* Jesus
Christ
Golden calf, Israel turns to, 48–49
Goliath, 17
Guilt, feelings of, 162

Hand of God, image of: frequency
of, 140; use of, in Book of
Mormon and Old Testament,
140–41; symbolic understanding
of, 141; parallels in use of, 142–
44; as being lengthened or
shortened, 144–45; instrument in,
145; modified use of, 144–47;
unique use of, in Book of
Mormon, 147–49
Hebrew language: Nephite language,
77; traces in Book of Mormon, 78;
construct state, 79; adverbial
phrases, 79–80; cognates, 80–81;
compound prepositions, 81–82;
conjunctions, 82–86; subordinate
clauses, 86–87; relative clause, 87;
extrapositional nouns and
pronouns, 87–88; interchangeable
prepositions, 88; comparison, 88–
89; naming conventions, 89;
possessive pronouns, 89–90;
unusual word use, 90–91

Helaman, Alma's exhortation to,
111–12
Henn, T. R., 195
History, repeating patterns of, 94
Homer's *Odyssey*, 114–15
Hunger, people murmur because of,
39–40, 95

Imagery in Book of Mormon: beauty
and meaning, 132, 139; patterns,
132–33; imagery illustrates
opposition, 133; fire, 133–34; light
and darkness, 134–35; captivity
and deliverance, 135–37;
wilderness or wandering, 137–38;
water, 138–39; dust, 139. *See also*
Hand of God, image of
Insignia of king's office, 213–14
Instrument in God's hand, 145
Isaiah: poetry of, 103–4; quotations
from, in Book of Mormon, 142,
198; prophecies of, regarding
fulfillment of covenants, 180–81;
Book of Mormon keys to
understanding, 197; prophecies
of, about latter days, 197–98;
types used by, 198–99, 202–3
Ishmael, 92–93
Israel: murmurings of, in wilderness,
39–40, 95–96; Zenos's allegory of,
61–62; ways of remembrance in,
172; Book of Mormon's concern
with, 186–87; reasons for
scattering of, 188–89; gathering
of, involves return to Christ, 189–
92; meaning of kingship in, 209–
13; festivals of, 230; covenant
renewal in, 232–34

Jacob: distinctive writing style of, 52,
58–60; descendants of, 56–58;
vivid vocabulary used by, 59–60;
favorite themes of, 60–62; birth
and childhood of, 62; pain of,
over divided family, 62–63; life of,